R. M. CROSK... W9-DGC-346

JAPAN'S LONGEST DAY

Compiled by

The Pacific War Research Society

KODANSHA INTERNATIONAL LTD.
Tokyo, New York & San Francisco

ACKNOWLEDGMENTS

The compilers and publishers are grateful to the following institutions and individuals for permission to reproduce the photographs in this book: Kyodo News Service, Kodansha Ltd., Asahi Shimbun, Bungei Shunju Ltd., the Imperial Household Agency, the Kantaro Suzuki Memorial Society, Mrs. Aya Anami, Mr. Okitsugu Arao, Mr. Masahiko Takeshita, Mr. Kazushi Oyama, Mr. Masataka Iwata, Mr. Yukio Nishihara and Mr. Morio Tateno.

Originally published in Japanese as Nihon no Ichiban Nagai Hi *by Bungei Shunju Ltd. in 1965. English edition published by Kodansha International Ltd., 2-12-21 Otowa, Bunkyo-ku, Tokyo 112 and Kodansha International/USA Ltd., 10 East 53rd Street, New York, New York 10022 and 44 Montgomery Street, San Francisco, California 94104. Copyright © 1968 by Kodansha International Ltd. All rights reserved. Printed in Japan.*

LCC 68-17573
ISBN 0-87011-422-0
JBC 0021-787909-2361

Second paperback edition, 1980
Second printing, 1980

Foreword

AT TWELVE NOON, AUGUST 15TH, 1945, two historic events occurred simultaneously in Japan: the people heard the voice of their Emperor, most of them for the first time, as he spoke over the radio to tell them that their country had lost its first war. This book is a detailed record of the twenty-four hours that preceded that broadcast—from the Imperial Conference, where the decision to surrender was made, to the broadcast itself. It was the longest day the people of Japan had ever lived through.

For us young members of the Pacific War Research Society, the idea of compiling this record was of overwhelming interest, for it seemed to us unlikely that we would live to see our country undergo so critical an experience a second time. August 15th, 1945, marked a climax in the hundred-year history of Japan since the Meiji Restoration. The whole future of the Japanese people and of Japan itself hinges on that single day.

Although I am the oldest member of the Pacific War Research Society, I was only a third-year student in middle school on the day of the Emperor's broadcast. Nevertheless, I had been making my contribution to the war effort; I had been drafted to work in a munitions factory that produced twenty-millimeter machine gun cartridges. The factory was virtually bombed out of existence by B-

29's, and many of my classmates who had been working with me were killed. The front had spread even to us and I continued to hope for a Japanese victory. Thus, my feelings, that mid-August noon, were a mixture of sorrow and anger, coupled with a sense of hopeless futility, for we had been told that with the occupation of Japan, we would be forced to lead the lives of slaves.

That day I smoked my first cigarette, an act which had been strictly prohibited by school authorities, and I determined to try anything that came along. Young as I was, there seemed to be too little time left to me—and yet I took no pleasure in anything I did. Those of us who survived the war, whether at home or on the front, had more or less been exposed to the horrors of war. Inevitably, we became hardened by the constant spectacle of man's inhumanity to man. Although August 15th put an end to some of that inhumanity, the fact of defeat had been, for the Japanese people, so catastrophic an experience, that it is difficult to measure its effect, even today. Japan has still not found the way to appease the souls of her war dead—and until she does, she cannot be said either to have forgotten the past or to be living wholly in the present. What had led all these hundreds of thousands to death? Some of the answers may be found in the thoughts and deeds of the chief actors in that twenty-four hour drama. That is one of the reasons we have written this book.

To die for one's country had always been regarded in Japan almost as a kind of religious duty. Twenty years are not, perhaps, a very long time for a nation to cast off an old and long-established belief, but it must be done if the people of Japan are to live in the world of today rather than yesterday. And maybe that is another reason we have written this book.

The difficulties of writing contemporary history, while some of the actors are still alive, are obvious, yet at the same time, a unique kind of history book may result. We interviewed every surviving actor in the final drama of Japan's defeat—with the sole exception of the protagonist, the Emperor himself—and while we read, naturally, all the published material, we based our report mainly on the interviews. Our reconstruction of actions, emotions and states of mind have all been substantiated by the men we interviewed.

However, it must be remembered that more than twenty years have elapsed since that climactic day. Emotions ran high, and so have inevitably colored memory. Memories fade. Men have reasons for remembering only what they prefer to remember or for repeating only what they choose to repeat. Then the historian must attempt to sift the true from the false—and must sometimes, inevitably, fail.

Many of the chief actors were old men at the time of the drama and have long been dead. Some died that very day. One has preferred not to speak: when we interviewed Marquis Koichi Kido, then Lord Keeper of the Privy Seal, he refused to break his silence.

Japan's struggle to surrender was a kind of earthquake whose aftershocks may still be felt today. To recount the tragic details of defeat must, necessarily, re-evoke unhappy memories, but it may also help pave the way to a new and better start. Perhaps that is the best reason of all for having written this book.

KAZUTOSHI HANDO,
The Pacific War Research Society

the Days Before...

IN 1931, THE IMPERIAL JAPANESE ARMY pulled the Manchurian Incident out of its cap and became, as a consequence, the dominant force in Japanese public life. By 1945, fourteen years later, the Emperor and most of his statesmen realized that Japan had lost the war—but their great, their seemingly insuperable problem was how to bring that war to a close. The still vigorous Imperial Army would admit neither defeat nor surrender—and it continued to insist that it, and it alone, knew what was best for the country. Thus Japan's final struggle was not against the enemy but against herself: and for a moment or two, during that long August day, the struggle looked as though it might prove fatal. If it was the Emperor around whom the struggle centered, it was the Emperor also who finally resolved it.

As far back as February, 1942, Marquis Koichi Kido, Lord Keeper of the Privy Seal, had realized that American preponderance over Japan must in the end be the deciding factor, and he had secretly advised the Emperor " to grasp any opportunity to bring about the earliest possible termination of the war." Others, as the war wore on, came to the same dangerous conclusion—dangerous, because the Army did not share it.

Clandestine attempts to end the war through an American O.S.S.

11

organization in Switzerland came to nothing; and many men, including the Emperor himself, preferred to pin their hopes on the "good offices" of the Soviet Union—until the day the Soviet Union declared war on Japan. The present Cabinet of Baron Suzuki was a far cry from that of General Tojo, one of the chief architects of the Army's plan to share the world with Germany. Suzuki's Foreign Minister, Shigenori Togo, headed the faction that believed acceptance of the Potsdam Proclamation, although too late by then to save the Japanese people much of their suffering, was the only means to avoid their total extinction.

Both groups—those who favored peace and those who favored war—were alike in their determination to preserve the essential structure of the nation and in their willingness to give their lives for their beliefs and for their Emperor. Japan without her sovereign was as unthinkable to one side as to the other: in this—and in very little else—they saw eye to eye.

Twenty days before the last day, the people of Japan had awakened to what seemed to them an ordinary wartime summer morning: heat and humidity were high, stomachs were empty and likely to remain so, and there was work to be done—the work of prosecuting the war, though it had grown ever more difficult with the passing days, with increasing malnutrition, accelerated air-raids that meant death for some and homelessness for more, and shortage of raw materials to hamper essential production. And all this in the muggy heat of a Japanese summer. Another day, thought the hungry, weary, but still undaunted people of Japan; a day like yesterday, and like tomorrow.

But they were wrong, and the government of Japan knew it, for at six that morning the overseas radio bureau in Tokyo had monitored a broadcast from San Francisco announcing a proclamation signed the day before by the President of the United States, the

President of the Chinese Republic, and the Prime Minister of Great Britain, who had conferred at Potsdam and come to the conclusion "that Japan shall be given an opportunity to end this war." The Foreign Office began to study the terms of the Proclamation while a translation was being prepared:

The time has come for Japan to decide whether she will continue to be controlled by those self-willed militaristic advisers whose unintelligent calculations have brought the Empire of Japan to the threshold of annihilation, or whether she will follow the path of reason.

Following are our terms. We will not deviate from them. There are no alternatives. We shall brook no delay.

There must be eliminated for all time the authority and influence of those who have deceived and misled the people of Japan into embarking on world conquest, for we insist that a new order of peace, security and justice will be impossible until irresponsible militarism is driven from the world. . . .

We do not intend that the Japanese shall be enslaved as a race or destroyed as a nation, but stern justice shall be meted out to all war criminals, including those who have visited cruelties upon our prisoners. The Japanese Government shall remove all obstacles to the revival and strengthening of democratic tendencies among the Japanese people. Freedom of speech, of religion, and of thought, as well as respect for the fundamental human rights shall be established. . . .

We call upon the government of Japan to proclaim now the unconditional surrender of all Japanese armed forces, and to provide proper and adequate assurances of their good faith in such action. The alternative for Japan is prompt and utter destruction.

The first man in the government to react positively to the San Francisco broadcast was the Vice-Minister of Foreign Affairs, Shunichi Matsumoto. He advised Togo that Japan must accept the terms as stated, that to reject them would be the height of folly, and he had, in fact, already begun to compose a draft of the Japanese acceptance, to be sent to Japan's ministers in Switzerland and Sweden and from there to be conveyed to the enemy, when Togo came into the room where he was working.

"Wait," said the Foreign Minister, "it's not going to be as easy as that." His voice sounded immeasurably sad, as though he was speaking from some lonely height where he felt far from certain of being heard. "The Army will never accept the Proclamation as it stands."

But, Togo felt, the fact that the Allies had softened their first demand in the Cairo Declaration for "the unconditional surrender of Japan" to "the unconditional surrender of all Japanese armed forces" suggested that more favorable terms, or at least a more favorable expression of the same terms, might be forthcoming, which the Army could accept and still save face. He concluded, therefore, that before replying, Japan ought to make one final effort to use Soviet "good offices."

Togo reached this conclusion despite the fact that all of Tokyo's negotiations with Moscow had so far been wholly inconclusive. Attempts to enlist the assistance of the Soviet ambassador to Japan had failed; the Kremlin had refused to give a definite reply to the Imperial desire to send Prince Konoye to Moscow as a special envoy; and Naotake Sato, the Japanese ambassador to the Soviet Union, had assured Togo that "there is no chance whatever of winning the Soviet Union to our side. . . ." What Togo did not, of course, know was that Roosevelt and Churchill had already, at Yalta, secretly agreed to major concessions in the Far East if Stalin, within two or three months after the end of the war in Europe, entered the war against Japan.

In spite of what he knew (and did not know), Togo was able to persuade not only himself but also the Prime Minister that the Soviet Union was not ill-disposed toward Japan and that the Kremlin's "good offices" might still be available.

At ten-thirty on the morning of July 27th the Supreme Council for the Direction of the War met to discuss the Potsdam Proclamation and the possibility of Soviet mediation. This Supreme War Council—or "inner Cabinet"—consisted of Japan's Big Six: the Prime Minister, the Minister of Foreign Affairs, the Minister of War, the Minister of the Navy, and the chiefs of the General Staffs of both the Army and the Navy. At the meeting Togo emphasized the importance of the shift from the unconditional surrender of Japan to the unconditional surrender of the armed forces and declared that he felt it would be "extremely impolitic" to reject the Proclamation. He was able, against considerable opposition, to persuade the Supreme Council to withhold the Japanese reply until after they had heard again from Moscow. This, then, despite those ominous words, "We shall brook no delay," was to be a period of "watchful waiting."

How best to inform the Japanese people of the existence of the Proclamation was another major problem, and in an attempt to solve it, a full Cabinet meeting was held in the afternoon.

Once again Togo took the lead. An arrogant man of sixty-two, inclined to be contemptuous of other people's opinions, he was far more outspoken than his Premier, Kantaro Suzuki, who was then over seventy-seven, deaf and drowsy, saying one thing today and its opposite tomorrow, willing to let other men hug the limelight while he dozed his way through meetings that never seemed to come either to an end or to a conclusion.

Togo asserted that since the Potsdam Proclamation was the sole basis for peace negotiations, he believed that no announcement of it should be made until the government was able to take a firm stand one way or the other.

The Welfare Minister, Tadahiko Okada, dissented. As the Proclamation, he said, had been broadcast throughout the world, the Japanese people could not fail to hear of it; before that happened, they ought to be officially informed by their government. The

Director of the Information Bureau, Hiroshi Shimomura, agreed, adding that postponement might be regarded abroad as evidence that the Japanese Government was unduly apprehensive about the situation.

All eyes turned now to General Korechika Anami, the War Minister, who spoke for the Army and so was still the most powerful man in the country, though he lacked the color and fire of some of his predecessors. At fifty-seven, he kept himself in trim by means of archery and fencing, and to the younger officers he was a dependable, almost a paternal figure: they believed they could count on him to go on waging the war Japan had undertaken, and in Cabinet meetings he persistently, and obstinately, nurtured this belief.

He now insisted that if news of the Proclamation was to be released, the government must simultaneously state both its objections to the terms and the attitude it wanted the Japanese people to adopt. Anami was seconded by the Army and Navy Chiefs of Staff.

In the end, a compromise was reached; since the government could neither ignore the Proclamation entirely nor publish it along with strong protests until it knew where it stood, the Cabinet agreed to release the news vaguely—almost as though the Proclamation had been promulgated in dreamland, not Potsdam. The government's own position was not to be announced; the newspapers were to downgrade the story as far as possible. They were allowed to publish an expurgated text of the Proclamation,[1] but without any editorial comment whatsoever.

The Japanese government intended, for the moment, to "ignore" the Proclamation. Despite Anami's insistence on some strong statement of protest, Suzuki agreed with Togo; the government, he said, will, in a word, in a now famous and tragic word, *mokusatsu* the Proclamation—will kill it with silence. *Moku* means "to be silent" and *satsu* means "to kill"; taken together, the word is defined

---

[1]For Notes to the Text, see Page 329.

by the Kenkyusha Dictionary as "take no notice of; treat (anything) with silent contempt; ignore [by keeping silence]." It also means: "remain in a wise and masterly inactivity," and that, no doubt, was the sense Suzuki had in mind—but unfortunately the other meanings sounded both more spectacular and more persuasive, and when the word appeared on the front page of Tokyo's newspapers the following morning, it was taken to mean that the government held the Proclamation in contempt—that the government, in fact, rejected it. So the word was understood in Washington, as well as in Britain and the rest of Europe—although it was in American diplomatic circles that *mokusatsu* exerted its maximum damage. The *Asahi Shimbun,* one of Tokyo's largest newspapers, that same Saturday morning characterized the Proclamation as "a thing of no great value." The Japanese people were apprised of the existence of the Proclamation and assured at the same time that their government found it unacceptable—which was hardly what the Cabinet had decided the afternoon before. But the people were not to know that—any more than they knew anything else that went on behind the closed doors of the ministries and the official residences or the moats of the Palace—and so they treated the Proclamation with the silent contempt which their government had told them was all it deserved.[2]

The following day, Saturday, July 28th, Premier Suzuki agreed to hold a press conference at four o'clock, at which he would discuss the Allied declaration. To the all-important, expected question, Suzuki replied that the Potsdam Proclamation was nothing but a "rehash" of the Cairo Declaration and that the government considered it to be a "thing of no great value." Then, suddenly, he added, "We will simply *mokusatsu* it," after which he announced the government's determination to continue prosecuting the war until victory was won.

Togo was furious when he heard about Suzuki's answer. He

protested that the statement was glaringly inconsistent with the decision that had been jointly arrived at by the Cabinet. At the same time he realized that there was nothing he could do: it was impossible to retract the Premier's words.

And the damage had already been done. Suzuki's statement was published in Japan on Monday, July 30th, and picked up by newspapers throughout the world, which reported that Japan had not even bothered to "reject" the Proclamation. In describing this moment later, the American Secretary of War, Henry L. Stimson, said that the United States

... could only proceed to demonstrate that the ultimatum had meant exactly what it said when it stated that if the Japanese continued the war, "the full application of our military power, backed by our resolve, will mean the inevitable and complete destruction of the Japanese armed forces and just as inevitably the utter devastation of the Japanese homeland."

For such a purpose the atomic bomb was an eminently suitable weapon.

Japan, meanwhile, continued to await a reply from the Soviet Union.

When the Japanese ambassador to the Kremlin cabled Togo that there was "no chance whatever" of persuading Russia to aid the Japanese, the Foreign Minister replied: "In spite of your views, you are to carry out your instructions. . . . Endeavor to obtain the good offices of the Soviet Union in ending the war short of unconditional surrender."

Togo had served for a time as Japan's ambassador to Moscow and was not, then, unfamiliar with the Soviet mind and the way it worked. His reasons for persistently pursuing this will-o'-the-wisp across the marshes of the war's end may be summed up in his own words at the time: "No matter how hard I may try to persuade the Japanese military to hold direct negotiations with the

Americans or the British, I have no doubt whatsoever that they will refuse to listen. Therefore we must attempt to negotiate through the Soviet Union because there seems to be no other way to terminate the war."

The Army did not believe it was possible to come to an understanding with the Soviet Union either. As early as mid-June, Anami had predicted that the Russians "would attack Japan just as the Americans were preparing to land their forces on our islands." He continued of this opinion to the very end; a few days before surrender, he told Home Minister Abe that if Japan held out a little longer and engaged the American forces at Kyushu, in the south of Japan, the United States would become so apprehensive about Russian occupation of the Asian mainland and northern Japan, that she would be eager to conclude a peace treaty and would therefore offer more advantageous terms. The Navy was of the opinion that the Soviets would enter the war after the battle of Okinawa: that is one reason the Navy wanted the Japanese forces to take the dogged stand that they did there, inflicting such heavy losses on the enemy.

Thus, although Russia had already announced its intention not to renew the Soviet-Japanese Neutrality Pact, and although Moscow's replies to Tokyo consisted mainly of equivocal silence, both the Supreme Council and the Emperor himself continued to pin their hopes on the "good offices" of the Soviet Union. The days passed as Japan waited for Stalin's reply.

It seemed almost as though the whole country was, at that moment, too bewildered to act. The Japanese had been taught that they had never lost a war, that surrender was dishonorable, that the only decent alternative to victory was death. It was difficult, it was impossible, to believe that what seemed to be happening was actually happening: it was the complete upset of all known and changeless values.

Contributing perhaps even more heavily to their state of shock

19

was the position of the Emperor, whom the Japanese believed to be not only of divine descent but divine himself and upon whose continued existence the continued existence of Japan as it had always been since time immemorial depended. It is impossible to guess what would have happened if the Allied powers had, at that moment, offered assurances that the Japanese polity, in the person of the Emperor, would be maintained: the war might have ended, the Army might have been forced to concede—and the Russians might not have been given the opportunity to enter Manchuria. But these speculations are idle; Japan, in her stunned state, followed the only path that seemed open to her; and the first few days of August passed in idle, not quite hopeless, watchful waiting.

On August 6th a reply came.

At eight o'clock Hiroshima radar operators detected two B-29's. A warning was sounded. The planes mounted to an extremely high altitude; the radio announced that they were on a reconnaissance flight. Most of the city's quarter of a million people didn't bother to seek shelter, anticipating no bombing. Many gazed up into the sky to watch the maneuver.

In the lead plane, the bomb bay doors opened. At eight-fifteen and seventeen seconds, many persons on the ground saw a cluster of parachutes drop from one of the planes.

In the next seconds there was a blinding white flash—and sixty-four thousand people were dead or about to die.

This then was the answer to Japan's waiting. Not, as expected, from the Soviet Union—but from the United States, who now delivered the first installment of her threat to visit "prompt and utter destruction" upon Japan.

A Domei News Agency dispatch reached Tokyo around noon, but details of the extent and character of the catastrophe arrived only in late afternoon, in the form of a report from Second Army headquarters transmitted through the Kure Naval Yard, and even then the details were scanty. All that Tokyo learned that afternoon was that a very few enemy planes had inflicted tremendous damage with a bomb of an unknown type. The next morning, at dawn, Lientenant Gèneral Torashiro Kawabe, vice-chief of the Army General Staff, was the recipient of a succinct dispatch which informed him that all of Hiroshima had been wiped out in the momentary explosion of a single bomb. Later, General Kawabe said he suspected the bomb to be atomic.

His fellow-officers were, in any case, not long in doubt. Broadcasts from Washington, picked up by the government in Tokyo, confirmed Kawabe's suspicions. "We have spent two billion dollars," said President Truman, "on the greatest scientific gamble in history—and won." If the Japanese, he added, "do not now accept our terms they may expect a rain of ruin from the air, the like of which has never been seen on this earth. . . ."

There was no longer any question in Tokyo about what had occurred at Hiroshima. "The source from which the sun draws its power," as Truman called it, could now totally eclipse the land of the rising sun, on whose throne sat a direct descendant of Amaterasu O-Mikami, the Goddess of the Sun. But Tokyo was indifferent to the irony. The situation demanded drastic action—and yet the curious lethargy that had held the Japanese capital in its grip continued to immobilize the men whose duty it was to make decisions.

On the following day, August 7th, the Army issued a communiqué in which it said that an attack on Hiroshima by "a small number of B-29's" caused "considerable damage" and that a "new type of bomb" had been used. "Details," said the Army, "are now under investigation. . . ." Later that same day Togo informed the Cabinet of Truman's announcement; no apparent action, however, was taken.

On August 8th, Togo advised the Emperor that Japan must

accept the terms of the Potsdam Proclamation as soon as possible, whereupon the Emperor commanded his Foreign Minister to indicate to the Premier that, in view of the "new type" of weapon that had been used, Japan was now powerless to continue the war and must make every effort to terminate the war with the least possible delay. Japan must accept the inevitable. According to Marquis Kido, Lord Keeper of the Privy Seal, His Majesty said that he considered his own personal safety secondary to the immediate termination of the war. The tragedy of Hiroshima, he insisted, must not be repeated.

Suzuki, thereupon, called for an emergency meeting of the Supreme War Council, but the meeting had to be postponed because one of the members was unavoidably detained by "more pressing business" elsewhere.

The Army, meanwhile, attempted to blanket enemy broadcasts from Manila and Okinawa and to nullify the effect of enemy leaflets dropped over Tokyo expressing the Allied desire to end the war without destroying Japan. In any case, the Army claimed, it was not really possible, even for the Americans, to manufacture and use an atomic weapon: it would be both too variable and too dangerous. At the same time, the government of Japan filed a formal protest through Switzerland against the government of the United States.

In Moscow, that same afternoon, the Japanese ambassador was conducted into Molotov's study. Molotov cut short Sato's attempts to make the meeting a friendly one and began reading a short note that ended with the following words: ". . . the Soviet Government declares that from tomorrow, that is from August 9, the Soviet Union will consider herself in a state of war against Japan." Within two hours the Red Army had entered Manchuria and begun its systematic annihilation of Japan's once invincible Kwantung Army.

The Japanese considered the Soviet action to be both unpardonable and unlawful, since the Soviet-Japanese Neutrality Pact did not expire until April, 1946; but Stalin, with Truman's help, made a legal case for his act; and Suzuki's government knew by now that the alternative to unconditional surrender was indeed, without any doubt, total annihilation.

And yet it almost seemed that the chance to be totally annihilated was exactly what the Army wanted. Peace that hot, sultry Thursday morning of August 9th must have seemed to Foreign Minister Togo like the cool, quenching water that men are said to see in the distance as they lie dying in the desert. By eight o'clock he was at Premier Suzuki's house in Koishikawa, in north-central Tokyo, angrily demanding that the meeting of the Supreme Council, which had been postponed the day before, be held at once. Valuable time had been lost: the war must now be ended as soon as possible.

Suzuki agreed, and to Hisatsune Sakomizu, Chief Cabinet Secretary, he said: "Let our present Cabinet take the responsibility of seeing the country through the termination of the war." Under normal circumstances, after the ignominious failure of his government's attempts to use the Soviet Union's "good offices," he and his Cabinet would have resigned *en masse;* Japan's circumstances, however, that Thursday morning were far from normal, and Suzuki was apparently determined to pull as many of Japan's chestnuts out of the fire as he could.

Togo then went to see Admiral Yonai, the Navy Minister, who agreed, as he had before, that Japan had no choice but to sue for peace. While still at the Ministry, Togo was questioned about the situation by Imperial Prince Takamatsu, a Navy captain; his reply was not hopeful. He said he believed it was now too late to negotiate substantially better terms than those of the Potsdam Proclamation, and while he would do all he could, he felt Japan could insist on nothing save preservation of the national polity.

Meanwhile, the symbol of that polity, the man who gave it both meaning and existence, the Emperor, had already conferred with Lord Privy Seal Marquis Kido, and had asked him to impress once again on Premier Suzuki His Majesty's desire that the war be brought to the speediest possible conclusion. Suzuki, who had just entered the Palace, agreed to call immediate emergency meetings of both the Supreme War Council and the Cabinet and to communicate with the former Prime Ministers who composed the body called the Jushin, or Senior Statesmen, and whose duty it was from time to time to advise the Throne.

At eleven o'clock that Thursday morning the world's second atomic bomb exploded over Nagasaki, one of the westernmost of Japanese cities, on the island of Kyushu. Just half an hour before, the Supreme War Council reconvened to continue its unhurried deliberations at the Imperial Palace in Tokyo, some six hundred miles away as the plane flies.

Premier Suzuki opened the proceedings. In view of Hiroshima, he said, and the Soviet invasion of Manchuria, it is virtually impossible for Japan to continue the war. "I believe," Suzuki concluded, "that we have no alternative but to accept the Potsdam Proclamation, and I would now like to hear your opinions."

The Supreme War Council was silent.

Finally Admiral Mitsumasa Yonai broke the spell that seemed to have bewitched the Councilors. Yonai was a quiet, pleasant man, with a cheerful smile, who had been Premier in 1940 and forced to resign because he opposed the alliance with Germany and Italy. He was conscious, like Suzuki and Togo, of the ever-present danger of assassination at the hands of the fire-eating young officers in the War Ministry. "We're not going to accomplish anything," he said now, "unless we speak out. Do we accept the enemy ultimatum unconditionally? Do we propose conditions? If so, we had better discuss them here and now."

With that, the other members of the Council began to state their positions, and it was soon apparent that there was unanimous agreement on only one point: the Imperial structure of the country must be preserved. Beyond that there was a sharp division that was to become sharper and more familiar as the days wore on.

Suzuki, Togo, and Yonai favored acceptance of the Allied ultimatum with the single proviso relating to the Imperial polity. The other three—War Minister Anami and the two Chiefs of Staff, Umezu for the Army and Toyoda for the Navy—wanted to propose other conditions: a minimal occupation force, trying of war criminals by Japan rather than by the enemy, and demobilization of Japanese troops by Japanese officers. Anami and the two Chiefs of Staff were unable, apparently, to accept the *idea* of either defeat or surrender, both of which went against all their training; these proposals, thus, were aimed at minimizing, perhaps even denying, the *fact* of both defeat and surrender.

Togo replied vigorously that Japan's position was so precarious that if she even attempted to propose a number of conditions, the Allies would in all probability refuse to negotiate at all. General Umezu, the Army Chief of Staff, contended that Japan had still not lost the war and that if the enemy invaded the homeland, Japanese troops were still capable of holding him back and perhaps even repulsing him; the cost, in enemy losses, would be tremendous. To this Togo replied that even if a first assault failed, Japan's power to defend herself would be even further diminished, and that a second enemy attack would almost certainly not fail. Japan, said Togo, must accept the Potsdam ultimatum *now,* demanding no more than the preservation of the Imperial House.

By then it was one o'clock. The Council had been in session for two hours, and although word had arrived of the bombing of Nagasaki and of the fact that Manchuria, for all practical purposes, was in Soviet hands, the Council was still not able to reach an agreement.

The line of demarcation was as sharply drawn as ever, with three on one side and three on the other. Suzuki proposed that the Council adjourn, to reconvene later in the day, after the afternoon's Cabinet meeting. That is how the Thursday morning session of the Supreme Council for the Direction of the War ended in Tokyo.

In Washington, President Truman, speaking of the bomb in the course of a radio address, declared: "We shall continue to use it until we completely destroy Japan's power to make war. Only a Japanese surrender will stop us."

Around the time that the Supreme Council adjourned, Hiroshi Shimomura, Director of the Information Bureau, was received in audience by the Emperor. The audience, which had been granted on an application by Shimomura's secretary to the Imperial Household Ministry, lasted a full two hours, although Imperial audiences usually took only thirty minutes at the most, and when it was over Shimomura said with a relieved smile to his secretary:

"It all went well. The Emperor has agreed to make a broadcast telling the nation whether we're to have peace or war."

If His Majesty were indeed to make the broadcast, it would mark the first time the people of Japan heard the voice of their monarch.

The Cabinet meeting to decide Japan's fate began at two-thirty that Thursday afternoon, August 9th, at the Premier's official residence. It was opened by Foreign Minister Togo, who related the events leading up to the Soviet declaration of war, including the government's attempts to persuade the Kremlin to mediate. Togo then described the nature of the catastrophe that had overtaken Hiroshima and Nagasaki.

The Minister of the Navy and the War Minister, asked for their opinions by the Premier, repeated very much what they had said earlier at the Supreme War Council.

"We might," said Admiral Yonai, "win the first battle for Japan, but we won't win the second. The war is lost to us. Therefore we must forget about 'face,' we must surrender as quickly as we can, and we must begin to consider at once how best to preserve our country."

"We cannot pretend," said General Anami, summing up the arguments on the other side, "to claim that victory is certain, but it is far too early to say that the war is lost. That we will inflict severe losses on the enemy when he invades Japan is certain, and it is by no means impossible that we may be able to reverse the situation in our favor, pulling victory out of defeat.

"Furthermore," Anami went on, "our Army will not submit to demobilization. Our men simply will not lay down their arms. And since they know they are not permitted to surrender, since they know that a fighting man who surrenders is liable to extremely heavy punishment, there is really no alternative for us but to continue the war."

The Ministers of Agriculture, Commerce, Transportation, and Munitions disagreed. They pointed out that Okinawa was already being used by the Americans as a bridgehead for their forthcoming invasion of Kyushu (called "Operation Olympic"); that the people of Japan were on the verge of exhaustion; that the present rice crop was the poorest since 1931; that air-raids and bombings had been increasingly devastating in recent weeks, and likely to grow more so; that enemy ships were already bombarding the coastal cities of Japan—that Japan, in short, had neither the strength nor the means to wage war any longer.

"Yes, yes!" cried Anami impatiently. "Everyone understands the situation . . . but we must fight the war through to the end no matter how great the odds against us!"

Here Genki Abe, the Home Minister, served notice that he could not promise civil obedience if the Cabinet decided to attempt to end the war through capitulation. He recalled the incident of February 26th, 1936, when a group of enflamed young officers had led some two thousand troops in an insurrection that resulted in several deaths, including an attempt on the life of the prime minister, and the wounding of the minister of finance, the Grand Chamberlain, and the Lord Privy Seal, all of them liberal statesmen whose influence the young officers desired to remove from about the Throne. The rebels had occupied the War Office, Tokyo police headquarters, and the residence of the prime minister before the Emperor himself was forced to intervene, commanding the minister of war to take action. Recalling the details of that incident, which had occurred less than a decade before, Abe advised against acceptance of the Potsdam Proclamation.

Here Foreign Minister Togo reported what had occurred at the Supreme War Council in the morning and gave it as his firm and considered opinion that the Cabinet must accept the Allied ultimatum with the sole condition that the Imperial structure be maintained.

When Suzuki asked for other opinions, two of the ministers announced that they agreed with Anami that Japan should insist on acceptance of the three other conditions as well.

At five-thirty, an hour's recess was called. At six-thirty, the ministers reconvened and continued their discussions. At ten o'clock, Premier Suzuki asked if there was a consensus. There was not, and since unanimity was the Cabinet rule, the meeting ended without any decision having been taken. The ministers bowed and made their uncertain way into the blacked-out streets of the ruined and smoking capital.

Suzuki and Togo held a brief and private conversation. Both men knew what needed to be done, and had in fact already paved the way for the sole move that appeared capable of breaking the disastrous stalemate in which both the country and its rulers were immobilized.

Yet it was a move that had never been played before: the rules made no provision for it. It was as though, to break the fatal deadlock, the chessboard king was to be not only allowed to place himself in check but also granted the freedom of movement of the queen. As long ago as June, 1944, Mamoru Shigémitsu, then Foreign Minister, and Marquis Kido, Lord Privy Seal, had envisaged a situation of this sort, where Japan, required to act and unable to act, might find salvation only by taking recourse in the mystic powers of the Emperor. Togo had discussed the subject with Suzuki earlier that Thursday and they had agreed that in the event of an impossible deadlock, the final decision would have to be left to the Emperor. With this in mind, they had asked Chief Cabinet Secretary Sakomizu to get General Umezu and Admiral Toyoda to sign a petition enabling the Premier to convoke a meeting of the Big Six, the Supreme War Council, in the Imperial presence.

Sakomizu's explanation had been that this would save time should a meeting with the Emperor have to be called suddenly. And the two chiefs of staff had signed, for the tradition was immemorial that the the Japanese government never approached the Throne with a problem until the government's own solution to the problem was unanimous. The Emperor himself neither took sides nor stated his own opinion: he merely approved what the government had already decided. His August Mind was not to be disturbed by party strife and political ambition; the responsibility for decisions made and actions taken was never his. To present him with a divided cabinet was unthinkable; normally, if a cabinet could not reach unanimity, it resigned. But Suzuki had already determined not to resign; he had decided that he and his Cabinet would assume the responsibility for ending the war. But they could not do it alone—they required the magic that only the Emperor possessed. This was one drama that could not be resolved without the descent of a *deus ex machina*. The time was out of joint beyond all doubt and there was now only one man in the country who could set it right.

The situation, however, was a perilous one. Both Suzuki and Togo, as they held their late-night dialogue, were desperately aware of the danger. If a stalemate was likely to prove fatal, the wrong move might be even more catastrophic—for the most powerful, and unpredictable, piece on the board was the Army. It was a piece that for many years had obeyed no rules but its own. If the Army could not have what it wanted, it was willing to resort to assassination, or even outright rebellion, always on the pretext (which it almost certainly passionately believed) that it was protecting the Emperor from his "traitorous" advisers. Both Suzuki and Togo had a deep-seated and perhaps well-founded fear that violent death would prevent their signing the document they were convinced was now Japan's only salvation.

Upon their arrival at the Palace that night, the Emperor received them in audience at once. Suzuki first asked Togo to report to His Majesty on the two meetings, neither of which had resulted in unanimity. Then Suzuki proposed that the Supreme War Council be reconvened that same night in the Emperor's presence. His Majesty had been prepared for the appeal and gave immediate consent.

Suzuki at once ordered a convocation of the Council and a full Cabinet meeting to follow. The Emperor, meanwhile, after the two ministers left, received Marquis Kido briefly: it was the Lord Privy Seal's sixth Imperial audience that Thursday, August 9th. If his ministers had at last shaken off their lethargy and decided to act, the Emperor had not been idle either.

The man who was summoned by fate to authorize his country's salvation was mild-mannered, retiring, shy in the extreme. Short, bespectacled, forty-four years old, he had, since his enthronement in 1928, lived the cloistered life his subjects expected of their Emperor. The white glare of public life beat less fiercely on him than on any other monarch in the world: it was enough for his subjects that he existed, that he was there, for he embodied in his sacred person that sacred entity called Japan. Without him, or his successor, there could be no Japan.

His life had always been a simple one, and had, since the war, taken on an austerity that not even the poorest of his subjects was likely to envy. He customarily rose at seven, shaved, and read the newspapers. After praying at the Kashikodokoro, the Koreiden, and the Shinden, he took a simple breakfast of black bread and oatmeal. He usually worked from nine-thirty to noon, then lunched on cooked vegetables and a dumpling soup. He then returned to his work and ended his day with a short walk in the Inner Garden. He neither smoked nor drank and he slept lightly.

Now the door opened quietly and, accompanied by an aide, he entered the little bomb-shelter where, before the night was out, his country's destiny was to be entrusted into his hands. The time was ten minutes to midnight. The Supreme Councilors, with their aides and two invited guests, had been waiting since eleven-thirty. They bowed and sat back in their chairs, keeping their eyes respectfully turned away from His Majesty. The Emperor's appearance had a hurried look. Indeed, if his last audience with Marquis Kido did not end until 11:37 p.m., as Kido's diary indicates, then the Emperor would not have had much time to prepare for one of the most critical hours in his own and his country's life.

In addition to the Big Six and their aides, two other men, Chief Cabinet Secretary Sakomizu and Baron Hiranuma, President of the Privy Council, were present at the invitation of the Premier. The room where the meeting took place, in the Emperor's underground bomb-shelter, was only eighteen feet by thirty and, being poorly ventilated, was a small inferno that hot, damp August night. The Councilors and their guests were all wearing either formal morning clothes or uniforms: the white handkerchiefs, frequently used, formed strange patterns against their sombre clothes and faces.

The ceiling of the shelter was supported by steel beams, and its walls were paneled in dark wood. The eleven men sat behind long, cloth-covered tables, facing one another, six on one side and five on the other. The twelfth man took his seat in a plain, straight-backed chair at the head of the room. Behind him was a simple screen. The Emperor's aide positioned himself near the door.

Premier Suzuki, standing at the Emperor's left, asked the Chief Cabinet Secretary to read the Potsdam Proclamation aloud. As no minutes were kept of this meeting, or of subsequent meetings held during those few days Japan underwent her agony of surrender, the actual words spoken are lost to history; accounts of what occurred can only be partial reconstructions, based on personal recollections of the men who were present and of those in whom they confided. Suzuki, then, after the reading of the Proclamation, repeated the account he had given the Emperor of the earlier, deadlocked meetings. He offered His Majesty an apology for requesting his presence at a time when his ministers were still not in agreement. (It has been suggested that Suzuki was also obliquely apologizing to the two Chiefs of Staff for having used their signatures to petition the Throne while opinion was still divided. The unprecedented nature of this midnight meeting had caught the two Chiefs of Staff unawares—but once they had signed the petition, and once the Emperor had commanded the meeting to be held, they had no choice but to obey the Imperial summons.) Suzuki reviewed the situation as of that moment: the Supreme War Council was divided three to three, while the Cabinet, which alone had the constitutional authority to approve Japan's surrender, was split three ways—six members favored acceptance of the Proclamation provided only that the Imperial House be guaranteed, three insisted on the four conditions Anami had outlined, while five advocated more conditions than one but fewer than the war-party's four.

The Premier called on his Foreign Minister. Togo recapitulated the familiar arguments in favor of surrender ending with an urgent recommendation that Japan accept the Potsdam Declaration without further delay, if assurances were given on the question of the preservation of the national polity.

Suzuki then turned to the unloquacious Minister of the Navy. Admiral Yonai rose. "I agree with the Foreign Minister," he said. He resumed his seat.

General Anami, the War Minister, leapt fighting to his feet. He expressed his absolute disagreement, saying he believed that the nation should fight on, that the outcome of the Battle for Japan could not be known until it was fought, but that, in any case, if Japan were to surrender, she must insist on acceptance of her four conditions, guaranteeing not only the integrity of the Imperial structure but also Japan's right to disarm her own soldiers, conduct her own war trials, and limit the forces of occupation. General Umezu agreed, adding that Japan was still more than a match for the enemy and unconditional surrender now would only dishonor the heroic Japanese dead. In the event of surrender, he, like Anami, would insist on the four conditions.

It was now the turn of Admiral Toyoda, the Navy Chief of Staff, to speak, but Suzuki called instead on Baron Hiranuma, who had been invited to the meeting in an attempt to involve the Privy Council in the proceedings, since constitutionally the Council was expected to ratify all foreign treaties. Hiranuma subjected the ministers to a series of precise and exhaustive questions about Japan's unfortunate Soviet experience, about the identity of the men likely to be classified as "war criminals," about the nation's ability to protect herself against raids and invasion, and about the probability of civil disorder in the event of immediate surrender. Hiranuma's conclusion was that, aside from the continuance of the Imperial polity, which went without saying, negotiation on the other three conditions was not necessarily doomed to failure.

Admiral Toyoda, given his chance to speak at last, repeated the arguments in favor of continuing the war and concluded with the remark that he could not guarantee the Navy's behavior unless its disarming was conducted by the Japanese themselves.

Now the Premier rose once again. It is evident, he said, that we are unable to reach an agreement; in view of that fact, therefore, and of the urgency of the situation, there seems to be only one thing to do. Turning at last toward the head of the room, he said, "Your Imperial Majesty's decision is requested as to which proposal should be adopted, the Foreign Minister's or the one with the four conditions."

The silence in the stifling little room was absolute. It is impossible, now, to say how many of the eleven men sitting at the long tables knew, or suspected, that Suzuki was going to take the step, unheard-of in modern Japanese history, of asking the Emperor to make a decision; or to say how many were shocked to the marrow by so untraditional a procedure. In older days the pronouncement of an Imperial command was known as the Voice of the Crane, the crane being an Imperial symbol. It is said that the sound of a crane may still be heard in the sky after the sight of it is hidden from view. Now, at two o'clock in the morning of Friday, August 10th, 1945, the Voice of the Crane was about to be heard again in the land.

Continuing the war, said the Emperor quietly, can only result in the annihilation of the Japanese people and a prolongation of the suffering of all humanity. It seems obvious, he went on, that the nation is no longer able to wage war, and its ability to defend its own shores is doubtful. "That it is unbearable for me," His Majesty said, "to see my loyal troops disarmed goes without saying. . . . But the time has come to bear the unbearable." There was no longer any need for the Emperor to put his decision into words; nevertheless, he went on, in that quiet, controlled voice: "I give my sanction to the proposal to accept the Allied Proclamation on the basis outlined by the Foreign Minister." He walked slowly from the room.

In the silence, the white handkerchiefs reappeared—perhaps to wipe away the sweat induced by the August heat in that little room, perhaps to wipe away the tears that welled in the eyes of men who were now bound to deliver their country to the enemy. "His Majesty's decision," said Suzuki, "ought to be made the decision of this conference as well." Continued silence gave consent.

However, the only body in the country that possessed the constitutional authority to effect the surrender was the Cabinet. (Whether the Privy Council's approval was also required was a question that would arise later.) The Councilors left the Palace, therefore, for Suzuki's official residence, where the Cabinet meeting was to be held. Discussion here centered not on whether to accept the Imperial decision—for there was no longer any doubt about that, despite the Home Minister's reluctance—but on the wording of the note of surrender. At last that too was agreed upon, around four in the morning, and within three hours cables had been dispatched to Switzerland and Sweden, for transmission to the Allied powers.

The Japanese Government [the note said in part] are ready to accept the terms enumerated in the joint declaration which was issued at Potsdam on July 26th, 1945, by the heads of the Governments of the United States, Great Britain, and China, and later subscribed to by the Soviet Government, with the understanding that the said declaration does not comprise any demand which prejudices the prerogatives of His Majesty as a Sovereign Ruler.

Japan's long night of August 9th was ended at last—but a longer day was still to come.

"Suppose," the War Minister, General Anami, had said, during the previous night's meeting, "the enemy refuses to give you any assurance that the Imperial House will be preserved—will you go on fighting?" Premier Suzuki, of whom he had asked the question, looked at him for a moment. Then, "Yes," he said, "we will continue the war." Anami asked the same question of Admiral Yonai, the Navy Minister—and received the same reply.

The next morning, Friday, August 10th, Anami ordered all personnel in the War Ministry above the chief-of-section rank to gather at nine-thirty in the Ministry's underground bomb shelter. When he recounted what had occurred at the Imperial conference, their reaction was one of disbelief and shock. Though they had anticipated that some action of this sort might be taken, the reality of it caught them unprepared. The Army, which for so long had been the most powerful force in Japan, which had run the government and disobeyed the Emperor when his commands seemed "ill-advised," was now about to cease to exist, to disappear entirely from the life of Japan. That this would be one of the consequences of surrender, all the officers knew; and many feared that Japan also would cease to exist—in any recognizable form, at least.

So many emotions seemed to be raging in the hearts of the young officers, so many strange blends of emotion—love and hate, fear and dismay, the horror of defeat, the terror of dishonor, bewilderment at seeing the total imminent collapse of everything they had lived and sworn by: it is not surprising, perhaps, that their passions were sometimes uncontrollable, that their actions, as they tried to fight their way out of a trap that had no exit, shifted from moment to moment, unvarying only in loyalty to the Emperor. Whatever the officers did, they were convinced, they did in loyalty; some, unfortunately, decided they knew better than the object of their loyalty how to be loyal.

The Minister's voice was firm, his attitude unequivocal. "We have no alternative," he said, "but to abide by the Emperor's decision. Whether we fight on or whether we surrender now depends on the enemy's reply to our note. No matter which we do, you must all remember that you are soldiers, you must obey orders, you must not deviate from strict military discipline. In the crisis that faces us, the uncontrolled actions of one man could bring about the ruin of the entire country."

A younger officer stood up. "The War Minister," he said, "has told us to obey his orders whether we fight on or whether we surrender. Is the War Minister actually considering surrender?"

A cold wind swept across the room, fanning the smoldering fires of rebellion.

There was a silence.

Then the crack of Anami's swagger stick on the table sounded as loud as a gunshot. "Anyone who isn't willing to obey my orders," said the Minister coldly, "will have to do so over my dead body."

Because of the thirteen-hour difference in time, it was around the same hour, that Friday morning, that President Truman held a conference in the White House to discuss the news of Japan's capitulation, which had been received over radio broadcasts beamed directly from Tokyo to the United States. Among those present at the early-morning meeting were the Secretary of State, the Secretary of War, the Secretary of the Navy, and the President's personal chief of staff.

The President questioned each of the four men as to whether he thought the Japanese note could be accepted as the "unconditional surrender" the Allies had demanded. The trouble, of course, lay in the phrase, "with the understanding that the said declaration does not comprise any demand which prejudices the prerogatives of His Majesty as a Sovereign Ruler," a phrase that Baron Hiranuma had successfully insisted on seeing written into the note. As originally envisaged, this "condition" had read: "with the understanding that the said declaration does not include any demand for a change in the status of His Majesty under the national laws." Hiranuma had insisted that the nation and its Emperor were contemporaneous, having existed simultaneously since the beginning, and that therefore Imperial sovereignty was in no way dependent on national law. The Japanese word that Hiranuma had successfully insisted on was *taiken;* and Toshikazu Kase, who translated the note into English, said that he "experienced a moment's hesitation in choosing the word 'prerogatives.'" Hiranuma's word "literally translated meant powers inherent in the crown."

To the President's question, Mr. Henry Stimson, the Secretary of War, replied that he felt the Imperial presence was essential not only to the Japanese but also to the Americans, to facilitate the process of surrender and avoid bloodshed between occupying and defeated troops. Mr. James Forrestal, the Secretary of the Navy, and Admiral William D. Leahy, the President's chief of staff, agreed. Mr. James F. Byrnes, the Secretary of State, was more doubtful; he pointed out that both Roosevelt and Churchill had insisted Japanese surrender must be "unconditional" and that since both Britain and China had signed the Potsdam Proclamation they ought to be consulted before the United States agreed to any "conditions" whatsoever.

The decision was made to await the arrival of the official version of the note.

That same morning Tokyo was heavily bombed; hundreds of B-29's showered incendiaries over the capital, while thousands of other planes bombed other Japanese cities. Although it was called "the most impressive and nerve-wracking demonstration of the whole war," it was by no means unique; air-raids had been steadily mounting in intensity, and by now millions of people had no houses to live in, no clothes to wear, and almost nothing to eat. The Japanese people were perhaps approaching the limit of their endurance: many other peoples might by now have gone beyond it.

The temperature rose as the muggy August day wore on. Government nerves were on edge now that the decision had at last been taken and the period of waiting had set in. The people of Japan were still unaware that their government had—with that one condition— accepted the Potsdam Proclamation, but it was obvious to them that some drastic change was imminent, for the Soviet declaration of war had appeared in Friday morning's papers, with its statement that "the proposal of the Japanese Government to the Soviet Union on mediation in the war in the Far East loses all basis. . . ." This was the first the Japanese people knew that their government had sought Russian "good offices"—and failed to win them.

So a secret or two had been spilled, but the biggest secret of all was still being jealously guarded. The Army had kept the people of Japan in the dark for so many years now about what was really going on that the government feared what effect a sudden announcement of surrender might have. Two meetings were therefore held during the day of the 10th to discuss this problem—one of the Jushin, or Senior Statesmen, a body composed of ex-premiers which had considerable influence; and one of the Cabinet itself.

Once again there was difference of opinion, uncertainty, a seemingly endless reiteration of on-the-other-hand's. Every statement appeared to have an equally valid counter-statement. If, for instance, announcement of Japanese acceptance of the Potsdam Proclamation was made at once, it would be possible to give the people an immediate directive and so perhaps minimize the destructive effects of the announcement. But, on the other hand, if preservation of the Imperial structure was not guaranteed by the Allies, Japan's will to fight might by then have been dissipated, perhaps forever.

The Cabinet decided, finally, to say nothing for the moment about either the Emperor's decision or the Japanese note of acceptance; instead, the Director of the Information Bureau was instructed to issue an ambiguous statement that would do no more than convey the suggestion that a momentous change might perhaps be announced fairly soon by the government.

The statement was prepared by the Information Bureau staff, revised by its director, Hiroshi Shimomura, gone over by Foreign Minister Togo, by Admiral Yonai, and especially carefully by General Anami, and then sent to the Tokyo radio station for the afternoon news broadcast.

At the same time, another statement was being prepared without either the knowledge or the approval of the Cabinet. When General Anami had spoken, that morning, to the officers of the War Ministry, Lieutenant Colonel Masao Inaba, of the Budget Branch of the Military Affairs Bureau, listened with particular care and particular dismay. He decided that until the surrender actually occurred, the Japanese Army must fight on with undiminished vigor, and so he began to prepare a statement to be broadcast to overseas troops, having first obtained the War Minister's approval of his idea.

After he had completed the first draft, he showed it to the Vice-Minister of War as well as to a couple of other officers, including Colonel Okitsugu Arao, of the Military Affairs Section. Following revisions, the officers wanted the Minister himself to read it, but he was busy elsewhere, working on the official Cabinet statement, so Colonel Arao agreed to take it to General Anami's official residence later in the day.

Shortly after Arao left, Lieutenant Colonel Masahiko Takeshita (Anami's brother-in-law) arrived at the Ministry with another staff officer to get Inaba's statement for the seven o'clock news broadcast. As Arao had the revised draft with him, Inaba changed his first draft, as nearly as he could remember, to conform with the revisions and gave it to Takeshita.

When the Director of the Information Bureau, Hiroshi Shimomura, reached his headquarters with the revised draft of the official Cabinet statement, which he and General Anami had been working on, he was told that the Army had ordered a "proclamation" over the name of General Anami to be read at the evening broadcast and printed in the morning newspapers. Shimomura telephoned Anami, and in the course of their conversation he got the impression that Anami knew little or nothing about the statement but that extremely strong pressure was being applied by the younger officers. Shimomura conjectured that if he refused to release the "proclamation," Anami might be assassinated.

In Washington, both the State Department and the War Department were drafting replies to the Japanese note. When the two were compared, the Secretary of War agreed that the State Department draft was more suitable, and the President, with the Cabinet's agreement, approved it.

The second paragraph was in reply to Japanese insistence on preservation of the Imperial polity:

From the moment of surrender the authority of the Emperor and the Japanese Government to rule the state shall be subject to the Supreme Commander of the Allied Powers who will take such steps as he deems proper to effectuate the surrender terms.

The next paragraph began, "The Emperor and the Japanese High Command will be required to sign the surrender terms. . . ."

Copies of the proposed reply to Japan were sent to London, Moscow, and Chungking.

At seven o'clock, on their regular evening news broadcast, the Japanese at home and overseas heard two statements.

The first, over the authority of War Minister Anami, said, in part, "We have but one choice: we must fight on until we win the sacred war to preserve our national polity. We must fight on, even if we have to chew grass and eat earth and live in fields—for in our death there is a chance of our country's survival. The hero Kusunoki pledged to live and die seven times in order to save Japan from disaster. We can do no less. . . ."

The Cabinet's statement was not so forthright. After announcing that the enemy was making use of a "new type" of bomb unparalleled in ruthlessness and barbarity, the statement concluded:

Our fighting forces will no doubt be able to repulse the enemy's attack, but we must recognize that we are facing a situation that is as bad as it can be. The government will do all it can to defend the homeland and preserve the honor of the country but it expects that Japan's hundred million will also rise to the occasion, overcoming whatever obstacles may lie in the path of the preservation of our national polity.

Perhaps it was fortunate that the Japanese people had put their minds away for the duration; otherwise they might not have known what to think.

Another broadcast was being beamed away from Tokyo that afternoon. Fearful of the Army, of its strict censorship and its violent reaction to frustration, the Foreign Ministry had been unable to prevent the release of the "Anami Proclamation"; nevertheless, it authorized the Domei News Agency to broadcast, in Morse code, the text of Japan's acceptance of the Allied declaration. The Foreign Office hoped, in this way, to forestall the third atomic bomb which rumor said was to be dropped on Tokyo on August 12th. It believed also that once the people of the world heard that Japan wanted peace, they would be so relieved their governments would be forced to accept Japan's sole condition even if they found it unacceptable.

The Army, which had neglected to censor Morse code broadcasts, was extremely annoyed when it learned of the Foreign Ministry's action, but to the Ministry's reply that it had, after all, only communicated what had already been commanded by the Emperor and approved by the Cabinet, the Army could make no open objection. It could, however, and it did begin to consider suitable retaliation.

London approved Washington's proposed reply to Japan with one exception. Attlee, Bevin, and Churchill all agreed that to require the Emperor to sign the instrument of surrender was not diplomatic and suggested instead that the note read: "The Emperor shall authorize and ensure the signature by the government of Japan and the Japanese General Headquarters of the surrender terms. . . ." Washington concurred at once.

Moscow attempted to delay giving its answer, perhaps because it wanted the war to go on a little longer, and when the answer finally came, it was unsatisfactory. Molotov wanted to see two Supreme Commanders, one American and one Russian; Averell H. Harriman, America's ambassador, replied that that was "absolutely inadmissible." After some further procrastination, Moscow backed down and Washington received the agreement it desired.

Chungking had sent immediate word of its approval.

By Saturday morning, August 11th, then, the United States had secured the concurrence of its fellow-signatories and was able to set about the business of replying to the Japanese government by way of Switzerland.

Both Stimson and Forrestal tried to persuade the President to stop all bombing of Japan immediately, but Truman decided that this might encourage the Japanese to attempt further negotiation. He ordered air and naval activity to continue.

Saturday morning, August 11th, in Tokyo, thirteen hours earlier, newspapers appeared on the streets with both Anami's proclamation and the official Cabinet statement. The people of Japan now had the opportunity, as the air-raid warnings howled in the background, to study these two contradictory declarations in greater detail. They were still wholly ignorant of the fact that their leaders were impatiently awaiting the Allied reply to Japan's "conditional" acceptance of the Potsdam Proclamation.

"I lived through what was literally a life of torture," wrote Toshikazu Kase, of the Foreign Office, describing that Saturday; and the

43

sentence describes also the state of mind of most of the people who were privy to the secret of Japan's momentous decision—but not of all: some, as it turned out, were not content with the passive act of waiting.

Ironically, the American Secretary of State, Mr. Byrnes, in describing that same day, wrote: "Never have I known time to pass so slowly!" But, because of the difference in time, the Saturday of which he wrote was half a day later than Mr. Kase's Saturday: it was after the United States had sent its reply to Japan.

Japan, meanwhile, continued in limbo: it still did not know whether it was at peace or war, whether it was to be hopefully reanimated out of its own ashes or whether it was to fight a last-ditch battle for survival against an immeasurably stronger enemy. Nor had its leaders been able to achieve a consensus on which alternative they preferred.

Two of the Emperor's younger brothers were officers in the Army, one in the Navy. The latter, Prince Takamatsu, invited members of the Imperial Family to a meeting at his house to hear Foreign Minister Togo's account of the situation. Prince Mikasa, the youngest of the brothers, an Army officer, had been visited by some fellow-officers who favored continuance of the war and who wanted the Imperial Prince's sanction. He refused, but he needed to know how things stood with Japan; Togo supplied the information.

Togo also conferred with Marquis Kido, the Emperor's Privy Seal and, in a sense, his spokesman. So did Premier Suzuki and Director Shimomura of the Bureau of Information. The Emperor received General Anami in audience, and the General—so his brother-in-law said later—reported that the Emperor had reprimanded him because of his "proclamation." Anami's explanation was that the Army would naturally have to go on fighting until the surrender became a fact. The War Minister was also questioned by the Cabinet on the same subject and gave much the same reply.

In a bomb-shelter at the War Office in Ichigaya, some fifteen officers met to decide what concrete steps needed to be taken to ensure the continued prosecution of the war. The "peace-faction," they decided, would have to go: Suzuki, Togo, and Kido were marked down for assassination. The Emperor might have to be "protected," even if that meant occupying the Imperial Palace.

Lieutenant Colonel Takeshita, who presided, assured his fellow-conspirators that they could count on the support of his brother-in-law, General Anami, the Minister of War. Once the biggest fish was in the net, the smaller fish would follow. If Lieutenant General Takeshi Mori, commander of the Imperial Guards, whose duty it was to protect the Emperor, refused to join the conspiracy, well, then he too would have to go.

Among the officers present at this meeting were Lieutenant Colonel Inaba, instigator of the "Anami Proclamation," and Major Kenji Hatanaka, who was later to figure far more prominently in the activities of this band of rebels. When at last they separated, it was on a note of optimism: there seemed no reason why their treasonous *coup d'état* should not succeed and once it did, of course, it would cease to be treason. The sacred honor of Japan and her Imperial Army would then remain unstained by surrender. Only death could cancel defeat; only more death could appease the souls of the already dead. The officers were not affected by the sufferings of the people—they felt themselves equal to the sacrifice of asking the people to go on suffering a little longer.

Both officers and people were on Marquis Kido's mind. He was aware of the danger of conspiracy, and he was aware also of the danger of a sudden announcement of defeat. He agreed that the safest—in fact the only—person to make the announcement was the Emperor himself, and the Emperor repeated his assurance that he would do whatever was deemed necessary.

Apprehension in both government and Army mounted as both

waited impatiently for the enemy's reply. Most hoped that the reply would be flexible enough to enable the government to secure peace—and the Army to accept it; a few fervently desired the opposite. No reply, however, came. Then, forty-five minutes after the day of waiting ended, the Foreign Office monitored a broadcast from San Francisco that answered its question.

The answer was disheartening.

The Foreign Office radio had picked up the broadcast at 00:45, and within the next couple of hours both the Navy and the Domei News Agency received the same broadcast. Soon everyone in Japan who had known of the government's offer to surrender—"with the understanding that the said declaration does not comprise any demand which prejudices the prerogatives of His Majesty as a Sovereign Ruler"—now knew also that the United States insisted that "the authority of the Emperor and the Japanese government to rule the state shall be subject to the Supreme Commander of the Allied Powers."

But the monitored broadcasts had been received in Morse code. Had they been correctly received? And if so, how was the phrase "subject to" to be interpreted? What, precisely, did it mean? The Foreign Office was well aware that the Army, though unfamiliar with both the English language and the language of diplomacy, would make its own interpretation and the interpretation would not encourage acceptance of the Potsdam Proclamation as clarified by Mr. Byrnes. The Vice-Minister of Foreign Affairs, Shunichi Matsumoto, as soon as he had studied the note, conferred with Hisatsune Sakomizu, the Chief Cabinet Secretary, on how to present the text to their superiors. They decided that "subject to" ought to be translated in the sense of "controlled by" rather than "obedient to," and after some further unhappy deliberation they agreed that the second-to-last paragraph did not compromise the Emperor's sovereignty, although they knew that the Army would use it as a trumpet-call for further battle. The paragraph read:

The ultimate form of government of Japan shall, in accordance with the Potsdam Declaration, be established by the freely expressed will of the Japanese people.

If the word "government" included the Emperor, then Japan was obligated to reject the American reply. But Sakomizu and Matsumoto decided that it did not; and on this decision they separated, one to present the case to Suzuki, the other to Togo.

The events of that crowded day of cross-purpose and back-stage manipulation, of shifting alliance and preparation for rebellion, of passion and apprehension are not easy to disentangle. No one's mood was of the kind to encourage accurate note-taking or sharp memory.

Apparently the Emperor was apprised by Marquis Kido, very early in the morning, of the monitored broadcast and of its contents. Kido, who was one of the chief targets of the pro-war faction, had now taken up permanent residence within the Imperial Palace grounds, so as to be less available to the assassin's bullet and more available to His Majesty. During the rest of the day, he was in constant attendance on the Emperor.

It was at eight o'clock in the morning that the Foreign Minister, having studied the note and its tentative translation, decided that Japan must accept it. Although by no means fully satisfied with the American reply, for he too of course foresaw the use the military would try to make of it, Togo believed that within its terms the Imperial polity could be preserved and that Japan, if she rejected the note now, was lost.

Around the same time, the Army and the Navy, personified by their younger, more fiery officers, decided that Japan must finally reject it. They stormed into the quarters of General Umezu and Admiral Toyoda and demanded a public announcement of rejection.

So insistent were they that the two Chiefs of Staff went to the Palace and at eight-twenty were received in audience. After they had expressed their objections to the note, the Emperor, who apparently could not make out whether they were speaking on their own behalf or on that of others, thanked them and said that no decision could be reached until the official text had been received and studied.

The two Chiefs of Staff had, it seems, asked for an audience without prior consultation with their superiors, and Admiral Yonai, the Navy Minister, was extremely annoyed when he learned of Toyoda's action. The War Minister, General Anami, was more favorably inclined, although he too was placed in an awkward position when, at ten o'clock, a dozen of the younger officers rushed into his room, all of them in a state of the highest excitement. Their spokesman, once again, was Lieutenant Colonel Takeshita, who announced, in a tone of cold ferocity, "The proposed surrender must not take place. If it does, the War Minister ought to commit suicide with his own sword." Anami stared at his brother-in-law, lips compressed, but remained silent.

At eleven o'clock the Emperor received Foreign Minister Togo, heard his interpretation of the Allied note, and agreed with his recommendation to accept it. He asked the Foreign Minister to relay his desire to Premier Suzuki.

But Suzuki was then being subjected to pressure by two visitors who had quite an opposite end in view. The visitors were the War Minister, General Anami, and Baron Hiranuma, the President of the Privy Council, who had come to a last-minute agreement on their desire to see the American note rejected and their belief that the weakest link in the chain around the Throne was the Prime Minister himself. Old, confused by the events of the past few days, and vacillatory by nature, he was soon persuaded that the American reply meant, in reality, the end of the Imperial structure. Hiranuma declared that since the Emperor was divine, there could be no question of the people deciding his status: this would constitute an inadmissible change in the national polity. Anami reminded Suzuki that they had agreed to reject the Proclamation unless the national polity was guaranteed. The old man agreed to stand firm with Anami and Hiranuma in defending the Throne.

After he left Suzuki, Anami went to call on Prince Mikasa, the Emperor's third brother. Because the Prince was considered to be unconventional, the War Minister perhaps thought he could enlist him on the side of the warriors, but His Imperial Highness told Anami brusquely that ever since the Manchurian Incident the Army had acted contrary to the Emperor's desire and were continuing to do so.

A little later in the day, Prince Mikasa and the other Imperial princes, with their families, convened at the Palace, where they pledged the Emperor their whole-hearted support in his decision to effect a peaceful settlement of the war.

At the same time, the Cabinet met in extraordinary session. After Suzuki had read a translation of the American note, Anami and Hiranuma reiterated their arguments of the morning, and Anami also demanded the reinstatement of two conditions that had been discarded. Togo leapt angrily to his feet. He declared that any further request would lead to a breaking off of negotiations, which was contrary to the Imperial decision, and that to ensure the continuance of the war in this manner was "senseless behavior." With that he left the room and telephoned Vice-Minister Matsumoto, who pressed him to have the meeting adjourned so as to avoid the taking of a vote. Togo returned in time to hear Suzuki say that since the Allied reply did not guarantee the preservation of the Imperial polity, Japan must ask further clarification—and be prepared to continue the war unless satisfaction was forthcoming. The Premier's statements, said Togo quickly, merited careful consideration; on the other hand, unless Japan had some chance of victory, she ought to sue for peace. "I therefore propose," he went on, giving no one a chance to speak, "that the meeting be adjourned and that the question be reopened after the official communication from the Allies has been received." The Cabinet rose.

Togo, furious, had a private conversation with Suzuki in which he told him bluntly that his attitude was incomprehensible in view of the fact that the Emperor himself had decided on surrender, and then he added a veiled threat that unless Suzuki voluntarily returned to his earlier point of view, Togo would ask the Emperor to command him to do so.

With that he left the Premier and reported the day's disasters to Marquis Kido, who assured Togo that he would do everything possible to bring Suzuki back into line.

The Metropolitan Police Department, as a result of the wild rumors that were flying between the War Ministry and the Navy Ministry, posted special guards at strategic points in the city and began keeping strict watch over the officers who were thought to be involved in the rumored conspiracy.

Togo's aide, Vice-Minister Matsumoto, got in touch with the Telegraph Section of the Ministry and ordered the officer on duty to date any official communication that arrived during the night as of the following morning. His idea apparently was to provide Togo and the rest of the "peace party" with a little time in which to reorganize their defenses. Thus, Byrnes' official communication, which reached Tokyo at 6:40 p.m., August 12th, was stamped 7:30 a.m., August 13th.

At nine-thirty that Sunday night, Premier Suzuki was called to Kido's office in the Palace. He listened in silence as the Privy Seal repeated, once again, the arguments they all knew so well in favor of immediate surrender. Kido painted a graphic—but not inaccurate—picture of the hundreds of thousands, and perhaps millions, of people who would be sacrificed if war continued. He concluded with the still more telling argument for Suzuki—that surrender was, in any case, His Majesty's desire. The old man agreed to stand firm with Kido and Togo in defending the Throne.

It was a clear night. General Anami looked across the plain toward the far distance, where the sharp, lovely silhouette of Mount Fuji was outlined against the still glowing summer sky. He would not see that view very often again. Silently he went through the gate. He had come to his house in Mitaka, just outside Tokyo, to say farewell to his family; he had a pretty clear idea of what the future was likely to bring.

During the night he was visited by Lieutenant Colonel Ida and Major Hatanaka, that delicate, pale young man who was one of the most fanatic of the younger officers in his determination to pursue the war to the end. Their purpose in this late-night call was to request the War Minister to do everything in his power to prevent acceptance of the Potsdam Proclamation. The General, torn between the desire of his superiors to end the war and the bellicose fanaticism of his younger officers, remained non-committal. His conferences with other aides continued.

Finally, around four in the morning of Monday, August 13th, he ordered Major Hayashi to take a verbal message to the Chief of Staff, General Umezu, saying that the War Minister was considering asking Field Marshal Hata to make an appeal to the Emperor, on behalf of the senior officers of the Army, to refuse the Allied surrender terms. The War Minister, said the Major, would like an opinion from the Chief of Staff.

Umezu was silent. He paced up and down the room for a time. Then, at last, he said, "You must forgive me—I favor acceptance of the Potsdam Proclamation."

This reply, which Hayashi brought back to the War Minister, was too surprising to be taken in immediately, for Anami had thought of Umezu as one of his firmest allies. He retired at last, to try to sleep over his problem for an hour or two at least.

During that same night a cable arrived at the Foreign Office from the Japanese Minister in Stockholm, saying that both Russia and China were opposed to the Emperor and that opinion in Britain was hardening in the same direction. The United States, said the Minister, was being pressed to change its mind, while the Soviet Union was driving forward as fast as it could in China: any delay in the acceptance of America's terms could only make the situation worse, if not downright impossible, for Japan. The Minister's message only gave further confirmation of what the Foreign Office already knew; it did not help to solve their problem.

At seven-ten that morning General Anami was being ushered into Marquis Kido's office. Pessimism, said the General, never won a war; and since he believed that a passionate defense of the homeland would lead to more acceptable Allied terms, he strongly favored a continuance of a state of belligerence. Kido pointed out that the Emperor himself did not object to the provisions the Army found so offensive and that in any case he had made his decision and the decision had been communicated to the Allies: if His Majesty now changed his mind, he would look like a fool or a madman. How could Anami desire to see the Emperor rendered so absurd? Anami smiled. "You don't know what it's like in the Ministry," he said, as he took his leave. But the General underestimated Marquis Kido, who had been the object of attacks by fanatics for some time and who realized how difficult Anami's position was. The War Minister was not a fanatic—but he was an Army man, he wanted to do his best for the sovereign and the nation he had sworn to defend but also for the Army whose leader he was.

He decided not to go back to his Ministry. At nine o'clock he joined the rest of the Supreme War Councilors at a meeting in the underground bomb shelter of the Prime Minister's official residence. To the surprise of no one present, the Big Six were still split three to three: Suzuki, Togo, and Yonai on one side; Anami and the two Chiefs of Staff, Umezu and Toyoda, on the other; immediate acceptance *versus* more favorable terms or continued war. Umezu had wavered, but he would not desert his chief. Toyoda refused to accept Togo's interpretation of "subject to," nor could he stomach the provision calling for the "freely expressed will of the people."

Toyoda and Umezu were now summoned out of the meeting for an audience with the Emperor, who pointed out that as long as Japan was negotiating diplomatically for a ceasefire, action against the enemy should be kept to a minimum. The two Chiefs of Staff, on behalf of Imperial Headquarters, gave the Emperor their undertaking to initiate no aggressive action whatsoever and to take only such defensive action as was necessary. They then returned to the Supreme War Council, where the deliberations continued.

The deliberations at Ichigaya were of a different order. The War Ministry was like a huge, disturbed ant-hill, with hundreds of warrior ants scurrying back and forth through the long corridors, their antennae raised to receive whatever emanations might serve to solve their dilemma. To act without the approval of the War Minister would be difficult, if not impossible, and yet Anami would say neither yes nor no. A forthright yes was what they most ardently desired. But a forthright no would free them, at least, to attempt to act without him. The warrior ants were driven almost by instinct to defend their ant-hill—though the result might well be the destruction not only of the hill but of the nest that sustained it and of most of its hundred million inhabitants as well.

The Supreme War Council, having still reached no conclusion, adjourned at noon for lunch.

In Washington, President Truman, although he was growing impatient, decided to trust the indications from Tokyo that acceptance was now only a matter of hours away. In his directive to General MacArthur, he said, among other things:

From the moment of surrender, the authority of the Emperor and the Japanese Government to rule the state will be subject to you and you will take such steps as you deem proper to effectuate the surrender terms.

In Tokyo, Admiral Yonai, released from the inconclusive meeting of the Supreme War Council, returned to his office at the Navy Ministry. He summoned his Vice-Chief of Staff, Admiral Onishi, the blustering and aggressive inventor of the Divine-Wind *(kamikaze)* suicide attacks that had caused such terrible destruction among the enemy. The Navy Minister had learned that Onishi had spoken so bitterly to certain members of the Cabinet about the Minister's lack of will-to-fight that the implication was almost present he considered Yonai a coward. When Yonai asked him how he had dared to talk in this disparaging manner of his own Minister, Onishi broke down and began to cry. He tried to apologize but couldn't speak through the sobs that choked him.

In the Ministry at Ichigaya, the warrior ants were in ferment again. They had set down the details of a plan they hoped would free Japan and her Emperor of the cowardly, peace-mongering traitors who wanted to deliver them both to the enemy. The officers went first to the Vice-Minister of War, Lieutenant General Tadaichi Wakamatsu, who listened to them in a silence they took to be antipathetic, and so they proceeded on to the Minister of War himself, General Korechika Anami. Present, in addition to Anami and Wakamatsu, were Lieutenant General Nukada, director of the Personnel Bureau, and Colonel Hiroo Sato, chief of the War Preparations Section.

One of the young officers began to present the project they had concocted, but Sato interrupted him. "With the situation as it is at present," he said, "I cannot agree to implement your plan."

The young officers were about to protest when Major Kenji Hatanaka, of the Military Affairs Section, burst into the room. Almost white with rage, he pointed a finger at Sato and shouted, "There is a traitor in the Army! Measures must be taken to relieve him of his duties!"

No one moved. To the silent men in the room it seemed that the explosion must come now.

Then the quiet voice of General Anami, the Minister of War, was heard. "At this point," he said, "the chief thing is that we all have confidence in one another." Then he smiled at Major Hatanaka, who was something of a protégé of his, and was about to leave the room on his way to a Cabinet meeting, when a spokesman for the group of young officers stepped forward.

"The officers in the Ministry of War," he said, "have determined to follow their Minister in whatever course he takes. Please be assured of that."

As Anami left, he noticed that the faces of the young officers were as flushed as though they had been drinking. He was about to confront the Cabinet, to insist on further assurances from the United States; and yet he knew that before very long he would have to confront the young men too—or fall in with their plans.

Not only were the young officers in this state of abnormal tension: small groups of youthful civilians were also determined to resist surrender actively. One such was the Students' Federation for Victory[3], composed entirely of third-year chemistry students of the Yokohama Higher Industrial School, who, after hearing a fiery talk by an alumnus of the school, Captain Takeo Sasaki, decided, late that Monday afternoon, to use what arms they had to continue their own prosecution of the war—no matter what the country's statesmen decreed.

In another part of Tokyo, a solitary motorcyclist carefully threaded his way across the crazy, pot-holed roads, the staccato of his engine beating against the silence of the partly deserted capital. The rider was Major Hidemasa Koga, staff officer of the Imperial Guards Division and son-in-law of General Hideki Tojo. It was toward Tojo's house in Setagaya, in the south-western part of central Tokyo, that the Major was now making his noisy way. Although his own house stood next door to Tojo's, Koga had been there infrequently of late, for he had been working on the construction of a new air-raid shelter for the Imperial Family and sleeping at Division headquarters. Today was his wife Makie's birthday —but other, more portentous matters were preying on his mind.

The roar of the motorcycle signaled his arrival, and his mother-in-law hurried out to meet him. After a brief greeting, he headed not for his wife but for the study of his father-in-law, the ex-premier of Japan. Major Koga, a handsome, dashing, young cavalry officer, contrasted sharply with General Tojo, who was short (less than five feet, five inches) and bald, with old-fashioned spectacles and an ill-kempt moustache.

The two men were not destined to speak that afternoon. Seeing his father-in-law engaged with a visitor, Koga continued on to the back of the house. "Mother," he said, "you haven't put the house in order yet, have you? Division Headquarters are all in order." Mrs. Tojo had no idea what to make of his words.

Abruptly he picked up his eleven-month-old son and said to his wife, "I want to talk to you alone." They went down into the cellar, to the family air-raid shelter, and when, after a very few moments, they came back up, he said to Mrs. Tojo's questioning look, "I came to ask Makie if she had my hair and nail clippings." These, in Japan, are legacies of the dead: Mrs. Tojo glanced at her daughter.

The Major continued, "I'll be going home soon now. Just remem-

*The Emperor in his coronation robes
(November, 1928)*

As a young child

With his father, Emperor Taisho (on the right); beside the young heir-apparent is his brother, Prince Chichibu

As a schoolboy, aged seven

As Prince Regent, toward the close of his father's reign

As Prince Regent with Princess Naga-ko (the Present Empress)

With his brother, Prince Chichibu

Reviewing the troops (1939)

At the fiftieth anniversary of the National Diet, November 19, 1940

Reviewing the students of a Seinen Gakko (youth school), May 22, 1941

The Emperor presiding over a meeting of the Supreme War Council

Inspecting bomb damage in Tokyo, March 18, 1945

In the Goseimu Shitsu

With his family on the beach at Hayama, 1946

With the Grand Chamberlain, Hisa-nori Fujita, visiting wounded soldiers

The Imperial car, a Mercedes Benz, with the royal emblem— a chrysanthemum

Major Kenji Hatanaka, chief conspirator

Lieutenant Colonel Jiro Shiizaki

Above: Lieutenant General Takeshi Mori, commander of the First Imperial Guards Division

Lieutenant Colonel Masataka Ida

*Lieutenant Colonel Masa-
hiko Takeshita*

*Takeshita as he appears today,
in the uniform of the Self Defense
Agency*

Above: Major Hidemasa Koga

Captain Takeo Sasaki

Sasaki as he appears today (holding book) with (left) R.B. Pal, one of the presiding justices at the Tokyo War Crimes Trial, and (center) former prime minister Nobusuke Kishi.

Naval Captain Yasuna Kozono (center)

Colonel Okitsugu Arao

General Shizuichi Tanaka, commander of the Eastern District Army

Colonel Tomomi Oyadomari

Oyadomari's wife and his two children

ber one thing—when a storm comes, don't turn away, keep your eyes open and your face up and walk straight into it."

With these words, Koga left. When, a little later, General Tojo's visitor had also departed, and the family was alone, the two women told the General about the strange behavior of his son-in-law. He headed, almost immediately, for the Ministry of War at Ichigaya.

The Cabinet met again that afternoon in an attempt to attain the unanimity denied to the Supreme War Council. Although the Chiefs of Staff were not Cabinet members, Anami was not alone in his opposition to immediate acceptance of the Potsdam Proclamation: the Home Minister declared that he did not believe the national polity could be preserved under foreign occupation, and the Minister of Justice affirmed that the idea of the people deciding their own form of government was incompatible with the Japanese structure. The meeting had begun at four. At seven Suzuki asked for a consensus. Although twelve ministers were in favor of immediate acceptance, three were opposed, and one was undecided. Inasmuch, said Suzuki, as we have failed once again to agree, I propose to ask His Majesty for a second Imperial decision. The Cabinet adjourned.

After the meeting, Anami asked the Premier a question. "Will you give me just two more days," he said, "before you go to the Emperor again?"

Suzuki shook his head. "I'm sorry " he replied. "Our opportunity is now—we must seize it at once."

After Anami left, a Navy officer who had overheard the conversation repeated the War Minister's request. "Couldn't you possibly wait just the two days?" he asked.

"Impossible," replied the Premier. "If we don't act now, the Russians will penetrate not only Manchuria and Korea but northern Japan as well. If that happens, our country is finished. We must act now, while our chief adversary is still the United States."

"General Anami," said the Navy officer, "will kill himself."

"Yes," Suzuki said, "that will be very regrettable." He too believed, as did Togo and Kido, that although Anami opposed them, he was doing what he could to prevent his officers from engaging in open rebellion. It seems that Chief Cabinet Secretary Sakomizu overheard, that very day, a telephone conversation in which Anami told his headquarters an outright lie—he advised patience, for the Cabinet, he said, is beginning to agree with us. Later, Suzuki declared that it was Anami's refusal to resign from the Cabinet that had made a peaceful termination of the war possible.

Now that the Prime Minister had announced his intention of seeking a second decision from the Throne, it was imperative for the "peace party" to move as quickly as possible, for the announcement would obviously spur the officers to more intense, and perhaps fatal, action. Sakomizu secured the signatures of the two Chiefs of Staff on the petition for an Imperial conference, but they made him promise that the petition would not be used until they gave their consent. They then requested a private interview with Togo.

Time was running out, and both factions were aware of it. At eight o'clock, ten of the young officers called on Minister Anami at his official residence at Miyakezaka. It was a little cooler than in the darkening, rubble-strewn heart of the city, but nevertheless the officers were mopping their faces as they entered the Minister's study. They had come to secure his approval of an Army *coup d'état*, to take place at ten o'clock the following morning.

Major Hatanaka said first that the advocates of peace were planning to assassinate General Anami if he persisted in his opposition to immediate surrender. Anami merely laughed and turned to Colonel Arao, chief of the Military Affairs Section of the Ministry. Arao was in almost as awkward a position as Anami himself: he knew that Anami would never support a *coup d'état* and yet here he was, acting as spokesman for the rebellious officers. He outlined the points that they considered crucial: Japan was not to surrender until she had obtained confirmation that her national polity would be preserved; although the Imperial decision had been made, there still remained to be determined to what extent the Emperor had been influenced by the men around him; Marquis Kido, Premier Suzuki, Foreign Minister Togo, and Admiral Yonai were to be imprisoned; martial law was to be proclaimed; and the Imperial Palace was to be isolated. Execution of the *coup* presupposed the cooperation of General Anami, the Minister of War; General Umezu, the Army Chief of Staff; General Shizuichi Tanaka, Commander of the Eastern District Army; and General Mori, Commander of the First Imperial Guards Division. It was Colonel Arao who had insisted that the four generals must come to an agreement before any action be taken.

Anami's reply was that the plan seemed insufficiently detailed to be effective. He did not say whether he favored it or not. When the officers pressed him for some definite word, he told Colonel Arao to return at midnight for another discussion. He refused to be urged any further at that time and bade the officers goodnight. When his aide, Major Hayashi, remonstrated with him for not having given the conspirators his outright refusal, Anami shrugged. "Well," he said, "I'll have another talk with Arao."

From nine till eleven that Monday evening, Togo was closeted with the two Chiefs of Staff, who tried in vain to change his mind about the terms of surrender. Just as the two generals were leaving, Admiral Onishi came unexpectedly into the room. He had another plan to offer the Foreign Minister. He was prepared, he said, if the Emperor approved, to sacrifice twenty million Japanese in *kamikaze* attacks. Onishi said there could be no doubt, under those circumstances, of victory; but the Foreign Minister rejected that generous offer too.

At midnight General Anami told Colonel Arao that he very much doubted the projected *coup* could succeed, but Arao departed, shortly thereafter, without having heard either yes or no from the Minister of War. Was the Army to attempt its *coup* or not? Anami promised a more positive answer in the morning.

"I don't know," he murmured, "whether Arao will interpret my remark to mean that I am opposed to the *coup*."

"I don't know either," said Hayashi.

Anami left his Ministry to try to get some sleep, but the Ministry itself remained awake. Several English-speaking Japanese born in America were busy in the information department monitoring Allied broadcasts and translating them into Japanese. Into their midst swept a cyclone called Colonel Tomomi Oyadomari, a member of the department, who had fought, and seen many of lators tearlessly receiving word of Japanese defeat was too much.

"Are you satisfied," he cried, "that Japan is losing the war? Does it make you happy?" He drew his sword. "I ought to kill you all!"

No one made any reply. No one knew what to reply.

"You're traitors, all of you!" Oyodomari shouted. Then, still shouting, still brandishing his sword, tears streaming down his face, he left the translators to their unprofitable tasks.

After only a few hours sleep, General Anami breakfasted the following morning, Tuesday, August 14th, with Field Marshal Hata, who had just returned to Tokyo to report on the situation at Hiroshima. He said that the city was indescribably pathetic and that the people who thought they had survived were now dead or dying of the painful effects of radiation; then he remarked that people who were underground seemed to have escaped. Anami asked him to be sure to report that fact to the Emperor: it might affect His Majesty's final decision.

At seven o'clock Anami went to Ichigaya, to his Ministry, and at seven o'clock Marquis Kido was shown a copy of a leaflet that the Allied powers were dropping by the millions over Japan, giving a Japanese translation of the government's note of acceptance, dated August 10th, and of Secretary Byrnes' reply dated August 11th. "One look," said the Privy Seal, "caused me to be stricken with consternation. . . . If the leaflets should fall into the hands of the troops and enrage them, a military *coup d'état* would become inevitable and make extremely difficult the execution of the planned policy. It would bring about the worst possible situation for our country." A few minutes later Kido was with the Emperor.

At Ichigaya the young officers insisted on seeing the Minister. Their projected *coup* was supposed to begin at ten o'clock, now only three hours away. They therefore required Anami's approval at once; they had already asked General Tanaka and General Mori to come to the Ministry for a special meeting. General Anami went with Colonel Arao to the office of the Chief of Staff, General Umezu, who declared that he was unalterably opposed to the projected *coup*—if for no other reason that than it was doomed to failure. The young officers, however, persisted in their demands on Anami, and Anami persisted in his refusal to be explicit.

Having shown the leaflet to His Majesty, Kido declared that the only way out of this most dangerous impasse was a second Imperial conference. The Emperor agreed and commanded Kido to communicate with the Premier. As he left the audience, Kido found Suzuki waiting for him. To Kido's question, whether he had called another meeting of the Supreme War Council, Suzuki replied, "I am having a hard time." The Army, he said, wanted him to wait until one o'clock, while the Navy wanted him to wait indefinitely. At eight-forty, Suzuki, accompanied by Kido, presented himself before the Emperor; twelve minutes later, the Emperor agreed to command an Imperial conference himself for ten-thirty.

At ten o'clock the Emperor summoned Field Marshal Hata, Field Marshal Sugiyama, and Fleet Admiral Nagano to an audience. He told them that he had determined to end the war and he commanded their support and that of the Army and the Navy.

At around the same time, Lieutenant Colonel Takeshita and Major Hatanaka received word that the Chief of Staff, General Umezu, had changed his mind about the planned *coup d'état*. This meant that if they now secured the War Minister's approval, the sailing would be clear. Highly elated, they rushed to the Imperial Palace only to find that Anami had already entered the underground bomb shelter where the Imperial conference, like its predecessor of five days before, was to be held.

By ten-thirty, the Cabinet members, the Supreme Councilors, and a few other high government officials were already assembled. They had been told not to wear formal court dress, but some, as the weather was typically hot and humid, had had to borrow ties and coats from their secretaries. The underground room was not only humid, it was downright damp, and water dripped from the walls of the stairway that led to it. By the time the Emperor arrived, twenty-five minutes later, the room was a little like a steam bath.

His Majesty, wearing a simple military uniform, walked directly to the front of the room and sat down on a plain, straight-backed chair at a small table covered in gold brocade. Behind him stood a gilded screen.

Chief Cabinet Secretary Sakomizu reported later that he had feared the Premier would not be able to carry the proceedings off, as he seemed particularly vague that morning and had not even prepared a speech, but Sakomizu's fears were groundless. Suzuki explained, clearly and succinctly, that His Majesty had called the conference so that discussion about acceptance of the Allied note might take place in his presence. He outlined the divergent points of view that had led to the deadlocked conferences of the past few days. Then he called on those whose opinions differed from the majority to express their differences. Umezu and Anami spoke briefly, Toyoda at length, all of them apparently under the stress of deep emotion. Toyoda had never spoken so well, but his arguments were depressingly, exhaustingly familiar to everyone in the room.

When the three dissenters from the majority opinion had finished, the Premier arose. He apologized to His Majesty for presenting him with a divided Cabinet and for soliciting once again an Imperial decision.

The silence in the crowded, sweltering little room was absolute. The twenty-four men who waited to hear, a second time, the Voice of the Crane were aware that they were ending an era, that all the death and destruction of the past forty-four months were now to have their harvest: the fall of the Japanese Empire. Hindsight told all of them now what some of them had known from the start—that Japan, less well endowed than her enemies in natural resources, productive capacity, and manpower, never really had a chance to win the war she had felt obliged to inaugurate. It was only the collective will of her people that had allowed her to prosecute the war this long; now that will was, hopefully, to be focused in another direction. The stains of the past were being washed away by the tears of the twenty-four men in that underground bomb shelter as they watched their Emperor rise and wipe his face with a white handkerchief,[4] before he began speak.

The tears of twenty-four men! In twenty-four hours, it would be the tears of the whole country: twenty-four of the longest, hardest, and perhaps most fateful hours in Japan's long history.

12 noon to 1 p.m.

"Anyone who disagrees will have to do so over my dead body."

General Korechika Anami

"I HAVE LISTENED CAREFULLY," SAID THE Emperor,[5] "to all of the arguments opposing Japan's acceptance of the Allied reply as it stands. My own opinion, however, has not changed. I shall now restate it. I have examined the conditions prevailing in Japan and in the rest of the world, and I believe that a continuation of the war offers nothing but continued destruction. I have studied the terms of the Allied reply, and I have come to the conclusion that they represent a virtually complete acknowledgement of our position as we outlined it in the note dispatched a few days ago."

The Emperor paused for a moment.

"In short," he said, "I consider the reply to be acceptable."

He wiped his eyes, then continued:

"Although some of you are apprehensive about the preservation of the national structure, I believe that the Allied reply is evidence of the good intentions of the enemy. The conviction and resolution of the Japanese people are, therefore, the most important consideration. That is why I favor acceptance of the reply.

"I fully understand how difficult it will be for the officers and men of the Army and the Navy to submit to being disarmed and to see their country occupied. I am aware also of the willingness of the people to sacrifice themselves for their nation and their Emperor. But I am not concerned with what may happen to me. I want to preserve the lives of my people. I do not want them subjected to further destruction. It is indeed hard for me to see my loyal soldiers disarmed and my faithful ministers punished as war criminals."

Here the Emperor paused again. As he went on, it was apparent that he was speaking with great effort.

"If we continue the war, Japan will be altogether destroyed. Although some of you are of the opinion that we cannot completely trust the Allies, I believe that an immediate and peaceful end to the war is preferable to seeing Japan annihilated. As things stand now, the nation still has a chance to recover.

"I am reminded of the anguish Emperor Meiji felt at the time of the Triple Intervention. Like him, I must bear the unbearable now and hope for the rehabilitation of the country in the future. But this is indeed a complex and difficult problem that cannot be immediately solved. However, I believe that it can be done if the people will join together in a common effort. I will do everything I can to help.

"I cannot express the sorrow I feel as I think of all who were killed on the battlefield or in the homeland and of their bereaved families. I am filled with anxiety about the future of those who have been injured or who have lost all their property or their means of livelihood. I repeat, I will do everything in my power to help.

"As the people of Japan are unaware of the present situation, I know they will be deeply shocked when they hear of our decision. If it is thought appropriate that I explain the matter to them personally, I am willing to go before the microphone. The troops, particularly, will be dismayed at our decision. The War Minister and the Navy Minister may not find it easy to persuade them to accept the decision. I am willing to go wherever necessary to explain our action.

"I desire the Cabinet to prepare as soon as possible an Imperial Rescript announcing the termination of the war."

The Emperor rose and left the little underground room.

Tears that had been silent in the Emperor's presence now became sobs of anguish. Some of the ministers and councilors lost all control, some slipped to the floor, where they knelt in sorrow and reverence. Perhaps, to many of them, more heartbreaking than the surrender itself or the fate of their country was the uncertain destiny of the small, mild-mannered, bespectacled man who had just left them. "I am not concerned," he had said, "with what may happen to me," but those twenty-four men in the underground shelter *were* concerned—for to them he was not a man, or a god, or even an emperor, he was the personification and image of the sacred homeland they had sworn to protect until death, the symbol of Japan's immortality. Knowing, cynical, hard-bitten as many of them were, to them, as to the simplest peasant tilling his little corner of land, the Emperor was sacred and inviolable; and now, by his own desire, he was about to make himself "subject to" the authority of a foreign Supreme Commander. Many of them had known for some time that this was a likely eventuality, yet now that it was almost reality it seemed too terrible to bear. But if the Emperor himself was willing to bear the unbearable, could his ministers do less?

And there was so much to be done, so many problems to be solved: and no matter how hard the ministers worked, how successfully they solved the problems that faced them, there was no honor in it. Or security either: none of those twenty-four men had any idea what was likely to happen to him when the enemy forces occupied Japan. Trial, imprisonment, death. . . ?

Silently they walked through the long underground corridor to the Gobunko, where cars took them to the Imperial Household Ministry. Here they separated, each to go about his difficult and thankless task, each with private thoughts and sorrows best not spoken.

The Imperial Palace, built for Emperor Meiji, had been destroyed in the May 25th air-raid, with the loss of forty lives, and the Emperor moved at that time to the Gobunko, the Imperial Library, which, as it was constructed of reinforced concrete, had withstood the raids. The bomb shelter, where the Imperial conferences had been held, was tunneled into the ground just beside it. People authorized to visit the Gobunko went first, on entering Palace grounds, to the Imperial Household Ministry, whence they were driven to the Gobunko. They returned by the same route.

Yasuhide Toda, the chamberlain who saw the ministers and councilors off, was so struck by the sorrow that seemed to envelop them like a black cloud, he could think of nothing to say. In silence he bowed to each, as they left the relative security of the Imperial Palace for the sweltering uncertainty of the defeated, bombed-out capital this August noon.

On returning to the Gobunko, the Emperor summoned his Lord Keeper of the Privy Seal, Marquis Kido. Kido had spoken with the Emperor briefly just prior to the start of the Imperial Conference and knew what course His Majesty had decided upon, but listening now to the Emperor recount the speech, he was struck with the true enormity of the decision. The same emotions that just minutes before had gripped the ministers and councilors listening to the Emperor speak now took hold of Kido and for a moment his steel-like composure slipped.

The Cabinet was to meet, immediately after the Imperial Conference, at Premier Suzuki's official residence to ratify the Emperor's "decision," which then, but not until then, would become a state decision. According to the Constitution, the Voice of the Sacred Crane, however loud and clear it spoke, required the unanimous approval of the Cabinet before it became the voice of the nation. In this case the approval was expected to be automatic.

Waiting impatiently at the Premier's official residence was Lieutenant Colonel Takeshita, who had with him a document titled "Employment of Troops—Second Plan." He had been hoping that the Imperial Conference would not be held until later in the day, which would have given him more time to put his plan in operation. When he learned that the War Minister had already taken his seat in the underground Conference, he had turned away in despair. The Emperor, he knew, would make a second decision confirming the first. "I have been deceived," Takeshita muttered, as he paced up and down, waiting for his brother-in-law, General Anami, the Minister of War.

Takeshita was not yet ready to admit defeat; he could neither retreat nor surrender; and he had not given up hope of persuading Anami and the other three top generals that his way of thought was the only correct one. How could the national polity be preserved if the country was to be occupied, its soldiers disarmed, and its "war criminals" tried by enemy forces? Togo and Yonai, who kept advocating unconditional acceptance of the Potsdam Proclamation, could offer no assurances.

Takeshita sat down for a moment, then jumped up again. His impatience mounted, as did his determination that the only correct course for Japan to follow was a fight to the last man. By inflicting heavy losses on the enemy, she could secure more favorable terms. Takeshita was not such a fool as to believe in Japan's ultimate victory, but he was increasingly convinced that only a last-ditch fight could ensure Japan's survival: survival in the teeth of death, with the Army standing implacably together and the War Minister at its head.

But what if the Emperor has already spoken out in favor of acceptance? His power was in theory absolute; his decision, once it was made, could not be revoked. Or could it? There might be a way, Takeshita thought, as the members of the Cabinet began to converge on the Premier's official residence in preparation for the meeting that was to ratify the Imperial "decision."

Chief Cabinet Secretary Sakomizu, who was the last to arrive, ran upstairs to his room on the second floor and asked at once for Michio Kihara, an ex-reporter of the *Nippon Times,* temporarily assigned to the Cabinet.

"The Emperor has made his decision," said Sakomizu.

Kihara managed a smile. "You didn't have to tell me," he said; "I knew by looking at you."

"Then that's that," said Sakomizu briskly. He knew he had far too much to do to allow himself the luxury of emotion: the tears would have to wait. The two men had been working on drafts of rescripts for two days in anticipation of this moment; now they would have to remold these around the Emperor's own words.

Sakomizu explained: "We'll need two Imperial Rescripts. I'll do one announcing the termination of the war, and I would like you to do one for the troops. Neither," he added, "will be easy."

As the two men sat down at their desks they felt the heavy weight of their responsibility, for on the drafts they were then composing would be based the last words of the Japanese Empire.

The Cabinet members had snatched a few moments' rest after the exhausting ordeal of the Imperial Conference. Now they were gathered together to have a bite of lunch, but—except for the Premier himself—they found that they could not swallow the whale meat and the black bread that were being served them. It was too much like trying to chew rocks. They pushed their plates away and rose, having agreed to meet at one o'clock.

After rising from the table, Anami and his adjutant, Major Saburo Hayashi, went to the wash room, where Anami suddenly brightened and said, "Hayashi! You've heard the rumor that the enemy has a huge landing force near Tokyo Bay. I want to hit that hard while we're still talking peace—then maybe we'll get the kind of peace terms we want."

Hayashi was astonished. "But the Emperor has already given us his decision," he replied. "Anyway, we don't know definitely where the landing forces are now—it's only a rumor that they're near Tokyo."

Anami shook his head. The animation left his face, and he said no more. He then joined his brother-in-law, Lieutenant Colonel Takeshita, in a small room—for the private talk that Takeshita had requested.

Although Anami's work was ended, although the Imperial decision could be interpreted as a vote of no-confidence in the Army by the whole country, the War Minister himself looked—to his brother-in-law—calm and unharried. His eyes were bloodshot, but otherwise he seemed fit and ready to do whatever had to be done.

Takeshita, as he spoke, drew strength from the Minister's composure. He asked Anami to take action, using his authority "to mobilize troops for the purpose of maintaining security."

"Furthermore," Takeshita concluded, almost calmly now, "there is a lot you could do at the Cabinet meeting. You have power, you could use it. As you know, the Chief of Staff has changed his mind. Why don't you?"

"No." Anami's reply was immediate. "The Emperor has made his decision. There is nothing I can do. As a Japanese soldier, I must obey my Emperor." Anami's tone was final. It seemed obvious that he had given up whatever plans he may have entertained in the past: he was ready to drain the cup of sorrow and humiliation.

But Takeshita was not. He looked at the ink-stone on the desk. Would Anami use it when he signed his name to the Cabinet decision approving the Rescript? He could use it first, Takeshita reflected, for a different purpose. If Anami refused to ratify the Imperial decision but resigned from the Cabinet instead, then the government would fall; and if it fell, how could it terminate the war? This, it seemed to Takeshita, was the one last way to avoid the humiliation of surrender.

"Admiral Onishi," he said, "told an officers' meeting that even if the Emperor decided to end the war, he himself, at the risk of being branded a traitor, would advocate continuing the war for the sake of a higher justice." Takeshita drew himself up and stood at attention. "General," he said to his brother-in-law, "will you agree now to resign from the Cabinet?"

Anami was silent for a moment. Takeshita's hopes rose, only to be altogether dashed by the Minister's first words: "The war will end even if I resign. That is definite. And if I resign," he added, with a smile, "I would not see the Emperor again."

The two men looked at each other. Takeshita realized that Anami's mind was made up and that nothing was likely to change it. Further conversation now was useless. His boots beat a harsh tattoo on the wooden floor-boards as he headed toward the door. But where was he going? He had no idea; he had no place to go.

Anami sat on for a moment before making his way, like the other members of the Cabinet, for his own Ministry.

Foreign Minister Togo, the chief advocate of peace, was content with the Emperor's decision. He called the Vice-Minister, Shunichi Matsumoto, into his office and began to dictate an account of the proceedings of the Imperial Conference while they were still fresh in his mind. His voice sounded vigorous and fresh; Matsumoto felt a surge of admiration for his victorious chief—victorious in defeat, as he wrote down the Emperor's words:

"I agree with Foreign Minister Togo that the enemy does not intend to change Japan's national polity. I believe that the Imperial structure will remain unchanged."

And how admirable, Matsumoto thought, was the Emperor himself, who had staunchly advocated peace and insisted on the termination of the war even if unconditional surrender jeopardized his own position. Matsumoto, as he inscribed the Emperor's words, felt himself in the presence of greatness.

We have won out, he thought. Our efforts have been rewarded.

Anami, the defeated general, defeated in defeat, was on his way back to the huge Ministry of War on the heights of Ichigaya. His thoughts were not enviable. It was his Ministry, and it was about to fall; it was his Army, and it was about to disintegrate. The last lines were being written to the seventy-year-old history of the Imperial Army.

It had always been General Anami's intention to lead that Army in a last battle for the Japanese homeland; now he was being forced to lead his six million men in the opposite direction, in a retreat to surrender. The responsibility was a heavy one, for if the officers refused to accept the surrender order, the country might be plunged into civil war, of which the certain outcome would be total destruction and the end of the Japanese nation. The responsibility was a heavy one, it lay heavily and squarely on Anami's shoulders, and once he had discharged it he could hope for no reward but the satisfaction of having consistently performed what he held to be his duty. The country must, above all, be saved.

As he entered his Ministry, Anami recalled the old battle maxim that said it was a good general who could conduct an orderly retreat. In his office he unbuckled his sword and leaned it against the back wall. He was about to sit down at his desk when a score of young officers burst in, trembling and pale in the intensity of their reaction to the news that the Emperor had, for the second time, decided on peace.

They wanted to hear what had happened at the Imperial Conference and what the Minister of War proposed to do. On him they pinned all their hopes for the future.

"The Emperor," the War Minister told them, "said he was confident our national structure will be preserved. We have no choice but to abide by his decision—it is based on his confidence in our loyalty."

The officers were silent, uncertain. They had agreed to do as the War Minister said largely because they were confident he would never give the command to surrender. The proclamation issued over his name on Friday called for continued war, not humiliating peace: "We must fight on, even if we have to chew grass and eat earth and live in fields—for in our death there is a chance of our country's survival. . . ." Now, on Tuesday, but four days later, were the officers to make a complete about-face and give up all their hopes and plans for a less humiliating end to the war?

Lieutenant Colonel Masataka Ida, of the Military Affairs Section, stepped forward. "Will the War Minister," he asked, "explain why he has changed his mind?"

"Yes," said Anami, "I will. The Emperor told me he understood fully how I felt. With tears in his eyes, he asked me to persevere, however difficult the duty. I can no longer oppose my view to the Emperor's decision." Anami did not speak the word "traitor" aloud, though it hung in the air. And yet how well he understood the feelings of those passionate young officers! He also, at one time, had considered the necessity of a *coup d'état* to remove the traitors from

90

around the Emperor and to insist on more favorable terms. But now the planners of such a *coup* could only be regarded as traitors. Anami felt compelled to make his position absolutely clear. "The Emperor has spoken his decision, and we have no choice whatsoever but to obey it. Anyone who disagrees," he said again, "will have to do so over my dead body!"

In the silence that followed Anami's affirmation, one of the officers could be heard weeping. The unabashed, unrestrained sobs of Major Hatanaka filled the room—and they expressed the despair of more controlled but equally disillusioned officers who, like Hatanaka, felt they could no longer trust anyone and who remained bitterly opposed to what was being done to their country—and their Army.

The officers and the Minister eyed one another in silence. Then Anami turned away to look at the stricken figure of Hatanaka—in whom, perhaps, he saw a reflection of his own youth.

It was a time of tears. In an underground shelter of the Premier's official residence, Hiroshi Shimomura, Director of the Information Bureau, was holding a press conference. (But it was not really a press conference, Shimomura's secretary thought, as he watched the old man, his chief, recount the events of the past few days, tears coursing down his cheeks: it was more like a wake than a press conference.) One of the reporters for the *Asahi Shimbun* said later that he realized he himself was weeping only when he saw the tears splash onto the paper where he was taking notes. Shimomura, gaunt and pale, looked as though he could hardly sit up.

Yet he talked on. He told the reporters, in detail, all that had happened since the past Thursday. He answered all their questions freely. He described the confrontation between Togo and Yonai on one side and Anami and the two Chiefs of Staff on the other. He gave a complete account of the Imperial speech. When it was ended, he told the reporters, there were no dry eyes in the conference room. And there were no dry eyes, by that time, in the press room either.

It was a time of tears.

Lieutenant Colonel Hiroshi Fuha, staff officer of the Eastern District Army, had come, in the line of duty, to the headquarters of Lieutenant General Takeshi Mori, Commander of the First Imperial Guards Division. Both men were cavalry officers; Fuha had taken instruction from Mori at the War College. They were almost like father and son, and now, it seemed, the son had come to pay his respects to a worried father.

The problem that was worrying General Mori was, quite frankly, what attitude the Eastern District Army would take if the Emperor had really decided on surrender.

"What kind of attitude do you mean?" asked Fuha.

"If the decision has been to surrender," said Mori sternly, "we must abide by it. We must not let ourselves be carried away. To tell you the truth, I have had a number of visits today from young officers in the War Ministry. They wanted the Imperial Guards to start an uprising, but I told them I wouldn't give orders to one single soldier without a command from the Emperor. I sent them all away."

Mori peered suddenly at Fuha, as if to determine whether he too had been badgered by the young officers. Then he smiled a tight little smile, and Fuha was reminded that Mori's nickname was Monk (Oshosan in Japanese). It seemed to Fuha that Mori had not only the look of a monk but also the manner: he was solemn, set in his ways, rather stubborn in fact.

"I have a feeling," he went on, "that I failed to convince them. They'll almost certainly come to see me again and—well, whatever they do to me, I will not change my mind. And I would advise the Eastern District Army to follow the same line, to do nothing contrary to the Emperor's decision. This, of course, is assuming that the Emperor has decided on surrender. . . ."

With that he rose and, using his sword as a walking-stick, crossed the room to the window. The glass was crisscrossed with tape, as a protection against bomb damage. Mori looked out through the openings at the waters of Chidorigafuchi Pond burning brightly in the noon-day sun, with the thick foliage of Fukiage Garden behind the pond. Here stood the Gobunko, the Imperial Library, where the Emperor had taken up residence, and Mori tried to picture the slight, troubled figure who must now assume the responsibility for the future of Japan and report on his success, or failure, to his divine Imperial Ancestors. He could not, Mori thought, unburden his soul to anyone else.

Mori did not know that the Emperor had already handed down his judgment and was, at that very moment, describing to Marquis Kido, the Lord Keeper of the Privy Seal, all that had been done and said a little while before in the Imperial bomb-shelter.

Fuha, feeling more cheerful after his talk with "Monk" Mori, stood at attention to bid his former teacher and present friend goodbye—for the last time. He was not to see him again.

1 p.m. to 2 p.m.

"The Emperor himself will speak!"
Hiroshi Shimomura

AT ONE O'CLOCK NINETEEN MEN TOOK their places at a large round table in an inner room of Premier Suzuki's official residence. These included, in addition to the various ministers who composed the Cabinet, the directors of the Information, the Legislative, and the Overall Planning Bureaus, as well as Chief Cabinet Secretary Sakomizu and the Premier's son Hajime, who acted as his secretary and aide, for Suzuki's deafness often prevented his hearing everything that was said in the rapid cross-fire of a Cabinet discussion. Aside from that deafness, however, Suzuki, who was the oldest man present, appeared to be also the healthiest. His son said that in spite of all the alarms and excursions that had so shaken the government during the past crucial six days, the Premier himself had slept well and eaten heartily. The others looked as though they had neither slept nor eaten: their faces were pale and drawn, their eyes were bloodshot, their expressions were those of men assisting at the last rites of someone they had loved.

Suzuki, as always, was impassive. He customarily sat motionless in his chair and said very little; when others spoke, he listened as attentively as his age and deafness permitted, but no trace of emotion crossed his face: the speaker was quite unable to decide whether the Prime Minister was in agreement or, indeed, whether the Prime Minister was hearing what was being said.

At the very beginning of the Cabinet meeting, he expressed his anger and annoyance at the fact that the August Mind of the Emperor had been troubled twice to decide between the two opposing factions within the cabinet. "It should not have happened," Suzuki said; "it was an affront to the Throne. It happened only because we did not try hard enough." He then relapsed into his customary impassivity as the Cabinet unanimously approved the Emperor's "decision." The Minister of War sat back in his chair, relaxed: it was the attitude of a man who had done all that could be done, who had no quarrel any longer either with his own conscience or with the world.

The main job of today's Cabinet meeting was to agree on the wording of the Imperial Rescript terminating the war, after which each minister would sign it and the four-year war would indeed be ended. The Chief Cabinet Secretary reported that the Emperor's own words were at that very moment being incorporated into the Rescript, so the Cabinet decided to take up for prior deliberation various minor matters that also required attention. The first, which was unanimously approved, was the relatively simple one of begging the Emperor's pardon before the promulgation of the Rescript. It was only then, perhaps, that the Cabinet realized to the full that their four months of disheartening deliberation were now drawing to an end.

When Baron Kantaro Suzuki, Admiral of the Imperial Japanese Navy, retired, was asked, in April, to form a cabinet, it was apparent to everyone—except the people of Japan and the officers of her Army—that Japan had lost the war. The minutes of the meetings of

Suzuki's Cabinet grew more and more discouraged, and discouraging, as the weeks wore on. Daily the Ministers of Transport and Munitions would report on the damage inflicted by the ever heavier enemy air-raids, while the Minister of Agriculture had nothing but bad news about the rice crop. Although the ration kept being reduced, it was apparent that by the end of this present month of August there would be no rice at all. Japanese who escaped death by bombing and fire would die of starvation. Meanwhile, the Minister of Education was forced to concern himself not with education but with mobilizing students for the war effort; the Home Minister concentrated on the maintenance of security and evacuation of children from devastated cities; the Minister of Welfare attempted the impossible job of rehabilitation as the Allies stepped up their incendiary bombing. So today's meeting, sad as it was, was almost like a release: the weary months of waiting for the end were over, the end had come. The physicians who had stood helplessly over the death-bed now had only to verify the fact that their patient, the Empire of Japan, had indeed ceased to exist.

A few minutes after one, the directors of the Japan Broadcasting Corporation (NHK) were ordered to appear at the Information Bureau. Three men—Hachiro Ohashi, the chairman of the corporation; Kenjiro Yabe, director of the Domestic Bureau; and Daitaro Arakawa, director of the Technical Bureau—were met at the Information Bureau by a Cabinet secretary.

"An Imperial Rescript ending the war," he said quietly, "will soon be announced. Shimomura says the Emperor himself will speak! He will read the Rescript over the radio. . . ."

There were audible gasps from the three NHK men, who had had no previous intimation of the plan formulated by Kido and Shimomura for an Imperial broadcast. It seemed incredible to them that their Emperor, a being whose divinity had never been challenged, should himself go before the lowly and familiar microphone to tell his people of Japan's tragedy. The three men felt a thrill of awe and sacrilege. The Emperor's decision was sublime, but the carrying out of it was somehow blasphemous: no other single act could have conveyed to the Japanese people the immensity and the horror of the experience they were about to undergo.

"The Cabinet," the secretary went on, in the same quiet voice, "is now considering the question whether the Emperor should broadcast directly or whether a recording should be made. You will be informed as soon as a final decision is reached. Meanwhile, will you make all preparations for either eventuality?"

Ohashi accepted the responsibility on behalf of NHK, and as the three men went back toward broadcasting headquarters, to make plans for this extraordinary event, Yabe recalled the harrowing incident of December 2nd, 1928.

Then head of the broadcasting department, Yabe was listening to a special program of a military review at the Yoyogi Parade Grounds to honor the enthronement of the Emperor, which had taken place less than a month before at the Imperial Palace in Kyoto. Suddenly Yabe leapt out of his chair: he was hearing the voice of the Emperor!

Although the microphones had been placed fully fifty yards behind the Imperial enclosure, the Emperor's voice, through some strange acoustical phenomenon, could be heard over the radio as he read a Rescript to the Army. Yabe went at once to the broadcasting station, to find the entire staff in a state of terror. "Never mind," said Yabe calmly. "If anyone from the Communications Ministry asks who was in charge of today's brodcast, tell them it was Yabe." But he was far from feeling as calm as he sounded: there was no telling what the Army was likely to do or what attitude the Imperial Household Ministry might take.

And indeed, as Yabe had expected, the situation grew extremely grave. The Army refused to accept any explanation, while certain people in the Imperial Household Ministry seemed to regard the incident as a clear-cut example of *lèse-majesté*. Then, at the moment when things looked darkest for Yabe, a military attaché to Prince Taka, uncle of the Empress, remarked to the Vice-Minister of War that Princess Ayako, Prince Taka's elder sister, had much enjoyed the broadcast. With that, the incident ended.

NHK had twice, since then, requested permission to rebroadcast the unintentional Imperial reading of the Rescript and had twice been refused. From that day to this, the Japanese people had never heard their Emperor speak.

The honor—and the responsibility—of making arrangements for the entire country now to hear the Voice of the Crane seemed almost too great to be borne.

The Cabinet had decided that it would be presumptuous to ask the Emperor to broadcast directly to the people and that he ought, therefore, to be requested to make a recording. Shimomura, Director of the Information Bureau, was summoned back from his press conference. With his agreement, the decision became final, and Shimomura was asked to take charge of all arrangements.

He got in touch immediately with Chairman Ohashi of NHK and told him of the Cabinet's decision. "Will you," he said, "be at the Imperial Household Ministry with your recording team at three?" Shimomura cautioned Ohashi to maintain absolute secrecy.

At the Imperial Household Ministry, the heads of the General Affairs Bureau and the General Affairs Section decided that the Imperial Administrative Office (the Goseimu Shitsu) would be the most suitable place to make the recording, while the technical equipment could be put in the adjoining room.

Chamberlain Sukemasa Irie had just returned to Tokyo from the

Imperial villa at Shiobara to report to Grand Chamberlain Hisanori Fujita on the present state of the Imperial princes and princesses then living outside the Capital. He could hardly believe that the Emperor had decided not only to surrender but to tell the people about it himself; he could hardly believe that the guns would at last be silent and the streets of Japan cleared of their rubble; as he threw himself into the task of helping to prepare for the Imperial broadcast, his mind circled ceaselessly about the future. He kept asking himself the questions that all Japan would soon be asking: Was there really to be peace at last? And what kind of peace would it be? Would Japan survive the occupation to become a new Japan?

At one-thirty Fujita met with Marquis Kido to pass on the report he had received from Irie. Kido then told Fujita that the Emperor had offered to go himself to the War and Navy Ministries to speak to the recalcitrant officers who still advocated a continuance of the war. Did Fujita, Kido asked, consider such a course to be either desirable or suitable?

The Grand Chamberlain and the Lord Keeper of the Privy Seal stared at each other in grief-stricken silence: that the Emperor should have had to make such an offer was horrifying, that he might actually have to carry it out was unthinkable. Fujita said quietly that the question was too important to be answered with a prompt and simple yes or no.

General Shigeru Hasunuma, chief aide-de-camp to the Emperor, gave Kido the same reply. Both he and Fujita said that too much depended on the reactions of the Army and Navy to be able to forecast whether the surrender would be orderly or whether there would be revolt, perhaps civil war, perhaps the total destruction of that very polity the rebels would claim they were fighting to preserve.

Yet it was inconceivable to let the Emperor take all the responsibility, to speak not only publicly to the people and the troops but

99

also privately to the rebellious officers. And yet, what else was there to do? To wait a bit longer, the three men agreed; to let the War and Navy Ministers continue to take the responsibility for the time being; to hear what public declarations they made. Then, at one-fifty, General Hasunuma said, "Let's send a messenger to Anami and Yonai and ask them what they intend to do before it's too late."

Or was it already too late?

Can a man resist the current of history? It may be that the men who have appeared to do so have in fact allowed themselves to be carried along by that very current, that they have floated where they seemed to be swimming. Was Major Hatanaka such a man?

That he was courageous and determined all his fellow-officers agreed; his loyalty was never questioned; but many thought him a fanatic; and while some admired his purity of heart and singleness of purpose, others saw the same qualities in a different light: to them Hatanaka was like a dray-horse tirelessly pulling a cart along a narrow path without sufficient imagination to raise his head and look around, at a changed environment. Yet he had great charm, he was vigorous and full of life, and it may be that his weakness was the very thing that made his vitality seem so attractive.

There is no question that Hatanaka was dangerous. Left alone by his fellow-officers, after Anami had announced his intention of abiding by the Emperor's decision, he continued to lament what he felt sure was the death of his sacred country; then he raised himself up and after a few moments of intense communion came to what was to be the crucial decision of his life.

Japan had another potential revolutionist on her hands that Tuesday afternoon, a mature and experienced commander, a man of quite a different stamp from Hatanaka. A little earlier he had sent long telegrams to the Minister of the Navy, the Chief of the Navy General

Staff, and a few other naval commanders, urging both continued resistance and the putting of pressure on the "weaklings" in the Navy. One sentence in his telegram might, to some of those who received it, have implied that he was also urging a *coup d'état:* "It is only natural that officers of the Imperial Army and Navy, who have been taught never to surrender, should come into conflict with those government officials who desire to accept the surrender terms." However, by the time his telegram was received, the Emperor had already made his decision and the Navy had agreed on its course.

He was not, however, a man to sit down and weep. Just about the time Hasunuma, in his conference with Fujita and Kido, suggested sending a messenger to the War and Navy Ministers, this man took a car and drove across the burning-hot, noon-day countryside to Atsugi, where the 302nd Air Corps was based. This corps was in possession of a number of new planes—Raiden, Gekko, and Suisei—and was kept on a twenty-four hour alert. The largest air base in Japan, Atsugi had an underground generator, a huge underground repair plant, and extensive quarters, also underground, for flight personnel. Aside from the main runway, there were special runways for a rocket fighter plane, the Shusui, and a four-engine bomber, the Renzan, to be used in attacking the American mainland. These planes were in trial production. The entire base was ringed by anti-aircraft guns and accommodated some seven thousand men and over a thousand planes; it had sufficient food and ammunition for another two years of war. The man who was driving as fast as he could toward Atsugi was the corps commander, Navy Captain Yasuna Kozono. His watch said two o'clock.

2 p.m. to 3 p.m.

"I will guarantee the good behavior of the Imperial Navy."

Admiral Mitsumasa Yonai

THE DAY WAS STILL EXCRUCIATINGLY HOT and humid. Not a breath of air disturbed the damp stillness. Ghosts walked the desolate streets, thin, drawn, silent ghosts. Did they wonder if the war was ever going to end? Or had they stopped wondering about anything? Was it enough—or was it too much—just to be alive? No one had had enough to eat in such a long time. The sun glanced piercingly off bits of tin roofing that lay scattered over bombed and burnt-out areas; the discomfort it caused undernourished eyes was only one more indignity. The people went their way like sleepwalkers, silent, unseeing.

In the Gobunko there was only slight relief from the heat. At two, the Emperor again summoned Marquis Kido and in an hour-long audience discussed with him procedures for the broadcast and the events of the morning.

Outside the sun beat down relentlessly.

Lieutenant Colonel Masataka Ida, of the War Ministry's Military Affairs Section, sat motionless in his chair, the collar of his uniform pulled open. He felt like a man who had lost all will. Only a couple of hours ago, he had been ready to fight; now he was unequal to the task of rising from his chair.

Yet his restless thoughts gave him no peace; they returned again and again to the one question that underlay all the others: was Japan not more precious to the Japanese than their own lives? If their country was indeed sacred and indestructible, as all Japanese believed, then how could the government permit the divine structure of Japan to be shattered by surrender? The authorities, Ida thought, were using the Imperial Rescript as a cover, in the hope that it would save their own lives; they were laying all the responsibility for the final judgment on the shoulders of the Emperor. Ida felt nothing but contempt for their baseness.

"Japan," he murmured, "unable to bear her sufferings any longer, is about to commit suicide."

But the thought of action was remote. The world was empty: how could one move in an empty world? Why, Ida wondered idly, should I go on living? I have no more reason to live. And tomorrow I shall be dead. Then why do I keep torturing myself about this, since tomorrow I am going to die like a dog?

Ida glanced contemptuously across the big room at his chief, Colonel Arao, busy at his own desk, facilitating the surrender.

What Colonel Okitsugu Arao was doing at his own desk was setting down, at the orders of Vice-Minister of War Wakamatsu, details of "the Army's policy," so that future generations of Japanese might understand why the Imperial Army had changed its mind and submitted thus tamely to dismemberment.

103

As Arao saw it, the Army under its Minister, General Anami, had consistently advocated resistance to the bitter end because it wanted to unify all the armed forces, with the people behind them, and by inflicting enormous losses on the invading enemy pave the way for a more honorable peace. But now the Army was ready to lay down its weapons. "Obeying a command is a virtue" was one of Anami's favorite sayings; the command the Army was now about to obey had been issued by the Supreme Authority in the country. Although defeat need not mean destruction, a civil war would; the only means of rehabilitation open to Japan now was to obey the Imperial command.

The policy of the Army, therefore, must be unquestioned; every officer and man must follow it. To make absolutely sure, Colonel Arao intended to secure the signatures of his most important superiors: Field Marshal Sugiyama, Commander of the First General Army; General Umezu, the Chief of Staff; and General Kenji Doihara, Inspector-General of Military Education. Arao called for a messenger and sent him to the Premier's residence to ask the War Minister, General Anami, for his approval of the plan.

The Cabinet was still in session, although interruptions were frequent. Shimomura had returned to his press conference; and Yonai and Anami had been called out to receive the message from Marquis Kido and Chief Aide-de-Camp Hasunuma: the Emperor had signified his willingness to go personally to the War and Navy Ministries to admonish the dissatisfied young officers; did the two Ministers feel this course of action to be necessary?

"I will guarantee the good behavior of the Navy," said Yonai.

There was only the briefest of pauses. "And I speak for the Army," said Anami.

Both Ministers, as they returned to the meeting, were agreed that they could not ask the Emperor to do such a thing.

The Cabinet was just about to consider a proposal by Sumihisa Ikeda, Director of the Overall Planning Bureau, to refrain from destroying overseas installations. Japanese military strategy had always called for the destruction of all installations, weapons, and ammunition, in case of retreat, so that they did not fall into the hands of the enemy. Ikeda's point was that these ought now to be left intact and used as part of future war reparations.[6] Ikeda emphasized that provisions implementing this decision must be taken simultaneously with the act of surrender or it would be too late: the military would already have followed its custom of total destruction. Both Yonai and Anami agreed to take the necessary steps.

Some Cabinet members were suspicious of this apparent docility of General Anami, who had been such a fierce advocate of continued resistance but who now calmly agreed to all the measures the Cabinet deemed necessary to effect the surrender under the most advantageous possible conditions. Was he only pretending to be a gracious loser, knowing all the while he held the trump card of resignation in his hand? Was this only the hush before the storm? If there was indeed a typhoon approaching Japan, then Anami, these ministers believed, must be its eye; and they looked at him, as he calmly announced his acquiesence, in an attempt to discover what lay behind his impassive features. But there was nothing to take hold of.

Less than a mile from the Prime Ministerial residence stood the tall NHK Building. Daitaro Arakawa, director of Japan Broadcasting Corporation's technical bureau, was in secret session with Iwao Kumagawa, one of his assistants. Kumagawa was informed when and where the recording was to be made but was cautioned, at the same time, to say nothing to any of his engineering staff. However, when engineer Shunichi Nagatomo saw Kumagawa's expression of tragic gravity, he immediately surmised where he was going to be sent with his recording equipment and what was he going to record. He felt a moment of panic at the tremendous responsibility involved in recording the Emperor's voice—but he realized that he had no choice but to bear his responsibility like any soldier in the ranks. Silently he turned and left the room, to prepare the necessary equipment.

Two K-type 14 recorders, two sets of recording amplifiers, and a Matsuda A-type microphone, the best then available in Japan, were to be used. All four members of the recording staff by now sensed that they were to be instruments of the government in its hopeful attempt to transform the desolation of the war and the turmoil of surrender into a peaceful reconstruction of the country.

Major Hatanaka and Lieutenant Colonel Shiizaki had quite a different end in view. They were then at headquarters of the Imperial Guards Division, conferring with two of the Division's staff officers, Major Ishihara and Major Koga, bellicose General Tojo's bellicose son-in-law.

The four officers found that they were pretty much in agreement. The men around the Emperor had put pressure on him to accept the Potsdam ultimatum—an ultimatum that could only result in the destruction of the national polity. Therefore the Emperor could not possibly have desired it in his heart: therefore he had been maneuvered into it; and therefore it was the clear duty of the Imperial Guards to protect him from the men who, under the guise of statesmanlike counsel, were betraying their country and their Emperor to the enemy. Then the whole Army would be free to follow the real intentions of the Emperor rather than those he had been persuaded into announcing.

They began now to consider what action their decision, thus logically arrived at, should take. Death, they agreed, was nothing. All four were ready to die if by dying they could contribute to the preservation of the Imperial state; they were ready to die even if they failed, knowing that what they had done was for the ultimate good of Japan. They would not even, they decided, care if they were branded with the name of traitor—so long as it followed a glorious death. Like the stalwart heroes of ancient Japan, they would know that their names were inscribed in the pages of their country's history and in the annals of her Army.

But the details of the *coup* still remained to be worked out, and it was this rather tiresome chore they now put their minds to.

General Anami had agreed to Colonel Arao's suggestion and had summoned to his private apartment in the Ministry the Army's most illustrious names: the Chief of Staff, the Director-General of Military Education, the Vice-Chief of Staff, the Vice-Minister of War, the two Field Marshals, and heads of departments, bureaus, and sections.

The Vice-Minister of War solemnly laid a document on the table. "The War Minister," he said, "requests that all officers here present sign this statement of the Army's policy."

The first to sign was the Minister himself; then the others followed. The document read:

The Ministry of War
August 14th, 2:40 p.m.

The Imperial Forces will act strictly in accordance with the decision of His Imperial Majesty the Emperor.

After the ceremony of signing and sealing ended, General Umezu said, "I believe it is essential to control the activities of the Air Force as well, and so I suggest we secure the signature of Commander Kawabe." This was also agreed to.[7] The policy of the Imperial Japanese Army was now explicit: those of its officers who deviated from that policy would be guilty not only of insubordination but of treason.

As Hatanaka and his fellow-conspirators strove desperately to rationalize their actions, and as the Army's top echelon signed their oath of allegiance to the Emperor, an American radio operator on Okinawa scribbled down a message beamed in English from Tokyo by the Domei News Agency:

> FLASH FLASH TOKYO AUGUST 14—IT IS LEARNED THAT AN IMPERIAL MESSAGE ACCEPTING THE POTSDAM PROCLAMATION IS FORTHCOMING SOON

The time was 2:49. It was the first indication to the outside world that the end was near.

3 p.m. to 4 p.m.

"Was it going to be another Nagata incident?"

General Shizuichi Tanaka

THE THREE NHK EXECUTIVES, WITH THE recording team, were on their way to the Palace in the two cars that the Imperial Household Ministry had sent to fetch them. The men had been silent all the way, and they continued silent as the cars entered the Palace grounds through the wooden Sakashita Gate.

Palace etiquette had been relaxed very little during the war, and to this very day, the day before the war ended, a strict watch was kept to see that those who entered the Imperial Palace were properly attired. Rules had, however, been waived for the men from the Japan Broadcasting Corporation, not all of whom might be expected to possess the striped trousers and the long morning coat that protocol demanded. The guard, therefore, permitted them to enter the grounds wearing only a *kokuminfuku,* the war-time uniform for civilians. Kenjiro Yabe, director of the Domestic Bureau, had borrowed his uniform from a much bigger man, and now he was afraid, as they approached the Imperial Household Ministry, that his over-sized, baggy suit would be considered a serious breach of etiquette in the presence of the Emperor.

At the Ministry, the NHK group was met by two department heads of the Information Board, both of whose uniforms, Yabe noted unhappily, were remarkably well-fitting. He may have failed to notice that they, like the men they had come to greet, all wore the same serious, even tense expression, for they were all conscious of, and deeply stirred by, the terrible gravity of the task they had been called to the Palace to perform.

They went upstairs to the second-floor room where the recording was to be made and began installing the necessary equipment as quickly as possible, for they had not been told at what exact time the Emperor would speak for the people and for posterity and they wanted everything to be ready well ahead of time.

Someone from the Imperial Household Ministry asked whether it would be possible for the Emperor to hear the recording as soon as it had been made. The chief engineer said that could be arranged, so he and an assistant headed for the Daiichi Insurance Company Building in Hibiya, where a secret underground broadcasting station had been set up in case the NHK Building was destroyed during enemy attacks. It was here that the only playback machine in Tokyo was kept.

As they drove under the shade of some trees, on their way toward the Daiichi Building, they felt a cool breath of air on their sweat-dampened faces. They recall how moved they were to realize that there were still green trees standing in the devastated capital.

Green trees still grew on Ichigaya Hill too, but the men in the huge building at its top were not in a tree-viewing mood. The imminent dissolution of their "invincible" Army affected some with despair and some with anger, some with lethargy and hopelessness and others with the need to act, however ill-considered and rash the action might be.

What had happened, wondered some of the older officers, to the *bushido* that had once vitalized their Army and made it the stern, sensitive instrument it had been? How far it had fallen, they thought, from the old *samurai* "way of the warrior" to this disappointed swarm of ambitious self-seekers who had regarded being sent to the front as a form of punishment yet who saw themselves as the natural leaders not only of their own men but of a hundred million Japanese civilians as well. The fate that had overtaken the Army, some of these old-fashioned officers decided, was perhaps no more than it deserved: instead of serving the country, it had tried to make the country serve it—and it had failed, as an army that sets itself above and beyond the polity must always fail.

To one elderly officer, the Japanese Army seemed like a ceramic jar so cracked it had altogether lost its original shape. He felt only contempt for many of the men he saw around him who had left the old Japanese way of the warrior; when *bushido* ceased to be the vitalizing force in the Army, he thought, the Army lost everything.

But one man at least tried to cling to the principles of the *samurai*, and that man was the Army's leader, War Minister Anami, who stood now at his window, looking down onto the green hill below and wondering how best to implement his promise to the Emperor. "I speak for the Army," he had said, meaning he spoke for its loyalty and obedience. How could he ensure them? How could he prevent his bewildered and reckless officers from shattering the cracked jar—and the whole country with it?

There was a little breeze here, high on the hill, but the day was still hot and muggy. With a sigh, Anami moved away from the window and called a conference of all officers of the Ministry's various sections. When, at last, they were all assembled, he climbed up on a small dais at the front of the room. He was not a man given

111

to great mobility of expression, and the officers who stood facing him could read what they liked in his once cheerful features—despair? anger? weariness? hope?—but they could not be sure that what they read was really there.

"When the Emperor," Anami said, "made his decision on Friday to accept the enemy proclamation, provided the structure of the country was guaranteed, no one could say what the future held, or whether Japan was to surrender or continue fighting. Our decision was dependent on the enemy's decision. I ordered you, therefore, to await developments and to be prepared for either eventuality.

"However, the situation is now clear and definite. Three hours ago the Emperor commanded that Japan accept the enemy terms. The Army will obey the Emperor's command. He offered to come here and speak to you himself. I replied that that would not be necessary." Anami looked around the room, from face to face, before he continued:

"The Army, I said, will, like the rest of the country, obey the Emperor's command. That is Japan's only hope of salvation. The Emperor is convinced that our national polity will be preserved, and he has expressed that conviction to the Field Marshals. Accordingly, the three leaders of the Army and the Marshals swore, a few minutes ago in this building, to follow the Emperor's lead. No officer in the Imperial Army will disobey the Emperor's command. No officer in the Army will presume to know, better than the Emperor and the government of the country, what is best for the country."

The silence in the room was absolute.

Anami's voice, as he went on, was sharp and clear; it rang with conviction. "Conditions today are, I agree, extraordinary, but that does not alter the fact that one of a soldier's chief virtues is obedience. The future of Japan is no longer in doubt, but neither will it be an easy future. You officers. . . ."

Anami paused. His brother-in-law, Lieutenent Colonel Takeshita, raised his downcast eyes. Anami ought to have said, "We officers—" and the fact that he did not convinced Takeshita that Anami had also reached a final decision.

"You officers," Anami went on crisply, "must realize that death cannot absolve you of your duty. Your duty is to stay alive and to do your best to help your country along the path to recovery—even if it means chewing grass and eating earth and sleeping in the fields!"

In the silence that followed, Lieutenant General Masao Yoshizumi, Chief of the Military Affairs Bureau, stood up and briefly recapitulated the main points of the Emperor's speech. But the thoughts of most of the men before him hovered still on Anami's words.

The officers realized that the Minister had issued one of his last commands: he had ordered them to refrain from suicide. But some wondered, like Takeshita, whether he might not himself choose that means of expressing to the spirits of the Imperial Army's vanished commanders his sorrow at being the man fate chose to put an end to the Army's seventy years of successful military history. The Army had been entrusted to Anami's care, and he had failed that trust, obeying what he decided was a higher duty. Nevertheless, he had failed.

The Vice-Minister of War stood up and—in a tremulous voice— assured Anami that all the officers present would obey his instructions.

Anami stepped down from the dais.

But not all the officers in Anami's command were present to hear either the Minister's instructions or the Vice-Minister's assurance that they would be obeyed. No roll call had been taken.

Lieutenant Colonel Ida, for instance, although he had known that the meeting was to be held, was resting in the Ministry's underground bomb shelter. Resting? No, he was lying down, still as death, but his anguished thoughts allowed him no rest: there was nothing in life for which he did not feel horror and disgust.

Nor had Major Hatanaka and Lieutenant Colonel Shiizaki been present at the meeting. As Anami mounted the dais, Hatanaka was mounting the stairs to the office of General Tanaka, Commander of the Eastern District Army, on the sixth floor of the Daiichi Insurance Building. (By a strange coincidence, the NHK engineers were, at that same moment, dismantling the playback machine in the basement of the building for use in the recording of the Imperial Rescript that was to figure so largely in Hatanaka's thoughts, and actions, later in the day.)

Hatanaka shouted his name from outside the door. The commander's adjutant put his hand to his sword. Young Major Hatanaka burst into the room, breathing hard, his face pale, his eyes bloodshot.

But General Tanaka gave him no chance to speak. "Why did you come here?" he cried, in a furious voice. "I know what's on you mind! I don't want to hear it! Leave at once! Get out!"

Hatanaka stood straight as a ramrod. His lips twitched; he tried to speak, but no sound came forth. He stared at the General, and the General's adjutant kept his hand on his sword. Then, at last, like a Bunraku puppet, Hatanaka saluted, turned on his heel, and left the office.

The General's adjutant, with a sigh, let his hand drop from the pommel of his sword.

Tanaka nodded. "Was it going to be another Nagata incident?" he said. "I think it came very close."

Tanaka was referring to a time, back in 1935, when the division between two Army factions became so bitter that Lieutenant Colonel Aizawa burst into the Ministry of War, drew his sword, and killed Lieutenant General Nagata of the rival faction.

But the situation this Tuesday afternoon was, as General Tanaka realized, far more serious. The Eastern District Army, which he commanded, was a defense force, and no one knew better than Tanaka himself that it was no longer capable of defending the country. The quality of the troops had deteriorated with the years, as had the determination of the people; almost all the munitions factories in the area had been destroyed. If the enemy were to invade the western part of Japan, at Kyushu, the defending forces might be able to hold their own or even, for a time, gain an advantage, but here in the east, in the Tokyo area, lived some twelve million people. How could they be evacuated if the enemy landed here? How could they be fed? Some Army officers believed the spirit of Japan burned so strongly in the people that they would gladly die in the defense of their homeland, but Tanaka wondered if the years of near-starvation, as food supplies dwindled, and the months of near-annihilation, as enemy bombing accelerated, had not too severely weakened that spirit. And as commander of a defense force, he was troubled by the fact that the unarmed civilians in his district were far more openly exposed to day-and-night enemy air action than his own soldiers. Tanaka had no doubt at all any longer that the only hope for the people of Japan was surrender; nor had he any doubt either that if a few fanatical Army officers gained control of the country, the Japanese people had no hope at all.

He understood the Army point of view, of course, as did every officer trained in *bushido:* no retreat, no surrender, and an eagerness to die in defense of the homeland. Three million troops scattered across Japan had been imbued with the same belief: how strong a breath would it take to fan their smoldering ardor into flame? It was a flame that might well scorch the entire country. Seven thousand planes were available to suicide squadrons: if these were put to use, would the enemy be tempted to show quarter?

115

The commander of the Eastern District Army was not the only man who realized how precarious the situation was; Marquis Kido, the Emperor's adviser, continued his hectic schedule. At three-twenty he was visited by Imperial Prince Mikasa; at three-forty he conferred with the Emperor's Chief Aide-de-Camp Hasunuma; he then spoke with Imperial Household Minister Ishiwatari; at three-fifty he was in conference with Kingo Machimura, the General Superintendent of the Tokyo Metropolitan Police Department; next he was visited by Prince Takamatsu. The object of all these discussions was to ensure the safety of the Emperor, the capital, and the country and an orderly termination of the war.

Hasunuma had been in contact with the War and Navy Ministers, and he reported to Kido that they were confident they could control their officers. "Don't worry about the public peace," said Machimura; "I can ensure it." He paused but did not put into words the condition present both in his mind and in Kido's: "so long as the surrender is effected swiftly."

They knew it was the Army that might interpose itself between Japan's desire to surrender and her ability to surrender. They too had heard the rumors flying about Tokyo on vulture's wings that a huge enemy force would land in the Bay the following morning and march on the capital, ripping weapons from the hands of the soldiers and insignia from off their uniforms. Fear of this humiliation would predispose the troops to action. In Kido's mind as in Tanaka's loomed the same frightening question: how strong a breath would it take to fan the smoldering ardor of the troops into flame?

Behind the War Ministry, on Ichigaya Hill, the flames needed no fanning. A huge pile of documents had been doused with gasoline and fired. The afternoon was still unbearably hot. The heat of the flames drove the soldiers back. They contented themselves with throwing more documents onto the bonfire from a safer distance.

116

But to the officers standing by the windows of the Military Affairs Section and watching the black, sooty column of smoke thrusting its way into the heat-hazy sky, this was a true bonfire and the body that lay stretched on the pyre was that of the Imperial Japanese Army.

"Yes, yes!" cried Lieutenant Colonel Ida, who had come up from the bomb shelter to watch the flames. "Burn it all! Then there is only one thing left for us to do! Do you know what it is? We must apologize to the Emperor for our defeat. And do you know how we do that? We must all, every one of us, every officer in the Army, cut our stomachs open. How else can we apologize to the Emperor?" He looked at his fellow-officers with burning eyes. "How else can we make our names immortal? How else can we express our belief that Japan is immortal?"

He paused. "I was down there alone," he went on after a moment, in a voice so low the other officers could hardly hear him, "down there alone in the bomb shelter, I did a lot of thinking. Do you know something? During the whole of the Great East Asia War, I didn't experience one single moment of deep emotion. Can you believe it? But now I know that by killing myself I can atone for my lack of emotion.

"I can offer my apology to the Emperor—and to myself."

4 p.m. to 5 p.m.

"No, I am fated to die tomorrow."
Lieutenant Colonel Masataka Ida

AFTER GENERAL ANAMI, THE WAR MINISTER, returned to the Prime Minister's official residence, the Cabinet meeting was resumed. To each Cabinet member, Chief Cabinet Secretary Sakomizu handed a mimeographed sheet containing a draft of the Imperial Rescript that—broadcast to the nation and the world by the Emperor—would terminate the war.

Hisatsune Sakomizu and Michio Kihara based their draft on what the Emperor had said at his two Imperial conferences—the one held the night of Thursday/Friday and the other a few hours back. The Rescript was not an easy document to compile from any point of view—least of all from the point of view of style.

Japanese is a highly stratified language: a Japanese-speaker uses words and verb forms that are determined by his relationship to the person he is addressing. The Emperor, toward whom all other Japanese stood in the relationship of subjects, did not speak, nor was he expected to speak, the kind of Japanese that might be heard in the streets, or the drawing rooms, or even the universities of the country; his language was formal, archaic, court Japanese. The Rescript that he was to sign and deliver to the nation was naturally couched in the language he was familiar with and was expected to speak. Sakomizu and Kihara, in compiling the Rescript, had used several reference works[8] and had also secured the advice of two Japanese authorities on the Chinese classics.

The men sitting at the round Cabinet table received the draft with a bow and settled down in silence to study it. The room was dark, for the windows were few and small, and although the summer afternoon was still bright, electric lights had been turned on in the meeting room. Some Cabinet members had put on their glasses.

Sakomizu stood by one of the little windows. Tape had been crisscrossed over the glass, but through the interstices he could see all too clearly the havoc that enemy air action had visited on the once victorious capital. Behind the Premier's residence there had stood, at one time, a Japanese-style building: now all that was left of it was a disorderly pile of partly burnt wooden pillars and beams. The Western-style houses that had been used by the Cabinet secretaries were now nothing but a series of crumbling and blackened walls. All the trees within view were burnt and dead, stunted black husks and dark, wintry-looking branches—though it was mid-summer.

Beyond the walls enclosing the ministerial grounds the scene was just as desolate: block after block of buildings gutted by fire, some still smoldering behind charred walls. Here and there stood a whole building, but it failed to brighten the melancholy scene. Although the American Embassy, standing alone on a hill across Tameike, looked intact, it too was only a shell; its roof had been burnt out.

Sakomizu turned back to the room, his arm brushing the black-out curtain that hung beside the window. The Minister of Education had prepared his own draft of the Rescript, but now he abandoned it. "I move," he said, "that we make this remarkable document the basis for our discussions."

Both the Minister of War and the Navy Minister, as heads of the two services whose dissolution would be one of the results of the Rescript, said that before they approved it they would like to have it read by competent persons in their own ministries. The Cabinet, understanding how the two men felt and still apprehensive of a surprise move by Anami, immediately approved, and a copy of the draft was dispatched to each of the two ministries.

It now seemed evident that discussion on the Rescript ought to end in about an hour. A hopeful directive was accordingly sent to the Imperial Household Ministry, asking that everything be in readiness for the recording to be made no later than six that afternoon. No one knew better than the men assembled in that dark and melancholy room that the sooner the Rescript was formally promulgated, the better were Japan's chances for an orderly, unbloody surrender.

Major Hatanaka had been pedaling his bicycle through the broiling heat of the summer sun from one end of Tokyo to the other. From the War Ministry he had gone to the Imperial Guards Division; from there to Eastern District Army headquarters; then back to the War Ministry. He entered Lieutenant Colonel Ida's room.

Ida, who was house cleaning in preparation for his projected suicide, looked at Hatanaka in surprise. Dust and sweat had caked his face, his uniform was darkened and stained with sweat, and his face was radiant. He was not the same man who had broken down and wept in the War Minister's room four hours ago. He seemed to have found a purpose in life, and when he asked Ida to join him on the roof of the Ministry, Ida, fascinated and curious, agreed. There, as the two men watched what little was left of Tokyo smolder into ruin, they held an intimate and revealing, if inconclusive, conversation.[10] Neither, in the end, changed the other's mind.

General Korechika Anami, Minister of War

Anami (standing) as a young boy   *Before entering Military Academy*

Anami's two favorite sports—archery and fencing

Anami as a lieutenant general

During war-time

Anami (third from right) following Premier Suzuki and Navy Minister Yonai on a visit to Meiji Shrine just before the war's end

The War Minister and his wife

Official residence of the War Minister, showing the corridor where he committed suicide

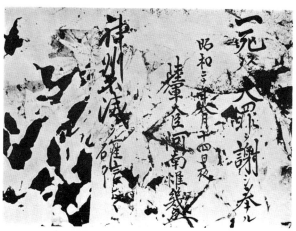

Anami's two dying statements, spattered with his blood; the one on the left is his death-poem; the other, his apology for his "supreme crime"

Asakusa Park, by the Sumida River, in September, 1945

Evacuation of school children

Tokyo: an aerial view of Chuo Ward at the war's end. Numbers refer to (1) Shin-Ohashi, (2) Mei-jiza, (3) Hisamatsu Police Station, (4) Hisamatsu Primary School, and (5) the Sumida River.

Tokyo: a family at prayer on All Souls' Day, July 14th, 1945

Tokyo: a mother and child in the heart of the city

Tokyo: a public bath

A B-29 flies low over the Diet Building

Prime Minister Suzuki inspecting war damage

Students at Meiji
Shrine, Tokyo

Departure

Children carrying the ashes of their fathers

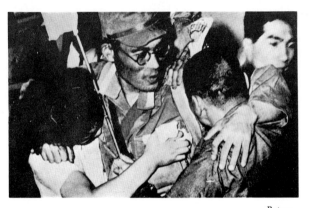

Return

Hiroshima, August 15th, 1945

Nagasaki, two weeks later

Hiroshima survivors

Mobilization of college students

Kamikaze (suicide) pilots about to emplane

抗戦を停止し母國を救へ

ビー廿九型超空の要塞重爆撃機の作戦に當る米國第二十航空隊司令官アーノルド大將は最近次の如く述べてゐる

日本帝國の版圖にして、一地區として現在我が航空隊の空襲圏外に存在するものはない

又た爆撃圏より遠隔の地にあつて爆撃を蒙らないといふ日本の軍需工場は全く無い

A leaflet dropped by American planes over Japan urging an end to resistance, to prevent the annihilation of the country. The photograph is United States Air Force General Arnold, commander of the 20th Air Corps.

國民抗戦必携

昭和二十年四月二十五日

大本營陸軍部

Cover of a pamphlet issued by the Army in 1945 calling on the Japanese people to fight to the end

The two men had been at the Military Academy together, and although Ida had graduated a year before Hatanaka, they had been close friends and had often spoken familiarly together—although never, of course, under such heightened circumstances. This was almost like a dialogue in a play—and it may be that the drama of the scene appealed to both the actors, who spoke their lines against the highly effective backdrop of the world's third largest city in smoking ruin.

Hatanaka began by asking Ida what he thought ought to be done, and Ida had no hesitation in replying that he believed only one righteous course lay open to the officers of the defeated Imperial Army: they ought all to commit suicide according to the code of the *samurai*. *Seppuku* was the word Ida used; *harakiri* was not considered a sufficiently elegant term for so elegant an action.

Hatanaka was startled for a moment. Then he cried: "Yes! It would indeed be a beautiful and correct thing to do—"

IDA: It is the only correct thing to do.

HATANAKA: But do you believe it would work?

IDA: Why not? Almost a quarter of the officers are with me already. . . .

HATANAKA: But will more join you? Some speak of going underground. No, in my opinion, your plan, beautiful as it is, is doomed to failure—

IDA: Then will you just stand around and do nothing? Wait for the enemy to break your sword?

HATANAKA: No!

IDA: Then what do you suggest?

HATANAKA: I don't know. I wish I knew! Is it better for us to obey the Emperor's decision or to fight on? How can anyone say? What human being can look into the future?

IDA: We must leave our fate to Heaven.

HATANAKA: Then I would rather take the course of remaining a

137

loyal Japanese—even if it means that in the end I must be called a traitor. *(Fervently)*: I would rather fight the enemy than entrust my Emperor and my country into his hands!

IDA *(clearly moved)*: But the Emperor himself has spoken. General Anami has ordered us to obey--

HATANAKA *(passionately, his eyes glistening)*: Heaven may favor either side—that is something no human being can say. But judgment is always affected by action, and if the mainspring of action is whole-hearted loyalty, then why need the actor feel ashamed even if he fails? No one may see the future of events till the future is past, but everyone may act in accordance with the dictates of his conscience.

IDA *(quietly)*: Have you a concrete plan of action as well as a justification for it?

HATANAKA: Yes, Colonel, I have. I want to occupy the Imperial Household Ministry, I want to cut the Palace off from all outside contact, I want us to concentrate all our efforts on helping the Emperor preserve Japan. Liaison with the Imperial Guards Division has already been made. Necessary preparations have been begun. If just a few officers start the uprising now, the whole Army will follow. And I have no doubt at all that we will succeed. Heaven will favor us. Join us, Colonel!

(IDA *remains silent.*)

Don't you think this is a more beautiful plan than cutting your belly open?

IDA: Success would be more beautiful. But the War Minister says there is no chance of success. The Emperor is determined to end the war.

HATANAKA: But surely every man who believes that Japan is eternal and indestructible—as I do, as you do—must make one final attempt to appeal directly to the Emperor to change his mind. The men around him—

IDA: But if the Army rises and fails, and a civil war follows, what will happen to Japan then? As you say yourself, there is no guaranty of success. Therefore I believe the Army must obey the Emperor's decision. Those of us who wish may choose an individual solution that does not endanger the country.

HATANAKA: But, Colonel—

IDA: No, Major Hatanaka, I cannot agree to your plan. A fire on which water has been poured will not burn again. That is the way of life.

HATANAKA: The Lieutenant Colonel speaks of success and failure. But how can he be sure that the Emperor's decision will succeed? Neither the Prime Minister nor the Foreign Minister can offer proof that our national polity will be preserved if we surrender. That is why I am determined to translate my plan into action.

IDA: I agree with you that we have no proof the Emperor's decision will preserve the country. But I am convinced an Army uprising now is doomed to failure: ordinary common-sense tells me that as well as my military training. The tide of time is flowing against us. Therefore I intend to commit suicide. Let the world witness that I do not tamely lower the fist I have raised to strike but instead take my sword in my hand and cut my stomach open.

HATANAKA: But the Imperial Guards have agreed—

IDA: Hatanaka, I admire your spirit, I admire it more than I can tell you. Perhaps I even envy it. So I say to you, go ahead with your plan, I won't try to stop you. But I won't join you either. . . . No, I am fated to die tomorrow. (Patting the other man's shoulder): Farewell, Hatanaka.

(Hatanaka bows and departs. He is less vibrant, less sure of himself than when he arrived. Clearly his interview with Ida has depressed him, but equally clearly he has no intention of abandoning his plan.)

To General Anami, Minister of War, sitting in Cabinet session at

Premier Suzuki's official residence, came his Ministry's judgment on the mimeographed draft of the Imperial Rescript that had been sent a little earlier. It came in the form of a proposal that the Rescript be approved by the Privy Council before promulgation, because legally acceptance of the Potsdam Proclamation was like the conclusion of a treaty.

The proposal was not unexpected. It was why the Cabinet had requested the presence of Baron Hiranuma, President of the Privy Council, at the Imperial Conference. However, now that the question of constitutional legality had been raised, the Cabinet could not dismiss it merely because Hiranuma had been present. The problems facing the Cabinet were suddenly multiplied geometrically. If the Army's proposal had legal validity, then the Privy Council must be called into session as soon as possible—but the time was now well past four in the afternoon, the Council could not be convened that day. Further delay, on the other hand, was out of the question. Insofar as both the situation within Japan and that outside it were concerned, surrender had to be effected within a matter of hours. Delay now would almost certainly frustrate the efforts of the Emperor and his ministers to put an end to the war without putting an end to Japan.

Chief Cabinet Secretary Sakomizu argued valiantly that there was no legal validity to the Army's proposal and that surrender could be effected without the approval of the Privy Council, but the Cabinet remained unconvinced and Premier Suzuki requested the Director of the Legislative Bureau, Naoyasu Murase, who was present at the meeting, to undertake an urgent study of the problem. He rose, bowed to the Premier, and left at once. The Cabinet took a brief recess.

This proposal, which had come from the War Ministry, was worrisome in the extreme. Did it mean that the Army was still not prepared to surrender? Was this only another delaying tactic to gain additional time for a military *coup?* Did the War Minister have a fateful letter of resignation hidden in one of his pockets? If so, he might produce it at any moment, and that moment the Cabinet would cease to exist; there would then be no constitutional body empowered to effect the surrender. Japan's danger was still ever-present. The ministers glanced surreptitiously at General Anami, but his face was as unreadable as ever: he seemed to be calmly awaiting the return of Murase, and nothing more. But if a man chose to veil his innermost thoughts, what colleague could hope to rip the veil aside? The other Cabinet members awaited Murase's return with more trepidation than Anami appeared to be feeling.

Most unusually, a battalion of the Second Regiment of the First Imperial Guards Division was then entering the Palace grounds to double the strength of the battalion already on guard duty.

There were three Imperial Guards Divisions, but the Second was then overseas and the Third was attached to the Eastern District Army, so protection of the Emperor was effectively in the hands of the First Division, whose two regiments guarded the Palace alternately. Today, Tuesday, August 14th, the Second Regiment was on duty. Normally, while one of its battalions was on guard, a second would be at command headquarters, while the third was either drilling or at rest. Yet for some reason a second battalion, under the regimental commander himself, was now entering the Palace to reinforce the battalion already on duty. What made it all more unusual still was that no air-raid alarm had been sounded.

The regimental commander, Colonel Toyojiro Haga, ordered his adjutant, Captain Otokichi Soga, to remain at Division Headquarters until he finished his work. Soga was at a loss to explain this order as well as the fact that Colonel Haga himself was commanding the auxiliary battalion. It was all so peculiar as to excite Soga's suspicions. He had heard a rumor on Saturday that Japan

141

had accepted the Potsdam Proclamation; but this seemed now to be untrue, and Soga did not know that the Emperor that very morning had issued a second decision confirming the first. Soga, unable to explain his commander's action, was quite frankly worried.

Director Murase of the Legislative Bureau had returned to the Cabinet meeting and was now listing his reasons for believing that it was unnecessary to obtain the Privy Council's approval of the Imperial Decision. Chief Cabinet Secretary Sakomizu glanced anxiously at General Anami, but the War Minister was listening calmly, and when Murase had finished, he nodded and did not insist that his Ministry's proposal be considered further.

Nor did he produce a letter from his pocket.

Somewhat less apprehensively the Cabinet resumed its discussion of the wording of the Imperial Rescript. Interruptions were frequent, however; ministers were constantly being called out of the room for private consultation; and deliberations as a result seemed interminable.

If the government was to achieve its aim of peaceful surrender, it was clearly going to have to get a move on.

8 月
AUGUST
14
火 曜 日

5 p.m. to 6 p.m.

"I am afraid of what may be happening at the Imperial Guards Division."
— *Prince Fumimaro Konoye*

IT WAS A LITTLE PAST FIVE O'CLOCK THAT Marquis Kido was shown into the presence of Prince Konoye, consistent though ineffectual advocate of peace, former Prime Minister, and therefore one of Japan's influential Jushin, or senior statesmen. Konoye had telephoned Kido a little earlier, hoping that he would be able to see him but fearing that the Privy Seal would be too busy. But when Konoye said there was something he would like to discuss with Kido but not over the telephone, Kido replied promptly that he would come around at once.

The two men sat facing each other.

"I have heard a rumor," said Konoye, "that I do not like the sound of at all. I am afraid of what may be happening at the Imperial Guards Division. Do you know anything about it?"

"Nothing," said Kido, shaking his head.

"Well, let's hope it ends as a rumor. . . ."

"May I know the source of it?" Kido asked.

Konoye laughed. "Well, rumors," he said. "But perhaps it would not be a waste of time to keep the Division under surveillance."

"Yes, of course," said Kido, "we will do that. But I believe the Division is loyal."

"I keep remembering the incident of February 26th," Konoye murmured. "And I am mindful of the fact that the Emperor has called a conference for this afternoon. . . ."

Then Kido told the Prince that the Imperial Conference had already been held—at noon that day. As Konoye held no official position— the Jushin were an extra-constitutional body who merely advised the Emperor when requested—he had not yet heard of the second Imperial Conference. Kido described the events that had led up to it, and gave an account of the conference itself, with what the Emperor had said, and by the time he finished, both men sat there with tears running down their cheeks.

After a melancholy silence, Kido rose.

Konoye repeated his advice to keep an eye on the Imperial Guards Division. Although throughout his public career, Konoye had feared a communist or socialist uprising more than an Army *coup d'état,* he now appeared to be in earnest: it may be that he feared the first might be a consequence of the second. In any case, Kido, as he left, repeated his assurances—though he still believed the Division to be both sound and loyal.

So did Imperial Chamberlain Yasuhide Toda. He could not help wondering, nevertheless, with a certain misgiving, why there seemed to be so many idle soldiers on the path between the Imperial Household Ministry and the Gobunko, where the Emperor was living. Obviously, thought Toda, rationalizing his fear, since surrender has been decided upon, the guards are here to cope with any emergency that might arise, yet there do seem to be an awful lot of them. . . .

There were. There were two battalions instead of the customary one—although after the Palace was destroyed by fire during enemy air action over Tokyo on May 25th, one battalion was more than enough to guard the Imperial Library, where the Emperor had taken shelter. Two battalions of guards, waiting for orders, did indeed clutter up the paths around the Gobunko. Toda's uneasiness returned as he walked past the armed and uniformed, but idle, soldiers.

In an upper room of the Imperial Household Ministry, the NHK men were still waiting. They had been ready to make the Imperial recording at three-thirty; now they were told that zero-hour would very likely be six. Their tenseness mounted as they looked at their watches every moment or two and, with nothing more to do, stood around and waited, as idle as the soldiers that surrounded the Palace they were in.

Although the NHK men did not know it, the one who was keeping them waiting was General Anami, the Minister of War. He insisted that one phrase, in particular, in the Rescript draft was unacceptable: "The war situation grows more unfavorable to us every day." This, Anami said, would mean that announcements made by Imperial Headquarters recently have all been lies. He could not sign his name to such a declaration. "In any case," he said, "we have still not lost the war—the situation has merely not turned in our favor." The tone of his voice—to some of the ministers—was maddeningly calm.

Admiral Yonai, the Navy Minister, rose. "Japan," he said, with passion, "is on the verge of destruction. Most regretfully we have lost the battles for Okinawa and Burma. Do you now speak of a last-ditch battle for the homeland? We will lose that too. We have been defeated, we have clearly been defeated."

"We have lost battles," said General Anami, "but we have not yet lost the war. That is the difference between the convictions of the Army and the Navy."

Admiral Yonai looked angrily at his calm, confident antagonist. Chief Cabinet Secretary Sakomizu was pale with apprehension: Japan was still not out of the woods; in fact she seemed, with the passing of every fateful moment, to be getting in deeper, and every glimmer of light from the outside was obscured as the path kept turning backwards. Sakomizu looked anxiously at his chief, but there was little reassurance there. The elderly Prime Mimister sat back in his chair with an abstracted look on his face: it seemed quite possible that he was not hearing a word that was being said.

Anami proposed that the sentence, "The war situation grows more unfavorable to us every day," be replaced by: "The war situation has not turned in our favor."

But Yonai as well as several other ministers demurred. They insisted that the original sentence was the correct formulation and that there was no need to change it. Anami, however, was adamant. The Cabinet was deadlocked on the phrasing of a sentence: the clock ticked on.

Sakomizu left the Cabinet meeting for a private consultation with Director Shimomura of the Information Bureau. They realized that the Rescript could not possibly be recorded at six and telephoned the Imperial Household Ministry to tell them so.

"I understand," said the director of the General Affairs Bureau. "But can you give me some indication of a likely time?"

"Well. . . ." Sakomizu paused. "Perhaps seven," he said. "Yes, I think seven o'clock will be all right."

He put down the telephone and turned to Shimomura. "I'm willing to cut my stomach open," he said, with a wry smile, "if the recording is made at seven."

Toshio Shibata, a political reporter on one of Tokyo's leading newspapers, the *Asahi Shimbun,* had waited for a while around the press room of the Prime Minister's official residence, after the press conference ended, but then he had gone back to his own office. He could not understand what was holding up the official promulgation of the Rescript ending the war. Although there had not been an air-raid all that day, Shibata knew that this unusual quiet would be shattered unless Japanese acceptance of the surrender terms was made official very soon. What was wrong with the government? Obviously, he thought, none of them is willing to assume the responsibility for defeat. They have been waiting for divine intervention or some incredible stroke of luck, and as a result tens of thousands of people have been needlessly killed in air-raids or had their homes and all their property destroyed. And now the government has shifted the responsibility to the Emperor, thus hoping to evade its own obligations. Shibata was astonished to discover that although he was a newspaper reporter, he was also extremely angry.

But then he decided that as he would very likely have to work the whole night through, without any sleep, he had better try to relax and get a little rest now, so he lay down on a collapsible cot in the office. He found, however, that he could not sleep after all: his mind kept returning to the strange, nearly fatal incident of yesterday afternoon.

His newspaper had received the following announcement:

Imperial Headquarters,
Four p.m.
The Imperial Forces have received new orders from the Emperor and have accordingly resumed operations against the forces of the United States, Great Britain, the Soviet Union, and China.

The same announcement had gone to all the other newspapers in Tokyo and to the Japan Broadcasting Corporation. As Tadashi Hase-be, one of the editors of the *Asahi Shimbun,* knew that the Cabinet was then in session to discuss the phrase "subject to" in the Allied reply, he was suspicious of the "Imperial announcement." Accordingly, he telephoned Shibata, who was waiting at the Prime Minister's residence and told him to find out about it. Shibata called Chief Cabinet Secretary Sakomizu out of the meeting, but Sakomizu had no knowledge whatsoever of the announcement. The time was then only a few minutes before four, the hour at which the broadcast was scheduled to be read over the radio. Panic-stricken, Sakomizu got hold of Anami and the Army Chief of Staff, neither of whom had had any prior knowledge of the announcement either; together, they managed to get it canceled. What would have happened if the Allies, who were watching for Japan's reaction to their official reply to her first surrender offer, had heard the broadcast? Would what little was left of Tokyo today still be here?

Shibata, lying on his cot in the newspaper office, shuddered as he thought of the possible consequences of that irresponsible announcement, and he knew that in the years to come he would recall with pride his own role in preventing the perhaps fatal announcement from being made.

General Korechika Anami was a man who had reached his present eminence because he was a capable administrator rather than a brilliant commander in the field. He had conducted one outstanding campaign—the taking of Luan Castle, in Shansi Province, in China—when he was commander of the 109th Division, but that Tuesday afternoon, August 14th, in the Cabinet room of the Prime Minister's official residence, he was conducting a far more difficult campaign than any he or other generals of the Imperial Army had waged in the field.

He was trying to make it possible for his insubordinate subornates to accept the Emperor's decision without feeling compelled either to commit suicide or to initiate a doomed but possibly bloody uprising: he must permit them an "honorable and glorious defeat." That was why he kept insisting that the wording of the Rescript be changed.

How could he blithely tell his millions of troops that "The war situation grows more unfavorable to us every day"—and therefore we are quitting? How could he tell it to General Okamura, commander-in-chief of the Expeditionary Forces in China, who had cabled, "We should fight for the realization of our war aims even if it means the death of all our troops"? How could he tell it to Marshal Terauchi, commander-in-chief of the Expeditionary Forces in Southeast Asia, who had sent him a similar message? How could he tell it to the eager, impatient officers in his own Ministry?

Anami had made his own decision to abide by the Emperor's word, but he knew that for many of his officers, despite their religious loyalty to the Imperial House, such a decision was virtually unacceptable. The undefeatable Japanese Army was being asked to admit defeat, and its officers who had been taught that surrender was dishonorable were being asked to surrender. If Anami now insisted that the Rescript read: "The war situation has not turned in our favor," it was because he hoped to end the seventy years of the Imperial Army's history without the letting of more Japanese blood.

Admiral Yonai, called out of the Cabinet room, whispered to Chief Cabinet Secretary Sakomizu, who was just returning: "Don't give in, hold out for the original wording." Sakomizu nodded, but as he took his seat at the table, the thought of engaging in a prolonged verbal battle with the War Minister was a dismaying one. Sakomizu was exhausted, the past five days had been almost sleepless, his vitality had reached its lowest ebb. Anami, on the other hand, sat calmly, monolithically in his chair; he seemed neither tired nor worried, ready to wait until he had gained his selfish point.

Then suddenly, perhaps because he *was* so tired, Sakomizu—in a sudden flash of understanding—caught a glimpse of what lay behind the War Minister's attitude. He might not have been able to put it into words, but suddenly he knew that the War Minister had no intention of submitting his resignation. Anami was not insisting on his own point of view out of mere obstinacy or gross egotism: it was because he knew that the Imperial Japanese Army had to be allowed to end its life with at least a semblance of honor. As the war situation had not turned in its favor, it must be allowed to perform its own act of self-destruction: it must be allowed to die as honorably as it believed it had lived.

Yet the War Minister could no more state this belief to the Cabinet than the Chief Secretary could put his flash of intuition into words. Sakomizu looked at the big wall clock. The session had begun at four. Now it was almost six. The ability to surrender seemed even more unattainable than ever.

At Kempeitai Headquarters, the commandant was addressing his officers. Kempeitai, the military police corps, was generally thought of as a secret police force: it was under the control of an officer who was responsible directly to the Minister of War. The commandant, having announced the Emperor's decision and his belief that the national polity could be preserved, called on all his subordinates to obey the Imperial command.

Among those who listened to these instructions was Lieutenant Colonel Makoto Tsukamoto, who now, as he listened, recalled the stirring words of the Emperor in his instructions to the armed forces: "If you will become of the same mind as myself and bend all your efforts toward the preservation of the country. . . ." Tsukamoto determined to obey the Emperor, to become of the same mind, and as he did, a face quite different from that of the Emperor appeared in his imagination. It was the face of a man who did not in his heart agree with the Emperor, a man who did not believe Japan's two millennia of history could be allowed to climax in defeat, a man who had himself spoken at one time of the need for an Army *coup*. It was the face of an old friend, Lieutenant Colonel Masataka Ida of the Military Affairs Section.

Tsukamoto decided he had better keep an eye on that old friend.

8 月
AUGUST
14
火 曜 日

6 p.m. to 7 p.m.

"In the present emergency we cannot be too cautious."
Chief Aide-de-camp Shigeru Hasunuma

THE AIR SEEMED A LITTLE FRESHER IN THE Fukiage Garden; the sun was a great glowing iron disc that had been taken from the furnace and set to cool on the horizon. The Emperor was having his regular evening walk, accompanied by Chamberlain Sukemasa Irie.

After a few moments of silence, His Majesty paused and asked about the Rescript.

It was not the first time the Emperor had asked that question that afternoon, and Irie was forced to give the same unsatisfactory reply: the Rescript had not yet been received at the Palace. The chamberlain bowed his head in sorrow; it was always painful to have to say things to His Majesty that one knew His Majesty did not want to hear—it was particularly painful today. Irie felt that he could sense how distressed the Emperor was, how earnestly he desired an end to the uncertainty and suffering and the beginning of a new life for his people.

The Emperor continued his walk. Irie suddenly looked around with a start: he had caught a glimpse of soldiers in the garden where he had never seen soldiers before. What on earth could it mean? It was strange, it was upsetting. . . .

Irie of course said nothing to the Emperor.

The Chief Aide-de-Camp was in conference with Lieutenant General Takeshi Mori, commander of the First Imperial Guards Division, at Hasunuma's official residence within the Imperial Household Ministry.

Mori first wanted to know whether there was any truth in the leaflets that American planes had been dropping over the city.

Hasunuma nodded. Did it seem strange to him that the commander of the Imperial Guards had not yet heard of the Imperial decision? Perhaps nothing that Tuesday afternoon would have seemed strange. "The Emperor spoke at noon today," he said. "The Cabinet is now approving the Rescript."

There was a brief silence.

Then, "What about the Imperial Guards?" Hasunuma asked in a worried tone, though as yet unaware that a second battalion had been ordered into the Palace. "Are you absolutely sure of them?"

"They're a little restless," Mori replied. "Considering all the rumors that have been flying around since Friday, it's not surprising. But I'm not worried about them."

"They say some of the young officers at the Ministry may be making trouble," Hasunuma went on.

"More rumors," said Mori. As commander of the First Imperial Guards, he was the man chiefly charged with securing the Emperor's safety. The tone of his voice was confident as he repeated, "Rumors, that's all."

Hasunuma sighed with relief, for he considered "Monk" Mori one of the most dependable of officers. So long as he was alive and well, the Emperor would be safe, the Palace would be protected. Before Mori left, however, Hasunuma added another word. "In the present emergency," he said, "we cannot be too cautious."

Mori agreed.

When the Emperor returned to the Gobunko, he was informed that Premier Suzuki had requested an audience. The request was immediately granted. But if the Emperor hoped that Suzuki had brought him the approved Rescript, he was in for more disappointment. Suzuki's purpose in asking for an audience was to report on the still deadlocked Cabinet and to apologize for the unavoidable delay.

After he had withdrawn from the Imperial presence, he headed back toward that dark and melancholy room where his Cabinet was still vainly trying to agree on the wording of surrender.

Meanwhile, orders relative to the termination of the war began going out from the Ministry at Ichigaya to the Eastern District Army command, which was responsible for the defense of the capital, and to the Imperial Guards Division.

Shortly after Mori had got back to his office at Division Headquarters, he received a telephone call from the Chief of Staff of the Eastern District Army ordering him to come to Staff Headquarters at once. There, in company with the commander of the Tokyo Defense Army and the commander of the First Anti-aircraft Division, he was officially informed by General Tanaka of the Emperor's decision to end the war.

Tanaka, who was commander of the Eastern District Army, went on: "The Imperial Forces will act in accordance with the Emperor's judgment. There is nothing further to be said.

"However," he added quickly, "we cannot anticipate what disorders may accompany the final termination of the war. Therefore we must see to it that public order is maintained and the laws of the country are enforced."

He turned to Mori. "At a time like this," he said, somewhat ambiguously, "many different people will try to protect the Emperor. There may even be violence if they fight for that honor. Your responsibility, therefore, is particularly grave."

His tone was a bit abrupt, and Mori understood that he was worried. But neither of the two men realized quite how much cause they had to be worried. They were in the process of ending the war, and their efforts would meet with final success, but neither of them was destined, after the famine, to taste the sweet fruit of peace.

Admiral Yonai came back from the Navy Ministry, but before returning to the Cabinet meeting went into the men's room. Nobumasa Kawamoto, one of Premier Suzuki's secretaries, was standing in a booth. When he saw the Navy Minister come in, Kawamoto bowed, but Yonai did not notice him; his eyes seemed to be looking inward, his face was clouded. He stood in the neighboring booth, wholly unconscious of the other man beside him. The splash of urine against porcelain was the only noise. Then suddenly Yonai sighed: the sound seemed to reverberate through the antiseptic little room like a cry of pain echoing through a cave. Kawamoto shivered; he had never heard a sound quite like that before.

When Yonai resumed his seat in the Cabinet session, he whispered something to General Anami, The War Minister nodded.

"On the question of the phrasing of the Imperial Rescript," said Yonai, "I would like to see it revised in accordance with the War Minister's desires."

Chief Cabinet Secretary Sakomizu was astonished. "But," he stuttered, "you told me yourself—"

Premier Suzuki broke his long silence. "Let it be done," he said.

The Cabinet took a deep breath, wiped the sweat from its forehead, and voted itself a brief recess. The members were glad to escape, if only for a little while, from the murky melancholy of the smoke-filled meeting room. One problem had been solved, but no one knew how many more lay waiting. Nor how much time they had before . . . before what? No one knew that either.

General Anami took advantage of the recess to go home and change his sweat-soaked clothes. The day was a bit cooler now; the sun had almost set; there was the beginning of a slight breeze. While Anami was changing and getting ready to return to the Cabinet meeting, he received two visitors: General Tojo, who had been Japan's Prime Minister on December 7th, 1941, and Field Marshal Hata, whom Tojo supported as his own successor in April, 1945.

Tojo came to the point of his visit at once. His eyes glittered behind his spectacles as he said: "After the surrender we will all of course be tried by a military court—as war criminals. That goes without saying. What we must do, when the time comes, is all stand together. We must be forthright in stating our belief that the Greater East Asia War was necessary. What we fought," said Tojo, with an echo of his former arrogance, "was a *defensive* war!"

Anami nodded. But did his nod mean that he agreed with Tojo? Or only that he had heard what the ex-Premier had said? Anami himself said nothing. Nor did he comment when Hata explained the purpose of his own visit: he would like, he said, to give up the rank of Field Marshal.

Anami returned to the Cabinet meeting. The cool breeze, for the moment, had died.

7p.m. to 8p.m.

"the Army's official policy and its real policy are the same."

Colonel Okitsugu Arao

THE NHK MEN, WAITING IN THE LARGE upstairs anteroom of the Imperial Household Ministry, checked their watches against the big wall clock. It was seven o'clock, and no further word had come from either the Cabinet or the Ministry as to when the Emperor was going to record the Rescript terminating the war. Chief Cabinet Secretary Sakomizu had said seven, but seven had come and gone, and the only activity in the room was the ticking of the wall clock. The men stared for a time at its swinging pendulum in hypnotized silence.

Then one of them said, "Do you suppose something has happened?"

"Something must have happened," said another. "But what?"

The men realized then that they had held this conversation before, and more than once before, during the hours they had been waiting, but the repetition did not seem funny. Their faces were tense; their apprehension mounted as they waited for word, and no word came. "But what *could* have happened?" said a third.

One thing that had happened was that the Cabinet was at last coming to an agreement about the wording of the Rescript. General Anami had won his two-hour battle: "the war situation," the Rescript now read, "has not developed to Japan's advantage."

Anami insisted also on the insertion of the phrase, "Having been able to save and maintain the structure of the Imperial State. . . ." The Cabinet agreed, and at the end of the same sentence agreed also to the deletion of the phrase "in preserving the sacred treasures." This might, said the Minister of Agriculture, lead to unnecessary and disagreeable enquiries by the occupying forces.

Copies of the approved Rescript were dispatched to the Imperial Palace. It had taken fifteen men over three hours to reach an agreement on these few, relatively minor changes in phraseology. If there seems to be little logic in the event, it may be that for these fifteen men the event transcended logic: it had entered a region where both logic and illogic ceased to exist.

At the War Ministry, Lieutenant Colonel Michinori Shiraishi had requested an interview with Colonel Arao, head of the Military Affairs Section. Shiraishi, a staff officer of the Second General Army, had accompanied Field Marshal Hata to Tokyo for the Marshals' Conference and was due to fly back to Hiroshima early the following morning. Shiraishi wanted to know whether the Army really intended to accept the decision to surrender or whether it had plans of its own. He surmised that if anyone could, and would, tell him, it was Colonel Arao, with whom he had served in Borneo and whom he believed to be in General Anami's confidence.

Smiling, Arao asked him to sit down; but Shiraishi could not believe in that smile: it looked too much like a mask. Nor could he believe in Arao's calm, unimpassioned voice, as he began to speak. "The Army's official policy and its real policy are the same," said Arao. "There is no conflict between the two."

Shiraishi asked if he might make a note or two of Arao's words, as he would have to report them to his junior officers in Hiroshima on the following day. Arao agreed and spoke on to the accompaniment of the hum of insects as they circled around the naked electric light bulb. There had been no air-raid warnings that day; the windows were opened to let in what little evening breeze there was.

Arao had done a lot of talking the last few days. His measured voice sounded hoarse as he recapitulated the reasons for Anami's original conviction that Japan must fight a final battle on the homeland and the reasons for Anami's change of mind. "They say that a good officer," Arao concluded, "must be able to command an orderly retreat as well as an orderly advance. Our Minister is a good officer, and we must follow his example, we must see that our troops continue to obey orders so long as there are any orders to be given and obeyed. There will lie the final glory of the Imperial Japanese Army."

Shiraishi was silent for a long time.

Then, "I understand," he said. "The country must come before the Army."

But that was not quite what Arao had meant. Or was it?

At the Imperial Household Ministry, Masujiro Ogane, the Vice-Minister of the Household, had handed out mimeographed sheets of the revised and approved Rescript to two officials to copy with brush on thick paper. One copy was to be signed with the Imperial seal; the other was to be used for the recording, and this one had to be done as quickly as possible. But the mimeographed sheet was so full of changes, of scratches and insertions, that it was almost

impossible to read. To make a fair, accurate, and hurried copy was
an extremely difficult task, yet it had to be done if Japan was ever
to find the peace she was seeking.

The Cabinet was now considering what would be the best time
to broadcast the Imperial recording. It was now too late to issue
it today, as they had originally planned. Foreign Minister Togo
then suggested seven o'clock the following morning, in which he
was seconded by Admiral Yonai; both ministers said they believed
that the sooner the announcement was made, the better it would
be for Japan on all counts.

General Anami disagreed. "We are going to have to issue orders
to the troops overseas," he said, "and we are going to have to
ensure that those orders are obeyed. In fact, we are going to have
to persuade the men to lay down their arms, and that will take time.
I request therefore that the Emperor's broadcast be delayed one
day."

But both Togo and Yonai persisted in their belief that since the
enemy had to be informed of Japan's capitulation as soon as possible, the people of Japan had better be too. The argument continued, but it lacked the animation of earlier discussions. Sensing
the possibility of a fairly easy compromise, Director Shimomura
of the Information Bureau declared that an early morning broadcast would not be entirely effective because many people—farmers,
for instance—would already be at work and out of reach of radios.
But since he agreed that if the broadcast was postponed too long,
there might be violence, he suggested that the best possible time
would be noon of the following day. The Cabinet agreed.

The Premier rose and turned to Anami. "Will the War Minister,"
he said, "make sure that advance notice of the broadcast is given to
all front-line troops?"

"I'll do my best," Anami said at once. The alacrity with which his agreement had been given both to Shimomura's suggestion and Suzuki's request filled some of the Cabinet with disquiet. They couldn't help wondering what trump card Anami still had hidden up his sleeve. Resignation? A *coup d'état*? Anything seemed possible, and Anami's sudden meekness seemed very suspicious.

But then so had his lack of meekness earlier in the day.

It was a quiet time as eight o'clock neared, perhaps too quiet. The Cabinet was calmly proceeding with its paper-work; there seemed to be no more dissension. In the Imperial Household Ministry, the two copyists were still quietly, industriously at work. The recording team had been told that the Rescript was already being copied; now that their long afternoon of waiting was about to end, they felt more relaxed, and chatted quietly in a corner of the big room. The Imperial chamberlains were having their dinner in turns, so that some would be on duty at all times. Eastern District Army headquarters had made its preparations for surrender and was now quietly waiting for the signal.

In his office at the Imperial Palace, the Chief Aide-de-Camp was talking quietly to some officers, among them Colonel Seike, another aide. Suddenly the door was opened, and two young officers entered.

"We've heard," said one abruptly, his voice bristling, "that the Emperor is to make a recording of his broadcast this evening. What time will it be?"

To Chief Aide Hasunuma's questioning look, he added that they were staff officers of the Imperial Guards Division and so had to prepare for the Division to be used if necessary.

Hasunuma made no comment.

"Has the recording already been made?" asked the other young officer, as immaculately turned out as his friend.

Colonel Seike felt that he had seen the faces of the two staff officers before, but he did not know their names. "No," he said, in reply, "so far as we know, the recording has not been made. We do not know when it will be made."

One of the young officers began to insist on a more explicit answer, but the other cut him short. "They're telling the truth," he said. "Let's go."

They saluted stiffly and left.

"Who on earth are they?" said Hasunuma.

"I think one of them," said an officer who had been watching, "is Major Koga."

"Who's that?"

"He *is* a staff officer in the Imperial Guards Division. That's true. And he's General Tojo's son-in-law."

8 p.m. to 9 p.m.

"I hope you have all decided to cooperate with me."

Navy Captain Yasuna Kozono

BY THE TIME HE GOT BACK TO THE BASE at Atsugi, early that afternoon, Navy Captain Kozono found that he was shivering and shaking and hardly able to stand, let alone lead a private war against the United States, Great Britain, the Soviet Union, and China, so he took to his bed. It was a recurrence of the malaria he had contracted in Rabaul; a man of a different stamp might have decided that fate was against him and abandoned his plan, but Captain Kozono, after a few hours' rest, found he was able to rise and by eight o'clock had put on his uniform.

He summoned to his office his deputy commander and the heads of the air force groups under his command.

"As I told you on Monday night," he said, his voice weak but resolute, "I am determined to fight to the end no matter what happens. I hope you have all decided to cooperate with me."

In the silence that followed none of the officers present found himself able to give the commander a negative answer. It may be that none of them wanted to, at least not single-handed, and it may be that the difficulty of saying "no" in Japanese was also a major contributing factor. In any case, after a few moments' silence, Captain Kozono said, "That's settled then." His satisfaction was evident, though the effort he was making was evident too.

"I have one question," said a group head. "How do we reconcile our policy with the order to obey the Emperor's decision—whatever it may be?"

It was the question Kozono had been waiting for and dreading; he knew it had to come and he knew he had to answer it: otherwise he could never count on his officers in a show-down. Yet at the same time, it was a question that could be discussed for hours and end in . . . nothing, in the same inaction in high places that Kozono so despised.

"That's an easy question to answer," he said gruffly. "How can we be disobeying the Emperor's decision if what we do is for his and the country's good?"

The officers nodded. They had been answered; at least, it seemed that they had been answered. Kozono gave them no time for further reflection. "Let's get down to work," he said, and with his staff he began to make plans for a dawn attack, using all his available aircraft.

Atsugi was not, as a matter of fact, the only base in Japan showing signs of preparation for action against the enemy. The men of the 27th Air Group at Kodama, for one, had received no intimation that Japan was about to surrender, but they had received orders to attack—so their personnel, made up of both Army and Navy airmen, were actually at that time warming up the engines of their thirty-six bombers (which had been converted into torpedo bombers, carrying one torpedo each). And other bases in Japan were effecting similar preparations for action against an enemy they assumed they were still at war with, having heard nothing to the contrary.

Two fair copies of the Imperial Rescript had now, at last, been brushed onto heavy paper, and Marquis Kido brought one of them to the Emperor, who had expressed a desire to see it. His Majesty, having read it, indicated five changes he would like to see made. Marquis Kido communicated these to the Cabinet, which was still in session, and the two copyists were told to make the changes.

Ordinarily the Rescript would have been entirely rewritten, but for the two men to make two fresh copies of the document's eight hundred and fifteen characters[11] would take another couple of hours each: this would delay not only the recording but also notification to the Allied powers of Japan's decision to accept the Potsdam Proclamation. The Foreign Ministry had hoped to be able to promulgate the Rescript by six o'clock that evening; it was now past eight; the Imperial Household Ministry decided not to have it rewritten.

The two copyists, therefore, who had been working in separate rooms, were now pasting small bits of paper over the characters to be changed; once the paper had dried, they would write in the new characters. They had the help of Yoshihiro Tokugawa, an Imperial chamberlain who had returned a short while before from the shrines of Kashima and Katori, where he had gone to pray on behalf of the Empress, and after reporting to her was now willingly assisting in the process of cutting and pasting bits of paper onto the surrender Rescript.

It was during this process that the phrase which had exercised War Minister Anami and the other members of the cabinet for some two hours received its final change and its final form: "the war situation has developed not necessarily to Japan's advantage. . . ."

And it was during this process also that an error was discovered in one of the copies. From the sentence:

Moreover, the enemy has begun to employ a new and most cruel bomb, the power of which to do damage is indeed incalculable, taking the toll of many innocent lives,

the final participial clause had been omitted. The copyist who had made the error paled when the error was pointed out to him; he could think of no excuse to offer, for indeed there could be no excuse that would mitigate so terrible an offense. Under ordinary circumstances. . . . but the circumstances grew less ordinary with every passing moment, and at last it was decided that against all precedent and tradition the omitted words might be written into the Rescript in small characters.

The completed Rescript was now brought by Tomoo Sato, chief of the Cabinet's General Affairs Section, to Premier Suzuki, who adjourned the meeting he was then attending, until nine-thirty, in order to proffer the Rescript to the Emperor and ask his approval. When he saw the blotched and pasted document he was expected to present to His Majesty, the Premier's lined, tired old face broke into a grimace—but observers could never agree whether the grimace concealed laughter or tears at the absurdity of the tattered document which was to end a long and disastrous war.

At eight-thirty the Emperor signed HIROHITO to the bottom of the Rescript, and the huge Imperial seal was affixed. The date given beside the Imperial signature and seal was "The Fourteenth Day of the Eighth Month of the Twentieth Year of Showa," Showa (or Enlightened Peace) being the name the Emperor had chosen for his reign.

It almost looked as though Japan was about to achieve the capitulation she had been striving for with such passion and chaos.

After Suzuki had bowed himself from the Imperial presence, Marquis Kido asked for a brief word with the Prime Minister. The Privy Seal repeated what he had heard from Prince Konoye—about the possibility of an uprising from the Imperial Guards Division—and also what he had heard from the Chief Aide-de-Camp: that General Mori had no anxieties where the Guards were concerned.

Kido himself believed that so long as Mori was in command, the Division was safe, but he would like to hear the Premier's opinion.

Suzuki was unusually forthright. "I know nothing about it," he said. "I have heard nothing, and believe nothing, of a projected *coup d'état*. The Imperial Guards are the last people in the world I would worry about."

Kido realized that to Baron Kantaro Suzuki, Admiral of the Imperial Japanese Navy, retired, it was unthinkable that the Emperor's command should be anything less than absolute to the very soldiers whose principal duty it was to guard his person. Kido himself, in fact, was of much the same opinion. He decided that perhaps Prince Konoye was a bit gullible, a bit too willing to put credence in unsubstantiated rumor.

Suzuki hurried off, to attend the meeting he had recessed until nine-thirty. There was still so much to do!

And so little time to do it in. Nobody realized that better than Major Hatanaka, who was in conference with Lieutenant Colonel Shiizaki and a few other officers. They feared that once the Emperor had recorded the Rescript, and it had been broadcast, there would be no time to act. Therefore they must act now, even though insufficient preparation might spoil everything.

They had already gone over the critical list of Guards officers. They had checked the names of Major Koga and Major Ishihara, who had already joined the conspiracy. A line was drawn across the name of another staff officer, Lieutenant Colonel Mizoguchi, who was in Karuizawa; and beside the crucial names of Colonel Mizutani, the Division's Chief of Staff, and General Mori, the Division's Commander, there still stood question marks. The conspirators were convinced that once they had secured Mori's participation, they would have Mizutani, and they thought that after they had the commanders of the first and second regiments, Mori would have no choice but to join them. Then all the other Guards officers, as well as the Eastern District Army, would fall in line: the government of Japan would, at last, be in the hands of men who understood the true meaning of Japan's sacred inviolability. These men had in mind no such simple aim as that which dominated the disastrous incident of February 26th: a change in governmental emphasis. What they envisaged was a structural change—or rather, as they saw it, a return to what Japan had been, and would be again.

They hurried off into the hot summer night. The revolt, it seemed to them, was almost won. And so was the war; it all followed.

Around the time that Premier Suzuki was crossing the still blacked-out streets of Tokyo, Captain Soga, of the Second Infantry Regiment of the Imperial Guards Division, received a telephone call from his opposite number in the Fourth Regiment. "I've heard there's a lot of unusual activity going on," said the latter, "all centering on the Palace. Do you know anything about it? Have you heard the rumor that an important Division order is about to be issued—and that it will be a forgery?"

Soga laughed. "It sounds like a joke to me," he said. "I haven't seen a sign of any 'unusual activity' in the Division."

Nevertheless, Soga decided to have a look around. At the Guards command post near Nijubashi (Double Bridge), he saw three unfamiliar officers: two lieutenant colonels and a major. (Later he identified the major as Hatanaka and one of the lieutenant colonels as Shiizaki.[12]) Although this was certainly "unusual activity," since no officers or men other than those of the Guards Division were permitted to enter the Imperial Palace, it did not seem quite unusual enough to Soga to warrant closer investigation. He continued on his way.

Soga, incidentally, had no idea that the Emperor and the government had decided to end the war; he was afflicted with the paralysis that had swept across the country as the Japanese waited for something—they had no idea what—to happen.

Toshio Shibata, of the *Asahi Shimbun,* found that he still could not sleep. He rose from the uncomfortable little cot, left the newspaper office, and went back to the press room at the Prime Minister's official residence. But it was empty, the Cabinet was taking a recess, Shibata was still alone with his thoughts.

They were concerned mainly with the rumors he had heard flying around the newspaper office: the Rescript was to be promulgated that night, a huge occupying force would take over Japan in the morning, the Emperor was to be exiled to Okinawa or some more remote place, the women of Japan would be subjected to methodical rape. The next generation of Japanese would hardly be Japanese at all.

Shibata, sitting alone in a dark corner of the press room, had no idea whether to believe these rumors or not. All he knew was that he could do nothing about them. He couldn't even get up out of his chair. He felt paralyzed.

9 p.m to 10 p.m

"It seems I've changed my mind."
Colonel ~~Toyojiro Haga~~

IN THE PRESS ROOM OF THE PRIME MINI-
ster's official residence, the *Asahi* newspaper reporter, Toshio Shibata, was still sitting in the same chair, as motionless as though he
had been turned to stone. He was waiting apathetically for official
word that the Rescript had been signed and was about to be promulgated. It was only a question of time, and he had nothing to do
but wait: there was nothing he wanted to do.

Automatically he listened to the nine o'clock news, which consisted, as usual, of announcements from Imperial Army headquarters. Then he heard a calm, official voice declare that an important
broadcast would be made at noon on the following day and that
everyone in Japan was expected to listen to it. That was all. The
program concluded with the customary martial music.

Shibata was one of the few of Japan's hundred million who knew
the nature of the next day's broadcast, who knew that on the mor-
row the hundred million would hear the voice of their sovereign
telling them that their country had lost its first war, that they must

lay down their arms, forget their animosity if they could, and try to rebuild a vanquished and desolated nation. Shibata could imagine the terror in a hundred million hearts as they realized they had lost the war they had given so much to win, as they tried, and failed, to keep out of their minds pictures of the depraved and brutalized forces of occupation pillaging the sacred soil of Japan and raping its womanhood.

Shibata felt two cool trails coursing down his cheeks in the still stifling heat of the August night. He had not realized that stones could weep.

Colonel Arao, his mind exhausted, his voice hoarse from talking to the procession of visitors he had entertained the previous day, suddenly became aware of the fact that this entire day, which was now drawing to a close, he had been called on but twice. That seemed to him a strange state of affairs for the chief of the Military Affairs Section of the War Ministry of a country now in the throes of trying to end the war that it had begun. Or was it so strange after all? Wryly he realized that the Japanese Ministry of War had suddenly become an extremely unpopular place.

A thick summer mist had wrapped itself around the heights of Ichigaya Hill. Within the empty, gloomy corridors of the huge central building of the Ministry, every noise seemed to reverberate from one end to the other before being sucked through the windows into the thick and silent mist. It was as though the Ministry had been isolated, padded against the world it had tried, and failed, to rule. Arao thought that in that deserted citadel he would sleep soundly tonight.

But first were there not things he ought to do? Was all his work altogether finished? He sat on, motionless, still torn between his conviction that the Imperial and governmental decision bound every soldier to obey it and his belief in the dogma that a soldier's duty

171

was to fight—that if Japan fought on now the terms of surrender might be made more favorable. But no, he had sworn to follow Anami, and Anami had sworn to follow the Emperor; there was no choice left, however much he might envy more resolute men like Major Hatanaka and Lieutenant Colonel Ida.

He ought, in fact, he thought, to go see Ida right away and try to dissuade him from rash action. He was Ida's immediate superior; he had a responsibility toward him. But he sat on a little longer, and soon his orderly came in to tell him that the Minister of War wanted to see him. Arao buttoned his uniform, strapped on his sword, and drove off into the misty night toward the War Minister's official residence. He did not know that Anami's car was just entering the Ministry grounds.

He did not know either that a couple of offices away from where he had been sitting, Lieutenant Colonel Ida was sitting too, quite alone, planning no rash act against the state, only the final, rashest act of all against himself.

A release, from the Information Bureau, on the Imperial broadcast scheduled for noon the following day now reached the city desks of Tokyo's newspapers—too late to be included in the first morning edition, which had already gone to bed three hours before. In any case, the release could not be used without permission from the Information Bureau, and permission would not be granted until the Rescript had been promulgated. The second edition of the newspapers would follow the Imperial broadcast.

The men from NHK were still waiting for the signal that the Emperor was ready to record the Rescript. Their fund of chatter, as they waited, had been depleted again; the ticking of the wall clock seemed louder.

General Anami noticed, with considerable surprise, that there were no sentries outside the front gates of the Ministry. He left his car and strode to the entrance of the main building: it too was deserted. Anami surmised that not only the entrances but the buildings themselves would be empty. It was only too clear what had happened. Anami had heard fresh rumors that American landing forces were waiting in vast numbers in Tokyo Bay and would launch an overwhelming attack in the morning. Then the unhealthiest place in Tokyo would be the War Ministry. The War Minister was in a position to ignore such rumors; his men, clearly, were not. And were these, he wondered, the troops the insurgent officers were depending on to deal a telling blow to the enemy? They had probably already changed into whatever civilian clothes they could muster. In a way, thought Anami, they were lucky that it was August, the hottest month.

As the Minister entered his office, his expression gave nothing away; no one could have told whether he regarded the desertion of his Ministry with contempt or sympathy; no one could have told, looking at him, what was in his mind.

Anami went to his desk and began straightening out the papers there, throwing some away, initialing others. When his adjutant offered to help, Anami asked him instead to call Lieutenant Colonel Takeshita. The adjutant went off in search of the Minister's brother-in-law, and the Minister himself continued his housecleaning. When the adjutant returned to say that Takeshita could not be found, Anami asked him to try to locate Arao; but Arao, because of a mix-up, was on his way to Anami's official residence, or perhaps by now on his way back.

The troops would, as the Minister knew, hear the Imperial broadcast at noon on the following day, but he would not feel that he had discharged his duties if he failed to give his officers and men orders from the Ministry itself. Accordingly he himself wrote out the following message, to be cabled to all troops in his name and that of the Army Chief of Staff:

. . . The Emperor has made his decision. The Army expects you to obey that decision and make no unauthorized moves that would put to shame the glorious traditions of the Imperial Army and its many distinguished military services. You must behave in such a way that you need never fear the judgment of posterity, and it is expected that your conduct will enhance the honor and the glory of the Imperial Japanese Forces in the eyes of the entire world. . . .

The Minister of War and the Chief of Staff dispatch this order with grief in their hearts, and they expect you to appreciate the emotions of the Emperor when he himself broadcasts the Imperial Rescript terminating the war at twelve noon tomorrow.

Then the War Minister wrote out a letter of resignation and put it in his pocket. His purpose in writing this letter was not to force the mass-resignation of the Cabinet, but merely to ensure that all his papers would finally be in order.

A wintry smile flitted across Anami's face. His work was now nearly done. He sat and waited for Arao. His office was still terribly hot and humid, a veritable steam bath; the black mist outside had done nothing to cool the air, though it seemed to seal the room in, almost like a prison cell—empty of all hope or the possibility of glory. Anami looked around: it was a strange place and a strange time for a man to be sitting alone, a man of fifty-seven who had given his life to the Army and been rewarded with the highest job that Army had to offer. As he awaited Arao, he adjusted his carefully trimmed moustache.

The Cabinet meeting was to resume at nine-thirty. Would he have to go without seeing Arao at all? But just at that moment, the Colonel's heavy figure appeared in the doorway. His eyes went to the War Minister's face; the men stared at each other for a moment in silence: a wave of sympathy and understanding passed between them.

Then, "Arao," Anami said, "I don't want our young officers to do anything foolish and heroic. The country needs them, I want them to go on living. No *seppuku,* eh? You can help."

"How?"

"Talk to them, tell them what I said, help them join the police force. . . ." There wasn't much, and both men knew it, that a young man trained to be part of a war machine could do when the machine stopped turning.

And an older man? "What about us?" asked Arao. "What will we be doing?"

Anami rose from his desk and walked slowly to the window. He stared out for a time, although there was nothing to be seen but blackness.

"Our people," he said, when he turned back, "are hard-working. Japan will surely recover. And although the Army won't be playing a part in this new Japan, its men can. You can, Arao. That is what I wanted to say to you—keep your energies for the tasks that lie ahead. They will be many, and they will be rewarding." He smiled. "Come along now, I've got to get back to the Cabinet meeting."

He picked up a box of cigars from his desk, wrapped it in a sheet of newspaper, and together the two men left the room, Arao towering over the shorter, but sturdy, Minister of War. They walked in silence down the stairs.

Then from the box he was carrying Anami took out a couple of cigars. "I'd like you to have these, Arao," he said. He smiled again. He said, "I'll be seeing you," as he went out through the front door of his Ministry into the black night.

At the Foreign Office, the Vice-Minister, Shunichi Matsumoto, had approved the text of Japan's acceptance of the Potsdam Proclamation. The Emperor had already signed the Rescript. Once the members of the Cabinet had added their names, the Foreign Office would cable the Japanese ministers in Switzerland and Sweden, the one to transmit the message to the United States and China, the other to Great Britain and the Soviet Union.

Matsumoto's message was as follows:

Communication of the Japanese Government of August 14, 1945, addressed to the Governments of the United States, Great Britain, the Soviet Union, and China:

With reference to the Japanese Government's note of August 10 regarding their acceptance of the provisions of the Potsdam Declaration and the reply of the Governments of the United States, Great Britain, the Soviet Union, and China sent by American Secretary of State Byrnes under the date of August 11, the Japanese Government have the honor to communicate to the Governments of the four powers as follows:

1. His Majesty the Emperor has issued an Imperial Rescript regarding Japan's acceptance of the provisions of the Potsdam Declaration.

2. His Majesty the Emperor is prepared to authorize and ensure the signature by his government and the Imperial General Headquarters of the necessary terms for carrying out the provisions of the Potsdam Declaration. His Majesty is also prepared to issue his commands to all the military, naval, and air authorities of Japan and all the forces under their control wherever located to cease active operations, to surrender arms and to issue such other orders as may be required by the Supreme Commander of the Allied Forces for the execution of the above-mentioned terms.

The war had begun for Japan fifteen years ago, with the Manchurian Incident; for the United States, four years ago, on December 7th, 1941: now, with the dispatch of this cable, the Japanese Minister of Foreign Affairs would be able to communicate directly once again with the American Secretary of State instead of depending on a man named Max Grässli, Chargé d'Affaires ad interim of Switzerland.

Meanwhile the Foreign Ministry sat and waited, and the world sat and waited, for word to come from the room with the round table in the Prime Minister of Japan's official residence.

The Prime Minister sat and waited too. The Rescript that had been signed by the Emperor lay spread out on the table. Beside it stood a new inkstone and a brush, ready for the Cabinet members to use. But only about half of them were present.

The Minister of War entered the room and bowed. Then he too sat down to wait.

Colonel Haga was commander of the Second Regiment of the Imperial Guards Division. For over an hour he had been listening to the persuasive arguments of Major Hatanaka and Lieutenant Colonel Shiizaki, who wanted him to agree to use the Guards to continue protecting the Emperor—but to "protect" him now from the "traitors" around him, in other words, to isolate the Emperor and the Palace from the rest of the world, during which time the Army would rise and the Emperor would be persuaded by that action to change his mind about surrender. And once the Emperor changed his mind, the Army would rise. The logic worked both ways. And in either event, there was no question that the troops, wavering between a dishonorable life and a glorious death, would now choose the latter. Japan would live again, and so would the Imperial Japanese Army.

Colonel Haga continued uncertain.

Then Hatanaka and Shiizaki let him in on a big secret: the Minister of War, the Army Chief of Staff, and the two commanders of the Eastern District Army and the Imperial Guards Division were all in on the plan. If Haga continued to refuse his cooperation, he would not only be missing his big chance, he might even be letting himself in for trouble.

That the Minister of War, the Army Chief of Staff, and the two commanders of the Eastern District Army and the Imperial Guards Division had all spoken out, unconditionally, against the plan did not unduly disturb either Hatanaka or Shiizaki. Ebulliently riding

177

the crest of their insurgent wave, they had convinced themselves that once they had Haga tucked into their pockets, and the Emperor isolated in his Palace, the four leaders of the Army would indeed join the conspiracy. They too would change their minds. The Emperor would change his mind, then the High Command, then the troops. It hardly mattered in which order these events occurred: although it is true that Hatanaka and Shiizaki had enough common sense left to realize that they had better get General Mori of the Guards on their side almost at once, or Colonel Haga would realize he had been tricked.

Meanwhile, he had obviously taken the bait. Was the hook firm? It seemed so to the two conspirators.

Colonel Haga summoned his adjutant, Captain Soga, into his office. Soga was surprised to see two unknown officers sitting there. They looked very like the officers he had seen only a little over an hour ago at Nijubashi. It seemed to Soga that the atmosphere in the room was rather odd; he couldn't quite put his finger on it, but the strange officers sat so tensely, with their swords between their legs and their hands resting on the pommels.

The silence in the room wore on for a moment or two. Then Colonel Haga broke it. "Soga," he said, "take down an order."

The adjutant prepared to write it out.

But no words came. Colonel Haga was deep in thought. All the officers remained silent. Soga kept his eyes on the regiment commander.

"All right," said Haga at last. "You may go. Thank you. It seems I've changed my mind."

Soga had no idea what it was all about. Neither, for the moment, did Hatanaka and Shiizaki.

The Cabinet meeting had been called for nine-thirty. It was now almost ten, and most of the members were present. The Prime

Minister decided to begin the signing of the Rescript. Wetting a brush with India ink, he bent over the document and signed the characters for SUZUKI KANTARO.

10 p.m. to 11 p.m.

"We'll kill if there's no other way to give the country what it needs."

Major Kenji Hatanaka

ONE OF THE INFORMATION BUREAU SECretaries, who was waiting for the Cabinet meeting to end, was called to the telephone by the head of the Bureau's broadcasting section. The secretary was told that everything was now ready for the Emperor's recording—save the signal to go ahead with it—and that the presence of Information Bureau Director Shimomura had been requested.

Obviously, a message had to be got to Shimomura that he was wanted at the Palace, but he was still in a meeting, and once the doors were shut on a Cabinet session, no one was allowed to enter or even communicate with one of the members except a certain old man named Yanagida, who, as long as anyone could recall, had been entrusted with this job. The Bureau secretary, accordingly, wrote out a message and gave it to Yanagida to take into the meeting.

The formal signing of the Rescript was still under way. The

Cabinet members looked exhausted and rather seedy; they sat in silence as the Rescript slowly made its round. When one Cabinet member received it from another, he straightened his back and bowed, then settled down to read the document as though he had never seen or heard of it before. Some members of the Cabinet read it several times.

Suzuki's signature had been followed by those of Navy Minister Yonai and Justice Minister Matsuzaka. The War Minister signed quickly, hardly even bothering to glance at the document that was to end the long domination of his uniform, the khaki uniform of the Imperial Army, over Japanese public life. Soon the only khaki to be seen on the streets of Japan would be that of its conquerors.

After Shimomura had signed the Rescript, he announced that he must leave the meeting in order to be present at the Imperial recording. Both he and his secretary, who accompanied him, were wearing *kokuminfuku,* the war-time work uniform; to this Shimomura pinned his decorations, and then they entered the waiting car in the company of an armed police officer, who was to see them safely into the Palace.

The night was black, and the pitted streets, so far as anyone could see, as the car wound its way through the ruins, were deserted. The mist seemed to have lifted, at least momentarily, and Shimomura's secretary looked up at the stars and found comfort in the reflection that they would still be there a thousand years from now, when Japan's defeat and degradation would have been long since forgotten.

A shooting star flared and was gone.

Time passed; nothing seemed to be happening anywhere in this defeated capital that was trying so hard, and so far failing, to surrender. Everywhere its streets seemed empty; no glimmer of light broke the still blackness. Occasionally a vehicle, like the car that was taking Shimomura to the Imperial Palace, threaded its careful way over the torn and dangerous streets. The citizens of the capital, their bellies empty and their spirits worn, holed in for another night, much as their long-dead ancestors must have sealed themselves into caves against the threatening darkness outside. Would the broadcast promised for noon tomorrow, they wondered, make any difference?

Even the ministries were dark and deserted, save for the Foreign Office, where a few people still waited wearily for the signal to start the chain of communication that would eventually let the world know the war had ended. In the Imperial Palace, the NHK recording team was still waiting too, in exhausted silence, for another signal, this one to start another chain of communication that would eventually let Japan know the war had ended. In a room next to the bedroom of the Chief Aide-de-Camp, double bunks had been constructed for two other aides, Seike and Nakamura; they were there now, getting ready to go to bed.

In the Military Affairs Section of the War Ministry, three lieutenant colonels—Takeshita, Shirai, and Eki—were sitting quietly in an almost darkened room drinking *sake*. They had been busy men, running a war; even if the war was latterly a losing one, it had taken running; and now it was all over: the three lieutenant colonels had nothing in the world to do but sit and drink *sake*. They did not even have anything to say, which is not a usual state of affairs in Japan; but tonight everything seemed to have been said already. And perhaps their minds were as silent as their voices, as the room they were in, the Ministry, the capital, the defeated country—and the radiant cities of Hiroshima and Nagasaki. Perhaps the three lieutenant colonels were only thinking how lucky they were to have some rice wine to drink when most other people in the country had not enough rice to eat.

Even at Atsugi air base, nothing much seemed to be happening. Captain Kozono had, to be sure, given orders to prepare for action, and his officers and men had by now completed their preparations, but no word came from the commander. He was invisible, behind the closed doors of his office; his men waited impatiently for the signal to attack, but the signal failed to come. And so they waited.

Behind his closed doors, Captain Kozono, weakened by the attack of malaria he had suffered that afternoon, was trying to draft a cable. He would write a sentence, then scratch it out, and write another—only to discover he had written the same sentence again. He would take a brief rest, but somehow the process seemed to repeat itself.

He muttered his exasperation at the illness that had so weakened him on this most important day of his life, for Captain Kozono had reached a momentous decision: he was going to assume command of the Imperial Navy. Let the Army surrender ignominiously! The Navy would fight on alone—under Captain Kozono. He was now drafting a preliminary cable, to be sent to all naval officers.

The captain wrote:

The order to cease fire, and the order to disarm that will follow, must inevitably mean the end of our national structure and of the Emperor. To obey such orders would be equal to committing high treason.

The captain wrote:

Japan is sacred and indestructible. If we unite for action, we will destroy the enemy. Of that there can be no doubt whatsoever.

He put down his pen. How tired he felt! His body ached, his head hammered in his skull. He made one last effort: he picked up the pen again and wrote:

I hope that you will agree with me.

Lieutenant Colonel Ida was not drinking *sake* with the other officers of his rank, he was asleep, in one of the rooms of the War Ministry, where he had been living the last few days.

He was awakened by Major Hatanaka and Lieutenant Colonel Shiizaki. Although Ida's annoyance was evident, the two young men offered no apologies. "I request the Lieutenant Colonel's approval!" cried Hatanaka, in an exalted tone.

"What's this all about?" said Ida, sitting up and rubbing his eyes.

"You turned Hatanaka down earlier in the afternoon," said Shiizaki. "Now he's come to make another request for your approval of his plan."

"The Imperial Guards are with us!" Hatanaka broke in. "All of them. Well, except Commander Mori. And he'll come around. Meanwhile, Colonel Haga is on our side, I assure you he is." And that was true. After his adjutant had left the room, Haga explained that he had changed his mind not about joining the conspiracy but about issuing an order that might be premature.

"But," said Ida, "without General Mori—"

"Exactly," Hatanaka cried excitedly. "But if the Lieutenant Colonel will approve our plan, then he is the obvious man to persuade General Mori to join us. The General was one of my teachers at War College—he thinks of me still as an immature boy. And Koga too is too young, although the General thinks highly of him. But if the Lieutenant Colonel will talk to him, I'm sure General Mori will come around to us. And once he does, our success is certain."

"But if he doesn't?" said Ida. "What then?"

"Then we must just accept that fact. But as I see it, the main question before us is not whether General Mori will join us or not, it's whether or not we should exert our maximum effort to the last."

In the silence that followed, Ida recalled their dialogue earlier in the day, when he had insisted that his own project for mass suicide was more suitable than Hatanaka's frantic but doomed conspiracy. He remembered Hatanaka's impassioned and curiously convincing arguments, his own despair. Now, as he looked at the flushed face

Suzuki's Cabinet, photographed June 9th, 1945. Members of the Cabinet (see diagram) are: (1) Kantaro Suzuki, Prime Minister; (2) Hiroshi Shimomura, Director of the Information Bureau; (3) Mitsumasa Yonai, Navy Minister; (4) Kozo Ohta, Education Minister; (5) Naoto Kobiyama, Transportation Minister; (6) Naoyasu Murase, Director of the Legislative Bureau; (7) Tadaatsu Ishiguro, Minister of Agriculture and Commerce; (8) Korechika Anami, War Minister; (9) Fujihara Yasui, State Minister; (10) Hisatsune Sakomizu, Chief Cabinet Secretary; (11) Sadajiro Toyoda, Munitions Minister; (12) Seizo Sakonji, State Minister; (13) Tsukizo Akinaga, Director of the Overall Planning Bureau; (14) Hiromasa Matsuzaka, Justice Minister; (15) Heigoro Sakurai, State Minister; (16) Shigenori Togo, Foreign Minister; (17) Hosaku Hirose, Finance Minister; (18) Tadahiko Okada, Welfare Minister and (19) Genki Abe, Home Minister.

Above: The Prime Minister, Baron Kantaro Suzuki

Hiroshi Shimomura, Director of the Information Bureau

Above: Admiral Mitsumasa Yonai, Navy Minister

Tadaatsu Ishiguro, Minister of Agriculture and Commerce

Above: Hisatsune Sakomizu, Chief Cabinet Secretary

Seizo Sakonji, State Minister

Above: Shigenori Togo, Foreign Minister

Hiromasa Matsuzaka, Minister of Justice

Hosaku Hirose, Finance Minister

Genki Abe, Home Minister

Meeting of the Supreme Council for the Direction of the War in the presence of the Emperor on August 9th. From left, clockwise: Lieutenant General Sumihisa Ikeda, Director of the Cabinet's Overall Planning Bureau; Vice-Admiral Zenshiro Hoshina, Director of the Bureau of Naval Affairs; Admiral Soemu Toyoda, Navy Chief of Staff; Shigenori Togo, Foreign Minister; Admiral Mitsumasa Yonai, Navy Minister; Baron Kiichiro Hiranuma, President of the Privy Council; General Shigeru Hasunuma, Chief Aide-de-Camp (behind Hiranuma); H.M. the Emperor; Baron Kantaro Suzuki, Prime Minister; General Korechika Anami, War Minister; General Yoshijiro Umezu, Army Chief of Staff; Lieutenant General Masao Yoshizumi, Director of the Bureau of Military Affairs at the War Ministry and Hisatsune Sakomizu, Chief Cabinet Secretary.

Marquis Koichi Kido, Lord Keeper of the Privy Seal

Baron Kiichiro Hiranuma, President of the Privy Council

General Yoshijiro Umezu,
Army Chief of Staff

Admiral Soemu Toyoda,
Navy Chief of Staff

General Shigeru Hasunuma,
Chief Aide-de-Camp

Above: Shunichi Matsumoto, Vice-Minister of Foreign Affairs

Sukemasa Irie, Imperial chamberlain

Yoshihiro Tokugawa, Imperial chamberlain

Yasuhide Toda, Imperial chamberlain

Nobukata Wada, NHK radio announcer

Morio Tateno, NHK radio announcer

Field Marshal Gen Sugiyama visiting the Meiji Shrine, 1945

Field Marshal Shunroku Hata, commander of the Second General Army

General Kenji Doihara, Inspector-
General of Military Education

Naoyasu Murase, Director of the
Legislative Bureau

*Sotaro Ishiwatari, Imperial
Household Minister*

Prince Fumimaro Konoye

General Hideki Tojo, then Premier of Japan, in December, 1941

staring at him, and at the dark, glittering eyes, he felt less certain that he was right and Hatanaka wrong. Was it not, perhaps, in the end, more honorable to die fighting for a righteous cause than to take one's own life in lonely splendor?

The fact that Hatanaka's superiors—although they knew, by now, all of them, of his frenzied efforts to foment an Army rebellion—refrained from taking any one of the many possible measures for stopping him was proof, perhaps, that they really did not want to stop him. In theory they disapproved, and they would disapprove in practice if the projected *coup* failed, but if it succeeded . . .?

How could it possibly succeed? Real, true success must end in final victory, and Ida knew well that victory was for Japan now an unrealizable dream—a tiny green island invested on all sides by the two mightiest nations on earth. It was hopeless. But perhaps, for that very reason, it was nobler to fight and die in a hopeless cause than to hopelessly die without having fought. . . .

In this state of continued, and tormenting, indecision, Ida rose. He went into the next room and woke another member of the Military Affairs Section, Lieutenant Colonel Shimanuki. Having sketched Hatanaka's plan briefly, Ida asked Shimanuki's opinion. "It's hopeless," replied the latter at once, echoing Ida's own words. "Hopeless. Out of the question. My advice to you is to forget the whole thing. And let me go back to sleep."

At that, Ida left him. "So you see," he said to Hatanaka, "if I can't even persuade the man who works with me and sleeps next door to me, how can I win over the commander of the First Imperial Guards Division? It seems to me very unlikely. So if General Mori doesn't approve your plan, what will you do then? I would like an explicit answer to that question."

"Heaven," said Shiizaki, "will reward our loyalty to our Emperor and our country. We are convinced of that. We are convinced our plan will succeed. As a last resort, however—"

201

"As a last resort," Hatanaka interrupted, his voice low and brusque, "we may have to kill. We'll kill if there's no other way to give the country what it needs. I think you had better make up your mind to that. Isn't Japan worth a death or two?"

Ida had been on the point of giving Japan his own life; it seemed a strange twist of logic to balk at giving her someone else's. And yet. . . . He decided that in his fatigue and despair he must be missing some essential point. He changed the subject. "How about the Eastern Army?" he asked. "You'll need that too."

"We don't know for sure whether General Tanaka is with us or not. However, I'm convinced that if the Guards take over the Palace, the Eastern Army will surely follow. There is no doubt in my mind whatsoever."

"Your whole plan, then," said Ida, "hinges on one action—the Guards taking control of the Palace and temporarily isolating the Emperor. Therefore, unanimity on the part of the Guards Division is essential to your plan—but you cannot achieve that unanimity unless the commander is with you. And yet you speak of killing General Mori *if necessary*. Do you really believe your plan could succeed if you kill the Guards commander? It's nonsense! And haven't you forgotten the true relationship between the Emperor and his subjects?"

"But I tell you—"

"It isn't your purpose merely to create trouble, is it? Political disorder? Chaos? To turn Japan into—"

"It's absolutely safe, I tell you! It's absolutely safe!" There were tears in Hatanaka's eyes. He continued solemnly: "I promise on my word of honor to forget the whole thing if the Lieutenant Colonel fails to persuade General Mori."

"May I believe you?" said Ida.

"I have given my word," replied Hatanaka.

Ida stared at him for a moment in silence. Suddenly he remembered the voice of Professor Hiraizumi, of Tokyo Imperial University, expounding what he called the "natural" basis of the relationship between Japan and her Emperor: the two were born simultaneously, and their relationship was fixed at that moment, and so is immutable—from the beginning of time to the end of time. The purity and simplicity of the theory were appealing, and Major Hatanaka had also fallen under the spell of Professor Hiraizumi, as had Lieutenant Colonel Takeshita, the War Minister's brother-in-law who was destined to become involved briefly in Hatanaka's *coup d'état*. The Emperor, according to this theory, is the possessor of Japan, and his subjects, in making use of what he grants them, must feel boundless gratitude toward him. How then could those subjects permit their Emperor to "surrender unconditionally" on their behalf? This was the most dishonorable ingratitude: it shamed forever the spirits of the heroic dead. "Very well," said Ida, "I'll do what I can."

Hatanaka's mobile face cleared and brightened; his smile was like the sudden reappearance of the sun on a cloudy morning. Impulsively he put out his hand; as Japanese shake hands infrequently, this gesture was perhaps more meaningful than it might have seemed to Western eyes. That's that, then, thought Ida: tomorrow the old Japan will be reborn again—or else we'll all be dead.

Hatanaka, echoing his thoughts, said: "One of the points to make with General Mori is that *we* are not the revolutionists. The revolutionists are the men who are forcing Japan to surrender. Japan cannot surrender! It is not part of her national polity. We're only trying to make sure that the old, natural Japan survives—we're not revolutionists, we're traditionalists. . . ."

The three men had left the War Ministry and now, in the treacherous blackness, began to bicycle toward headquarters of the Imperial Guards Division. It was slow going, across the dark, ruined streets, and Ida's mind was elsewhere. He had suddenly remembered a story he had read long ago, in the second or third year of middle school, about a young man of the Ogaki clan who had refused to abide by his clan's decision to side with the Emperor in a quarrel between the Imperial House and the Tokugawa Shogunate. This young *samurai* felt he owed a debt of gratitude to the Shogunate, and so he left his clan and joined the rebel army.

Now why on earth, thought Ida, am I remembering that story now? Then suddenly of course he knew: he too had left his clan, the War Ministry, and taken up arms—no matter how Hatanaka phrased it—in a rebel cause. If the cause succeeded, then he would be a rebel no longer but a champion of the Emperor, a defender of the "natural" relationship between the country and its ruler. Suddenly the chain of his thoughts was broken by an ear-splitting explosion.

But it wasn't a bomb, it was only one of his bicycle tires that had burst. They were all old and fairly useless, anyway. The journey to isolate the Emperor, reanimate the Army, and vanquish the Allied Powers had to be interrupted, then, a few minutes before eleven, while the three conspirators repaired Lieutenant Colonel Ida's dilapidated bicycle tire.

11 p.m. to 12 Midnight

"Anyway, everything has come out all right in the end."

Shigenori Togo

THE EMPEROR WAS ABOUT TO LEAVE THE Gobunko, where he was then living, for the Imperial Household Ministry, to make his recording of the Rescript. Waiting for him were Director Shimomura of the Information Bureau and Chairman Ohashi of the Japan Broadcasting Corporation, as well as members of the recording team. An air-raid warning sounded.

The Emperor indicated his intention to continue on to the Ministry, but Chamberlain Irie pointed out that he had better wait in the underground shelter until the targets for that night's enemy air action were known. The Emperor agreed.

In the Premier's official residence, the Transportation Minister had wet the brush that lay waiting on the table. He was the only Cabinet member who had not signed the document; once he did, the Rescript would become official, Japan would have agreed to unconditional surrender, although the rest of the world could not know it yet. An air-raid warning sounded. He signed his name.

The head of the Cabinet's General Affairs Section received a signal that he might enter the room. All the waiting secretaries knew what that meant. One of them telephoned the Foreign Office and spoke to Vice-Minister Matsumoto, who immediately instructed the chief of the cable room to send the prepared and waiting messages to Switzerland and Sweden for transmission to the four belligerent powers. Now the world would know it soon.

Meanwhile another copy of the Rescript was being made for publication in the Official Gazette, which, although it had suspended printing because of war-time shortages, would officially proclaim the Rescript in a brief supplement. The head of the General Affairs Section did not use customary channels but instead summoned the director of the Official Gazette and handed him the specially prepared copy of the Rescript in person.

The Japanese Empire had now breathed its last breath—but the Japanese people remained to be informed of the death.

Lieutenant Tsune Fujii, of the Eastern District Army, informed Shinjiro Okamatsu, head of the Imperial Household Ministry's Air Defense Section, that the enemy planes which had triggered the warning did not seem to be headed in the direction of Tokyo. Okamatsu relayed this information to Chamberlain Irie, and shortly after, the Emperor, wearing the uniform of a generalissimo, prepared to leave the Gobunko, where a car was waiting to take him to the Goseimu room of the Imperial Household Ministry.

The Premier and his Cabinet, greatly fatigued but also greatly relaxed, now that their last major piece of business was done, were considering the form of their resignation, to make way for a new "peace-time" Cabinet.

General Anami belted on his sword, went over to Foreign Minister Togo, and made him a fifteen-degree bow. "I have seen the text of the note the Foreign Office is sending," he said, "to accompany our acceptance of the Potsdam Proclamation, and I would like to thank you for it."

Togo smiled, for what he had done, after all, was no more than what he had always said he was willing to do—that is, to *ask* the enemy for the concessions that Anami had wanted to insist on. The second point in this Note read:

Disarming of the Japanese forces, being a most delicate task as it involves over three millions of officers and men overseas and having direct bearing on their honor, the Japanese Government will, of course, take utmost pains [sic.]. But it is suggested that the best and the most effective method would be that under the command of His Majesty the Emperor, the Japanese forces are allowed to disarm themselves and surrender arms of their own accord.[13]

"I am most grateful to you," Anami continued, "and feel I owe you an apology for some of the things I may have said in the heat of argument."

Togo returned the bow and, smiling, said, "Anyway, everything has come out all right in the end."

The two former enemies laughed and parted.

Now the War Minister picked up his small, newspaper-wrapped package and strode to the Premier's private office next door to the conference room. As Anami, wearing white gloves, with his sword hanging at his side, entered the room, the elderly Prime Minister was sitting exhausted in a chair behind his desk. Chief Cabinet Secretary Sakomizu and a few other men were in the room.

"I beg your pardon for disturbing you," said Anami. He stood at attention in front of Suzuki's desk.

Suzuki rose.

"When the problem of terminating the war came up," said Anami,

"I expressed the opinions I held as representative of the Army. I may have expressed them over strongly at times, but my intention was always to assist the Prime Minister to the best of my ability. I fear that as things worked out, I was not always successful, and I would like to apologize for that. I would like the Prime Minister to realize that my chief aim has always been the preservation of our national polity. That, and nothing else, has been my prime motivation. Please believe me."

Suzuki came from behind his desk. "I do believe you," he said. He put his hand on the War Minister's shoulder, as though the younger man was his own son. "I am grateful to you for the frankness with which you expressed your beliefs, and I know that it was patriotism that motivated you, nothing else."

The War Minister nodded, like a dutiful child.

"Set your mind at rest," the Premier went on. "The Imperial House will be preserved. The Emperor is safe. He will soon be praying to the spirits of his ancestors."

"I trust he will be safe," said Anami.

"Nor am I unduly pessimistic about the future of Japan," Suzuki went on.

"I agree with you," Anami said. "I believe that if the Emperor and the people are together, Japan will recover."

After a moment's silence, Anami brought out his little newspaper-wrapped package and handed it to Suzuki. "I would like you to have these," he said. "They're cigars from the southern front, and since I don't smoke, I think the Prime Minister should make use of them." He saluted and left without another word.

The Chief Cabinet Secretary saw him off, then returned to Suzuki's private office.

"I think the War Minister," said Suzuki, "came to say goodbye." The room relapsed into silence.

The lights in the Goseimu-shitsu seemed almost intolerably bright after the blacked-out darkness outside.[14] Director Shimomura of the Information Bureau escorted the Emperor into the room. Waiting by the window were the Imperial Household Minister and the Grand Chamberlain. When the Emperor entered, accompanied by two chamberlains, Mitsui and Toda, everyone in the room bowed deeply. In the adjoining room, its doors opened, stood Secretary Kawamoto and men from the Information Bureau, the Japan Broadcasting Corporation, and the Imperial Household Ministry. These too all made deep bows as the Emperor made his entrance into the Goseimu room.

As the Emperor approached the microphone, which stood in the center of the room, he asked, "How loudly should I speak?"

Shimomura replied that the Emperor's ordinary tones would be adequate. He stepped forward and raised his white-gloved hand, the signal to begin the recording.

In the second before the Emperor began to speak, the Imperial Household Minister, standing beside the window, recalled how the Emperor, just two days before, had said, "I am doing my utmost to effect peace, but I don't know whether I'll succeed or not, or if I do, what may happen then. I would like to see the Dowager Empress once more. Who knows whether I shall ever see her again?" Yet the Emperor's voice gave no hint of his uncertainty as he began to read the Imperial Rescript of August 14th, 1945.

TO OUR GOOD AND LOYAL SUBJECTS:

After pondering deeply the general trends of the world and the actual conditions obtaining in Our Empire today, We have decided to effect a settlement of the present situation by resorting to an extraordinary measure.

We have ordered Our Government to communicate to the Governments of the United States, Great Britain, China and the Soviet

Union that Our Empire accepts the provisions of their Joint Declaration.

To strive for the common prosperity and happiness of all nations as well as the security and well-being of Our subjects is the solemn obligation which has been handed down by Our Imperial Ancestors and which lies close to Our heart.

Indeed, We declared war on America and Britain out of Our sincere desire to ensure Japan's self-preservation and the stabilization of East Asia, it being far from Our thought either to infringe upon the sovereignty of other nations or to embark upon territorial aggrandizement.

But now the war has lasted for nearly four years. Despite the best that has been done by everyone—the gallant fighting of the military and naval forces, the diligence and assiduity of Our servants of the State, and the devoted service of Our one hundred million people—the war situation has developed not necessarily to Japan's advantage, while the general trends of the world have all turned against her interest.

Moreover, the enemy has begun to employ a new and most cruel bomb, the power of which to do damage is, indeed, incalculable, taking the toll of many innocent lives. Should We continue to fight, not only would it result in an ultimate collapse and obliteration of the Japanese nation, but also it would lead to the total extinction of human civilization.

Such being the case, how are We to save the millions of Our subjects, or to atone Ourselves before the hallowed spirits of Our Imperial Ancestors? This is the reason why We have ordered the acceptance of the provisions of the Joint Declaration of the Powers.

We cannot but express the deepest sense of regret to Our Allied nations of East Asia, who have consistently cooperated with the Empire towards the emancipation of East Asia.

The thought of those officers and men as well as others who have fallen in the fields of battle, those who died at their posts of duty, or those who met with untimely death and all their bereaved families, pains Our heart night and day.

The welfare of the wounded and the war-sufferers, and of those who have lost their homes and livelihood, are the objects of Our profound solicitude.

The hardships and sufferings to which Our nation is to be subjected hereafter will be certainly great. We are keenly aware of the inmost feelings of all of you, Our subjects. However, it is according to the dictates of time and fate that We have resolved to pave the way for a grand peace for all the generations to come by enduring the unendurable and suffering what is unsufferable.

Having been able to safeguard and maintain the structure of the Imperial State, We are always with you, Our good and loyal subjects, relying upon your sincerity and integrity.

Beware most strictly of any outbursts of emotion which may engender needless complications, or any fraternal contention and strife which may create confusion, lead you astray and cause you to lose the confidence of the world.

Let the entire nation continue as one family from generation to generation, ever firm in its faith in the imperishability of its sacred land, and mindful of its heavy burden of responsibility and of the long road before it.

Unite your total strength, to be devoted to construction for the future. Cultivate the ways of rectitude, foster nobility of spirit, and work with resolution— so that you may enhance the innate glory of the Imperial State and keep pace with the progress of the world.

"Was it all right?" asked the Emperor.

The question was relayed to the chief engineer, who replied, in a voice so low he could hardly be heard, "There were no technical errors, but a few words were not entirely clear."

The Emperor then said to Shimomura that he would like to make another recording, as he was aware that his voice had been too low.

Shimomura conveyed the Emperor's desire to the recording team, raised his white-gloved hand, and once more the Voice of the Sacred Crane was impressed into the grooves of a record. This time the Emperor sounded somewhat more tense, and his voice, instead of being pitched too low, was now a bit too high. He even, in this rereading, missed a word. The head of the Information Bureau's First Division said later that he distinctly saw tears in the Emperor's eyes.

There was no question that many of the other men in the room were crying: tears mingled with sweat, for the room was crowded, and it was a hot, still mid-August night. Even could the windows have been opened, it would not have helped much: there was hardly a breath stirring outside.

The Emperor apparently feared that the second recording was inadequate. "I am quite willing to make a third," he said.

Conversation within the Imperial presence was, apparently, an intimidating experience. The head of the General Affairs Section meant to ask the Chief Engineer whether he was ready to make a third recording. What the Chief Engineer understood by the question was whether a third recording was necessary; he replied that it was not. The head of the General Affairs Section was about to repeat his demand when Shimomura intervened. He had conferred briefly with the Imperial Household Minister and the Grand Chamberlain, and they had all agreed that it would be too much to ask the Emperor to undergo so trying an ordeal a third time.

Accompanied by Chamberlain Irie, His Majesty re-entered the car that had been waiting for him. He spoke not a word during the brief trip back to the Gobunko, where he was to sleep that night, while the Foreign Ministry's cables took their devious route to Washington and Moscow, London and Chungking.

After he reached his official residence in Miyakezaka, General Anami requested his adjutant, Major Hayashi, to see if he could find him a couple of sheets of heavy Japanese paper, by then very difficult to come by. Hayashi left on his errand, and Anami's maid asked if the Minister was ready for his injection. He had been taking a nightly course of vitamins in an effort to combat the fatigue resulting from long hours of work and short hours of sleep. Anami looked perplexed, almost surprised, for a moment; then said, "Yes. Why not?" He seemed almost to be laughing.

In the staff room of the Imperial Guards Division, Lieutenant Colonel Ida was meeting a fellow conspirator, Major Koga, for the first time. The introduction was performed by Major Hatanaka. Present also were Lieutenant Colonel Shiizaki, Major Ishihara, and Captain Uehara, of the Air Academy.

Ida and Hatanaka had requested an interview, some while back, with General Mori, but the General was in conference and could not be disturbed. They sat there waiting, while Koga and Ishihara studied Hatanaka's plan of action. It seemed hopeful to them, and perhaps even more than hopeful when they learned that the Division's battalion commanders had not only agreed to the plan but had already stationed troops in strategic positions around the Palace.

However, the crux of the matter, as Ida recognized, was General Mori, the Guards commander. If he was officially informed of the plan and failed to approve it, there was no guessing what action he might take. Ida shrugged; perhaps anything was better than cutting one's own belly open. It hardly seemed to matter. Ida's enthusiasm was dying with the long wait.

Captain Kozono had called all the officers of the 302nd Air Corps into his office, where he told them, for the first time, that the Emperor had actually decided to surrender. His manner and tone of voice left little doubt in their minds that he expected to be asked again whether he intended to abide by the decision; his reply was also anticipated.

"As long as I am commander here," he cried, "the Atsugi Air Corps will never surrender! There is a supply of food underground that will permit us to hold out for two years. And I personally intend to do so. Are any of you with me?"

The enthusiasm was immediate. "Yes, yes!" they all cried. This time there seemed to be no silent voices.

"Let them call us traitor!" cried Kozono. "It doesn't matter. Surrender is not only against our traditions, it's against our law. Japan *cannot* surrender! Are you with me?"

"Yes, yes! Banzai! Banzai! Banzai!"

The Imperial Japanese Army, muttered Captain Sasaki, of the Yokohama Guards, has no such word as "surrender" in its vocabulary. Japan must fight! It has the men and the will to fight—why should it surrender? There is still a huge Japanese army on the Chinese mainland, and Japan still holds 350,000 Allied prisoners of war. Why should Japan surrender?

Sasaki was on his way to the Guards headquarters behind Sojiji Temple in the Tsurumi section of Yokohama, where one battalion was always stationed. His plan was to issue arms to the men—and then an emergency order to kill the Prime Minister. It seemed to him that this was the best way to begin his private war against surrender.

Japan may perhaps be counted fortunate, as midnight struck, that Captain Sasaki was unaware of either the conspirators in the Imperial Guards or those at Atsugi Air Base—and that neither of the latter was in contact with the other. Even together they could not, of course, have held back the irresistible tide of history, but they might have succeeded in seeing their little island inundated by it.

12 Midnight to 1 a.m.

"Do you call yourselves men?"
Captain Takeo Sasaki

ANOTHER AIR-RAID WARNING SOUNDED throughout the Kanto plain. At Kodama, thirty-six planes of the 27th Air Corps took off to engage the enemy, who had been sighted off Boso. The citizens of the town had come out to the airfield at the first wail of the siren. They stood waving flags and shouting *banzai* as the planes with the rising sun painted on their sides took off into the night. The war may have ostensibly ended, but it was not over yet.

Tokyo was completely blacked out. Although the residents of the capital had got used to enemy raids by now, and even to the havoc of incendiary bombing over a largely wooden city, there had been a different thought in their minds ever since Hiroshima and Nagasaki and the rumor that Tokyo was next. Was this it? they wondered, as they huddled in their crowded little rooms and tried to anticipate what the planes might be bringing tonight in the way of destruction.

Colonel Arao, bedding down cozily in the War Ministry, hoped

215

it was something big and final. Colonel Arao would have liked to die that night.

In the Imperial Palace, the Emperor had returned to the Gobunko and was about to retire for the night. Chamberlain Irie said he would report to His Majesty if anything happened. His Majesty merely nodded and disappeared into an inner room. Irie doubted whether anything much would happen the night the war ended.

The NHK men in the Imperial Household Ministry had just listened to the Emperor's two recordings; they agreed that the first was the superior recording and proposed to Chief Motohike Kakei, of the Ministry's General Affairs Section, that it be used for the noon broadcast.

The two sets of records (two records to a set) were put into metal cases, but the lids didn't fit very well, so the broadcasting people asked Kakei if he could supply any better means of securing the records. After a moment's thought, he came up with two khaki-colored cotton bags, around eighteen inches square, that were used to hold air defense uniforms. After the records had been put into the bags, the question arose of where they were to be kept for the next twelve hours. To the Imperial Household Ministry it seemed reasonable that the Japan Broadcasting Corporation should take charge of them. But the Japan Broadcasting Corporation felt it would be disrespectful to the Emperor to bring the records to the station in the middle of the night. They pointed out, further, that in view of the sinister rumors about Army activity that were flying about, the records would be safer in the Imperial Household Ministry. The Ministry agreed.

But Kakei, having accepted the records, had no idea where to keep them. He could think of no suitable place in the General Affairs Section, so he asked the two chamberlains who happened to be present, Yoshihiro Tokugawa and Yasuhide Toda, if they would take charge of them. Tokugawa said he would, and accepted the two bags from Kakei. This, as it turned out, was probably one of the wisest moves that was made that night in Tokyo.

Tokugawa went into an office used by a member of the Empress's retinue. Although it was unheard of to keep objects relating to the Emperor in any but designated places, Tokugawa recalled that there was a small safe in this office and decided that that would be the best place to keep the records until morning. After he had locked the safe, he piled a lot of papers in front of it, to hide it from sight.

Once Director Shimomura of the Information Bureau had seen the two khaki-colored bags handed over to Chamberlain Tokugawa, he telephoned the Premier's official residence to report but was told that Suzuki was already on his way to his private house. Shimomura asked to speak to Chief Cabinet Secretary Sakomizu.

Sakomizu left the press conference he was holding in the underground bomb shelter of the Ministerial residence and came to the telephone.

"It's all over," Shimomura said. "The Emperor has made the recording, and there hasn't been any trouble. We're in the clear."

"Let's hope so," said Sakomizu. "But the night isn't over yet."

While he waited for the Chief Cabinet Secretary to return, *Asahi* reporter Shibata re-read the Imperial Rescript. The language was formal and unfamiliar, and Shibata had not been able to understand all of it in a first reading. It seemed to him now, studying it more carefully, that the little document possessed a strange power—the power to inspire Japan to recover from her defeat, to accept surrender without losing hope. It was something more, Shibata felt, than a Rescript terminating a war.

Sakomizu returned to the conference. He repeated, what he had said earlier, that no hint of the Rescript was to be printed until after the noon broadcast; he impressed on the editors and reporters present that no extra edition was authorized until after noon. The already enflamed Army, he said, might use the paper as an excuse for violence, with disastrous consequences for the nation. Newspaper men never like to sit on news, particularly news as momentous as this, but they acceded to Sakomizu's demands: the Emperor, they agreed, was the man to break the news to his hundred million subjects.

At Tsurumi, in Yokohama, Captain Sasaki stood in fury before his four company commanders. They had absolutely refused to obey his emergency mobilization order to assassinate Japan's cowardly elder statesmen. First, they said, politely but firmly, they would require orders from Major General Susumu Harada himself, commander of the Third Brigade of the Tokyo Guards, from whom the Yokohama Guards depended.

Captain Sasaki quivered in exasperation. He wanted to explain to them why true loyalty, in the present situation, called for action, not surrender; but he realized there was no time for lengthy arguments, and rebuttals, and more arguments. "We need action now!" he cried. "The very existence of the Empire is in question. Do you call yourselves men?"

"Say what you like," one of the four men replied quietly. "We're not going to follow your orders."

What Captain Sasaki did not know was that General Harada had issued secret instructions that Sasaki's orders were under no circumances to be obeyed.

"Isn't it our duty," cried Sasaki, more furiously still, "as officers and men of the Imperial Army, to preserve the Empire?"

"We're not doing anything without orders from General Harada."

"All right, then, don't!" cried Captain Sasaki. "But don't try to

stop me either, if you know what's good for you!" He stomped off
into the night.

It turned out that General Mori's long-staying visitor was his
brother-in-law, Lieutenant Colonel Shiraishi, who had called on
Colonel Arao at the War Ministry earlier in the day and who was
now taking his leave of General Mori before going back to Hiroshima in the morning. Finally, around twelve-thirty, word was
brought in to the waiting officers that General Mori would see
them. Hatanaka, who had been pacing up and down muttering,
"There's no time, there's no time," now suddenly cried, "I've
remembered something I've got to do!" He left just as suddenly,
taking Captain Uehara with him, and so Lieutenant Colonel Ida
had no choice but to interview General Mori with only Lieutenant
Colonel Shiizaki to back him. He would have preferred the more
volatile and inspiring Hatanaka and felt momentarily let down as,
with Shiizaki, he took his seat facing General Mori. Lieutenant
Colonel Shiraishi, Mori's brother-in-law, stood behind him.

In any case it appeared that Mori was not going to let the conspirators speak. He must have known the purpose of their midnight visit
and chose this means of telling them he was not with them and
preferred not to hear what they had to say. He began to talk at once,
slowly and calmly, monkishly, expounding his philosophy of life,
as though no war had just been fought and lost, as though no conspiracy was in the air, hopefully to turn defeat into victory like some
magician's sleight-of-hand. Whenever Ida tried to speak, Mori would
say, "Hold on a minute," and expose another of his views on life.
His office was small—only four and a half mats, less than nine feet
square—and hot, and Ida's exasperation mounted as Mori talked
affably on.

It seemed like hours. In fact, it was only about fifteen minutes.

Exhausted by four busy days and sleepless nights, Lieutenant Colonel Takeshita was trying to rest in his quarters at Surugadai, when Major Hatanaka burst into his room. Hatanaka declared that the plan was proceeding nicely. "The Second Regiment of the Imperial Guards," he said, "is already inside the Palace. They will take over at two o'clock." He looked at his watch. "In just over an hour," he said. "General Mori is the only one who's not with us so far—and I'm sure he will be by two. But we need Lieutenant Colonel Takeshita too."

Hatanaka's appeal was not without attraction. Takeshita had finally chosen the observer's role, but he still felt that in making that choice he was letting down not only his comrades but himself. Am I so cowardly, he thought, that I am afraid to be called a traitor? Am I so coldblooded I can say no to men who have fought and bled beside me? But the Emperor. . . . Anami. . . .

Takeshita had once been flagbearer of the Second Regiment of the First Imperial Guards. He would have given his life for it. Now his banner was flying over the grounds of the Imperial Palace and he was being asked to give perhaps something more than his life for it: his honor if he failed. Could he in all honor say no? But the Emperor. . . . Anami. . . .

"Isn't it better," said Takeshita, "to take the point of view that everything has ended? We've failed to win over the four most important officers in the Army—"

"Because they're bewildered," Hatanaka interrupted. "Just like their men. They don't know what to do. If we show them the right path to take, they'll follow. Once there's a state of real emergency, they'll all be with us."

"Not General Anami. Whatever happens, he'll stick by his word."

"He won't once we take over power. You're the only man who can explain the situation to him. No one but the Lieutenant Colonel can convince the War Minister!"

The impassioned voice ended. Takeshita found himself staring into those black, almost hypnotic eyes. Hatanaka's delicate young face seemed to glow with the fire of his conviction.

"Well," said Hatanaka, with a smile, "I must get back to the Guards. There isn't much time." He rose. "Maybe after our plan is already working, the Lieutenant Colonel will join us." He started for the door.

"Wait a minute," said Takeshita, who was already pulling on his uniform, "I'm coming too."

"Where?"

"You know where I'm going." Takeshita smiled. "To the Minister of War."

Hatanaka laughed, and the laughter sent a chill down Takeshita's spine. It was the most remarkable sound he had ever heard: it seemed to be the sum total of a man's happiness, the climax of his whole life. It was the laughter of a madman or a saint, and for a moment Takeshita felt himself elevated to a region too rarified for his more stolid blood.

Lieutenant Colonel Ida had been given, or had seized, a chance to speak at last. He expounded his belief in the "natural" unity of the Emperor, who is a living god, with all his subjects; this, he said, is not only Japan's national polity, it is her national faith. To accept a surrender, therefore, which leaves the Imperial House only outwardly intact while destroying its inner cohesion with the people is tantamount to the obliteration of Japan: it is both cowardice and treason.

"Whatever truth there may be," said General Mori, "in your words, the fact remains that the Emperor has spoken his decision. As Commander of the Imperial Guards, I must obey that decision, and I must insist that my men obey it."

His tone seemed final, yet Ida persevered. "The tiny country of

Paraguay," he said, "in South America fought a five-year war and lost eighty per cent of its people. And look at Finland, look at China. Yet we, though we boast that Japan is sacred and indestructible, are willing to surrender without engaging the enemy on our homeland. It is the height of selfishness, it is a betrayal of the spirits of the heroic dead. General, I do not believe that any honest officer can subscribe in his heart to such baseness. This is the moment for a regeneration of the Japanese spirit—and the Imperial Guards are the ones to lead us."

Ida fell silent. He was covered with sweat. His darkened uniform clung to his body, as he waited for Mori's reply.

1a.m. to 2a.m.

"What precisely are you asking the Eastern Army to do ?"
Major General Tatsuhiko Takashima

THE ROOM WAS SO QUIET LIEUTENANT Colonel Shiraishi, who was standing behind General Mori, could hear the ticking of his watch. He looked at it: the minute hand stood exactly at twelve, the hour hand at one.

"I sympathize with you," Mori said. "I appreciate your objectives and—confidentially—I respect them. I might even say that under other circumstances I would share them. But that is no longer possible: I am sworn to abide by the Emperor's decision. . . .

"However," Mori went on, "and I speak now as a plain, ordinary Japanese, my present intention is to go to the Meiji Shrine. Prayer may give me the answer to my problem."[15]

Ida bowed his head. He had faced the same dilemma himself, the same conflict between sworn duty and a loyalty that seemed to spring from a deeper source, from the very marrow of the bones— a loyalty that finally, at least in Ida's case, overruled all lesser obligations. Ida had decided that he could best serve the Emperor by disobeying him and the state by rebelling against it. He was convinced that if General Mori prayed at the Meiji Shrine, not as Commander of the First Imperial Guards Division but as "a plain, ordinary Japanese," he would reach the same conclusion.

Ida sighed, satisfied that even if Mori's final answer was no, and the attempt failed, Ida's own supreme effort had not been wasted. He had done all that he could. His body felt suddenly cooler, as though the sweat in which he was bathed had begun to dry, as though his temperature had dropped back to normal.

Just at that moment Colonel Mizutani, Chief of Staff of the Division, looked into Mori's office. "Hold on a minute," said Mori. "I think Lieutenant Colonel Ida would like a word with you."

"I'll be in my office," said Mizutani, withdrawing.

"See what Colonel Mizutani thinks of your idea," Mori said to Ida.

Ida bowed, left Mori, and was just about to enter Mizutani's office when the two conspirators, Hatanaka and Uehara, returned to headquarters. They were both breathing hard and covered with dust and sweat.

Ida, smiling, told Hatanaka to wait for him in General Mori's office. Then he continued on to have his talk with Mizutani. Hatanaka apparently interpreted Ida's smile to mean that all had gone well.

Every time that Ida expounded his own personal beliefs, and his basic agreement with Hatanaka's plan of action, his conviction became clearer and more certain in his own mind; so it was now in a tone of quiet assurance that he began to explain the situation as he saw it to Chief of Staff Mizutani.

He did not get very far. A pistol shot shattered the thick, muggy quiet of Guards headquarters. The shot seemed to come from General Mori's office. The two men leapt to their feet. As they did, they heard an agonized groan, then the heavy tread of boots across the floor.

Ida, perhaps, already suspected what had happened, but Mizutani could not have guessed as he followed Ida out into the corridor. At that moment, the door to Mori's office opened and an ashen-faced Hatanaka emerged, his pistol still in his hand.

"There was just no time," he said, in a thin, inflectionless voice. He looked almost pleadingly at Ida. "There was no time to argue, so I killed him. What else could I do?"

He moved aside.

Ida and Mizutani looked unbelievingly into Mori's office. The tableau is fixed for all time: Uehara was wiping his bloody sword, Shiizaki sat dazed in a chair; on the floor lay the hacked, bleeding bodies of General Mori and his brother-in-law, Lieutenant Colonel Shiraishi, who was to have gone back to Hiroshima in the morning. Blood was still spouting from their wounds; Shiraishi had been completely decapitated. The walls were splashed with his blood; the floor looked dark and slippery.

Ida turned away in horror and disgust, only to find Hatanaka still standing there behind him and still holding his pistol in his hand. The two men looked at each other, but there was nothing to say.

In a flash of intuitive understanding, Ida realized what must have happened. Hatanaka had taken Ida's smile to mean that Mori was in agreement with the plan; Hatanaka had spoken out in his wild, melodramatic way; Mori had replied disapprovingly; and Hatanaka's astonishment at this rebuff had ended in death. "Monk" Mori, presumably, had been impervious to the young major's charm.[16]

Hatanaka and Uehara saluted the dead bodies, then got down to work. Their time schedule had put zero hour at two o'clock: it would now, after what had just happened, have to be advanced. The two conspirators did not bother to consider whether the assassination of the Division Commander rendered their plan wholly unfeasible; they merely set about making use of his murder to facilitate the *coup d'état*.

Even Lieutenant Colonel Ida, who ought to have perceived that Mori's death must mean the death of the revolt, could see nothing to do now but carry on. He said he had better go to Eastern District Army headquarters and Hatanaka—tears in his eyes—agreed. Were they tears of sorrow or tears of entreaty? Or tears of exaltation? How was one to tell? Ida only knew that Hatanaka now wanted him to go to the Eastern Army and make a final effort to convince headquarters to join the uprising.

Ida and Mizutani, still in a state of shock, got into a staff car and drove off. While they were on the way Ida came to the more reasoned, and sobering, conclusion that the revolt was over before it began. Success depended on the Eastern District Army, and Mori's murder had put the Army's cooperation out of the realm of probability. Ida could see nothing but certain failure for Hatanaka and the other conspirators, to be followed by suicide—which was, after all, Ida's original solution to the problem.

Major Hatanaka had already examined the document produced by Major Koga and Major Ishihara called "Imperial Guards Division Strategic Order No. 584." It was dated August 15th, and the time that was originally planned for execution of the *coup*: 0200. The order read:

1. The Division will defeat the enemy's scheme; it will protect the Emperor and preserve the national polity.

2. The commander of the First Infantry Regiment will occupy the East Second and East Third garrison grounds (including the surroundings of the Eastern District Army strategy room) and the environs of Honmaru Baba, thus guarding the Imperial Family from this sector. The commander will also order a company to occupy Tokyo Broadcasting Station and prohibit all broadcasts.

3. The commander of the Second Infantry Regiment will use his main force to guard the Imperial Family at the Fukiage district of the Imperial Palace.

4. The commander of the Sixth Infantry Regiment will continue present duties.

5. The commander of the Seventh Infantry Regiment will occupy the area of Nijubashi Gate and prevent any contact with the Imperial Palace.

6. The commander of the Cavalry Regiment will order a tank force to Daikan Avenue to await further orders.

7. The commander of the First Artillery Regiment will await further orders.

8. The commander of the First Engineers will await further orders.

9. The commander of the Mechanized Battalion will guard the Imperial Palace at its present strength.

10. The commander of the Signal Unit will sever all communication with the Imperial Palace except through Division Headquarters.

11. I shall be at Division Headquarters.

Hatanaka took the dead commander's private seal from his desk and affixed it to copies of the order, which were then sent by messenger to the officers involved, of whom four battalion commanders and one regiment commander had already agreed to Hatanaka's plan. They may or may not have known that Strategic Order No. 584 was forged.

If Ida succeeded with the Eastern Army and Takeshita with the War Minister, Hatanaka reasoned, his plan was certain to come off, but in any case he could delay no longer in carrying out his own share of the *coup*. As the spurious orders were being delivered, he and Lieutenant Colonel Shiizaki, who two hours before had been wearily, dustily pedaling bicycles from the War Ministry, rode boldly into the precincts of the Imperial Palace in a staff car flying the insignia of the First Imperial Guards Division.

They made straight for Commander Haga's Second Regiment headquarters. There they informed Commander Haga that they had been appointed staff officers of the Imperial Guards Division to

227

ensure that special orders implementing the security of the Imperial Palace were carried out. Just then an adjutant arrived with a copy of the orders, which he handed to Haga.

Knowing that an insurrection was in the air, Haga supposed that the entire Army was part of it and that its sole aim was to persuade the Emperor to change his mind; he had no idea, apparently, that this *coup d'état*, in which he was about to become an actor, was in actual fact a revolt *against* the Army. He thus, in accordance with instructions, proceeded to take steps to quarantine the Palace. The conspiracy that was to restore the Emperor to his people in their natural unity and cohesion had begun by isolating him from them and from the world.

Although the Eastern District Army was charged with the defense of Tokyo and the whole Kanto Plain, there was very little activity at its headquarters early that Wednesday morning despite the continuing air-raid alarms. When the telephone rang, a staff officer, Lieutenant Colonel Hiroshi Fuha, answered.

"Major Koga speaking!" cried a highly excited voice, continuing at once: "The Imperial Guards Division refuses to accept surrender! It is in revolt against the government! Will the Eastern Army join the revolt? I repeat, will the Eastern Army join the revolt? This is most important! The Guards are in revolt against the cowards in the government. Will the Eastern Army join? Will the Commander please give a personal order immediately? This is most important. I repeat, the Imperial Guards Division. . . ." The near-hysterical voice broke.

After a moment Colonel Fuha heard the receiver being replaced.

He had no idea what to make of Koga's words. Like all highly placed Army men, he had heard rumors of an insurrection, but he had also heard his commander, General Tanaka, refuse to discuss the subject; and the day before, he had heard General Mori declare unequivocally that he proposed to follow the Emperor's decision and that he would tolerate no nonsense within the Guards Division. So long as Mori was in command, then, Fuha refused to believe that the Guards could be engaged in any insurrectionist activity.

All the same, he decided, he had better report Koga's words to the commander. General Tanaka was still in his office and, when Fuha entered, was talking to his Chief of Staff, Major General Takashima. Tanaka made no comment after Fuha had finished his report of Koga's telephone call. Quite obviously he put no more credence in it than Fuha had; he too knew General Mori well enough to harbor no doubts of either his loyalty or his sanity. Fuha went back to his own office, and so, a few minutes later, did Takashima, without any action having been taken by Eastern District Army headquarters.

The Chief of Staff was just sitting down at his desk when there came a knock at the door. Before he could say anything, the door was thrust open; Colonel Mizutani and Lieutenant Colonel Ida almost fell into the room, both of them pale and obviously agitated.

Takashima's premonition was confirmed by Mizutani's first words. "Mori's been murdered!" he cried. "The Guards are occupying the Palace. I've come to the Eastern Army for instructions and. . . ." And with that Mizutani fell to the floor in a faint.

Major General Takashima called some men to look after him, and he was stretched out on a couch in the next room. "Now then," said Takashima, "what's this all about?"

The heart was gone out of Ida. As they entered Eastern Army headquarters, he had had some wild idea of getting Tanaka's approval of the *coup d'état* while at the same time concealing, for the moment, the fact of Mori's murder. Mizutani's sudden declaration had rendered that stratagem useless; Ida was faced with the knowledge that he had indeed come on a fool's errand.

And yet, like a child on a merry-go-round, he knew no way to stop his meaningless gyrations until the music ended.

Faintly he began once again his exposition of the likely results of an uprising by the whole Army: an Imperial change of heart, a continuance of the war, victory or at least peace with honor, Japan's honor and the Army's honor, intact.

It was obvious that at that drab hour of the morning he believed what he was saying no more than Takashima did. "However," he went wearily on, his head aching, his nerves almost at the point of exhaustion, "the Eastern Army must act at once, it will be too late after the noon broadcast. If the Eastern Army takes a stand now, the national polity will be preserved, the natural relationship between the Emperor and the people will be restored, the old Japan. . . ." Ida's voice trailed away, his head drooped.

"What precisely," said Major General Takashima, "are you asking the Eastern Army to do?"

"To approve the action that the Guards have taken." Ida's voice was thick. "And to send some men to join the Division forces."

"I can do nothing," said Takashima, "without an order from General Tanaka. I suggest you discuss the matter with Lieutenant Colonel Itagaki while I report to the Commander."

The chief of staff left and was replaced by a lieutenant colonel, Itagaki. But there was no fight left in Ida. He had reached the limit of despair. Everything has failed, he thought: the Emperor's voice is all-powerful, it has extinguished the fighting spirit of the Japanese Army like a man blowing out a candle. As easy as that! Then isn't it my duty, Ida thought, to try to stop the insurrection, so as to prevent Japanese soldiers from killing one another? Ida wondered, foggily, whether he had the strength to carry out his new mission.

The Imperial Palace was now entirely in the hands of the insurgent Guards. The Palace police had been disarmed, the grounds surrounded, and all entrances blocked—but no one in the Imperial Household Ministry was as yet aware that the Emperor was in the hands of men who had sworn to protect him with their lives but who had decided to obey a more compelling obligation.

Director Shimomura of the Information Bureau, having seen the Imperial records safely consigned to the care of Chamberlain Toku-gawa, had had a relaxing cup of tea with the Imperial Household Minister, Sotaro Ishiwatari. It had been a long day for Shimomura, from the Imperial Conference, through Cabinet meetings and press conferences, to the Imperial recording completed not long before; but he decided to call in at the Prime Minister's official residence.

Accompanied by his secretary, Nobumasa Kawamoto, he got into a car and was about to leave the Palace through the Sakashita Gate when the car was halted by a soldier carrying a rifle and bayonet.

The air-raid warning was still in effect: presumably, thought Shimomura, that explained the soldier with the fixed bayonet.

The man looked in through the opened window of the car. "Are you the Director of the Information Bureau?" he asked.

"Yes," replied Kawamoto, who was sitting on the nearer side of the car.

At that, soldiers jumped onto both running boards. Having dis-armed Shimomura's bodyguard, they told his driver to back up and then directed him into the pitch blackness. Kawamoto was convinced that the soldiers were going to drive the car alongside the Palace moat and push it into the water. However, after the car stopped at the top of a little hill, Shimomura, with his secretary, bodyguard, and driver, was told to get out. On a dilapidated hut the words, "Guards Corps Battalion Headquarters" had been scrawled on an old piece of wood. In front of the hut stood two rows of soldiers with drawn bayonets.

"I'll lead the way," said a corporal.

The four men followed. It was a small, bare barracks, about twelve feet by fifteen, with a row of cots and a table with a bench on either side: an average Army barracks, in fact. Shimomura and the three others were told to stand up and not to talk. The corporal stood guard. Within moments they were joined by Hachiro Ohashi, Chairman of the Japan Broadcasting Corporation; Kenjiro Yabe, of the Domestic Bureau; and Daitaro Arakawa, of the Technical Bureau. Shortly after that came the six-man recording team of Engineer Nagatomo, who had been stopped as they were leaving the Palace under the escort of Chief Kakei of the Imperial Household Ministry's General Affairs Section. Kakei himself had boldly refused to be put under guard and had walked back to his own apartment within the Imperial Household Ministry.

"No talking!" the corporal repeated angrily, as the men greeted each other and tried to find out what had happened.

Eventually there were sixteen men in all imprisoned in the barracks, waiting in silence and watched by an armed guard. The windows were shut and covered with heavy curtains; the room soon grew unbearably hot.

"Can we at least take our coats off?" asked Kawamoto at last.

"No, you can't," barked the corporal. "And that's an order."

A soldier came in and threw a pencil and a piece of paper onto the table. "Write your names and official positions," he said. "And see that you don't make any mistakes."

Kawamoto took the pencil and listed those who were connected with the Information Bureau. Then someone from NHK wrote down the names and duties of the radio people. Last came Shimomura's bodyguard and driver. The soldier took the paper away.

A second lieutenant entered. "You are not allowed to talk," he said. "And you are not allowed to smoke. You may sit down."

But the benches were not long enough for all sixteen men. Some of them stood. The second lieutenant slammed the door shut behind him. Two sentries stood by the door with fixed bayonets. The NHK technicians had the customarily accurate watches of their profession: all agreed that it was two o'clock.

2 a.m. to 3 a.m.

"It looks like February 26th all over again."

Sotaro Ishiwatari

THE CITY DESKS OF TOKYO'S MORNING NEWS-
papers received two stories almost simultaneously. One came from
their reporters at the Prime Minister's official residence, with details
of the signing of the Imperial Rescript terminating the war and accompanied by the government's proviso that no mention of the
Rescript might be made in any newspaper until after the Imperial
broadcast at twelve noon. The other story was an announcement
that the Imperial Japanese Army was in revolt against the submissive
and cowardly government that had persuaded the Emperor to terminate the war.

The two conflicting stories put Tokyo's editors into something of
a quandary. Which were they to believe? Which was it safer to believe? And most important of all, which was it safe to publish?
The editors could not resolve the conflict as they had that of the previous Saturday by publishing both stories. On Saturday they had

printed the War Minister's bellicose proclamation alongside the Information Bureau's hints that the government might possibly be about to consider the Potsdam Declaration. But they could hardly publish side-by-side stories that said Japan was both at peace and at war, that she had accepted unconditional surrender and at the same time was about to attack the enemy with renewed vigor.

The fact that the air-raid was still in progress and that the supply of electric power to the capital had been cut did not make the editors' task any easier. By the light of a few candles, they read and re-read the two dispatches and tried to decide not only what was happening but what they could do about it. Some believed that reports of the Army *coup d'état* must be true because obviously the Imperial Japanese Army would not submit tamely to surrender. Others said promulgation of the Rescript was an Army ruse to entice enemy troops to Japanese shores and then annihilate them. But this could hardly be true, pointed out a third group, because it was the government that was about to promulgate the Rescript, not the Army.

And how could anybody guess what punitive action the Army might take against a newspaper that published the wrong story and failed to publish the right one? The *Asahi,* still by the light of a few candles, was preparing two newspapers: the one that was not needed could be destroyed as soon as confirmation came; while the *Yomiuri Hochi* was stymied by realization that the dilemma that faced it was the dilemma that faced the country itself: were they to have peace or war?

At the official residence of the Minister of War in Miyakezaka, General Anami was talking quietly to his brother-in-law, Lieutenant Colonel Takeshita. They were sitting at a table, in the General's twelve-mat living room, drinking *sake* and nibbling at the pungent tidbits that often accompany the warmed rice wine Japanese find so comforting, even on a hot summer night. At one end of the room, on a raised platform, some quilts had been laid for the General's bed.

Takeshita had already been with Anami for over half an hour. He had come at the promptings of a dual and, in a sense, antagonistic affection: that for an old friend, Major Hatanaka, and that for his brother-in-law, General Anami. Although Takeshita felt no longer any strong desire to play an active role in the proposed *coup d'état*, he had not only given tacit approval to Hatanaka's plan, he had promised to come and see the War Minister. But the fact is, he had wanted to see Anami anyway—to be with him, during what must be Anami's darkest hour. He determined, as he arrived at the War Minister's residence, that at his first sight of Anami's face he would decide whether to speak about the Army revolt or not.

But before he saw Anami's face, he saw the faces of his guards and his maid, and they confirmed Takeshita's premonition: Anami was contemplating suicide that night. The maid's expression of release from terror when she saw Takeshita was an indication he could not ignore.

He requested permission to enter the living room and heard the War Minister ask, in a kind of mutter, why on earth Takeshita had come. Then he heard the Minister's raised voice: "All right. Welcome! Come in." Anami was sitting at a low table, with some papers on it, drinking *sake* out of a small cup.

It was hard for Takeshita to believe, looking at the calm, healthy, ruddy face of his brother-in-law, that here was a man who had spent days in the exhausting and dispiriting business of trying to secure the best possible terms for his vanquished army, and who now, having done so, was considering when to kill himself.

"Sit down, sit down," said Anami, and told the maid to bring some taller glasses—as though Anami felt too impatient, that night, to deal with the thimble-sized *sake* cups that a man may not even fill for himself; etiquette demanded that he lift the cup while a companion filled it for him.

He folded the papers that lay on the table and put them away in a small cupboard behind him.

After he had poured some *sake* for his guest and himself, he said, "As you probably know, I decided some time ago to commit *seppuku*. I intend to do it tonight."

"Yes," said Takeshita, "I knew this afternoon that you had decided. Under the circumstances, I will not attempt to dissuade you."

"I am glad to hear it," said Anami. "When I heard that you had come so unexpectedly, I was afraid you might try to stop me. I am glad I was mistaken. I bid you welcome—you have come at an opportune moment."

Anami refilled the glasses and talked genially on. He seemed content that he had done his best for the Army entrusted into his care and for the country he had sworn to defend. He seemed satisfied that his work was done, relaxed, almost jovial.

Takeshita, on the other hand, as Anami talked on, grew sadder and more apprehensive. He was thinking of Hatanaka, and of the revolt that had been planned for two o'clock; he felt guilty that he was doing nothing to stop what could only end in defeat—and more death. But now that Anami, in grandeur and tranquillity, had made up his mind to die, could Takeshita bring him back to earth again with details of a sordid little insurrection in the Army that Anami had fought, and was now preparing to die, for?

Anami laughed. "You know, I had my vitamin injection tonight the same as I always do. When the maid asked me, I could hardly say I didn't want it because I was going to die. Could I now?"

Takeshita shook his head. "Did I interrupt you when I came in? You were writing something, weren't you?"

"Oh, that. No, I'd finished." Anami reached behind him and took two sheets of heavy Japanese paper from the cupboard. After a moment's hesitation, he handed them to Takeshita.

Both were written in thick black India ink and in the familiar,

236

heroic hand of the War Minister. The first was a poem:

After tasting the profound benevolence of the Emperor, I have no words to speak.

General Korechika
The night of August 14th,
1945.[17]

The other contained three lines of Japanese characters:

For my supreme crime, I beg forgiveness through the act of death.

Korechika Anami, Minister of War
The night of August 14th,
1945.

It seemed to Takeshita that he understood the distinction Anami was making in the two signatures he had employed. Though, as War Minister, and representative of the Army, he had opposed the Imperial decision, he was taking on himself the full responsibility of the Army for having brought the country to the edge of destruction. Yet his final, private word must be of love for the Imperial Family.

But it was not his final word after all. Suddenly he added some water to the block of ink, and taking up his brush, he wrote, on the back of the last testament of the Minister of War:

I believe in Japan's sacred indestructability.

"It's true," he said. "The dead are dead, the living face hardships that are beyond our power to foresee, but if they work together, and if each does what he can, I believe that Japan will be saved."

The two men were silent for a moment. Anami drained his glass of *sake;* then, as Takeshita filled it for him, he said, "I know, I'm out of date—it's after two o'clock, and today is August 15th, but I intend to die as though today were still the fourteenth. I had thought at first of dying on the twentieth, since that is my second son's birthday, but I'm afraid the twentieth will be too late, and since the fourteenth is the anniversary of my father's death, I have chosen that.

237

Besides, the broadcast of the Emperor's recording will be made at noon tomorrow—I could not bear to hear it."

Takeshita nodded but said nothing. He would have preferred that there were no tears in his eyes, but such things are beyond the power of most men to control.

The War Minister unfolded another sheet of paper, and with a smile he said: "I am going to date my letter of resignation the four-teenth too. . . ."

The War Minister's official residence was one corner of a triangle in the center of which stood the Imperial Palace. The other two corners were headquarters of the First Imperial Guards Division and headquarters of the Eastern District Army. While the chief of the Army, General Anami, was in quiet conversation with his brother-in-law and sharing warmed *sake* with him, the other two corners of the triangle were rather more active.

At Guards Headquarters, the commander of the First Infantry Regiment, Colonel Watanabe, had been informed orally of Strategic Order No. 584 by Major Koga. Not knowing that the order had been illicitly issued with General Mori's seal after Mori's death, Watanabe set about implementing his share of it. He ordered his troops to occupy the areas assigned to his command, including the Tokyo Broadcasting Station.

At Eastern Army headquarters, Major General Takashima, the Chief of Staff, having shifted the burden of handling Lieutenant Colonel Ida to Lieutenant Colonel Itagaki, had himself gone to report to General Tanaka, the commander of the Eastern District Army. As soon as Tanaka heard the details of Ida's story, he decided to go personally to the Imperial Palace to prevent the insurgent officers from going on with their plan.

Takashima was strongly of the opinion that Commander Tanaka ought to wait a bit longer, until the situation became clearer and

Eastern District Army headquarters was in a better position to know exactly which officers were involved and precisely what they had done. Tanaka reluctantly agreed, asking Takashima to make every effort to get the required information as soon as possible.

Takashima returned to the staff room and issued orders immediately to Colonel Inadome, who had come from the air defense strategy room at Takehashi; to Lieutenant Colonel Fuha, who had taken the initial telephone call from Major Koga; and to Lieutenant Colonel Itagaki, who had by then persuaded Lieutenant Colonel Ida to return to the Imperial Palace and, as a friend of Hatanaka's, to do what he could to put an end to the rebellion.

It was at this point that Colonel Teisaku Minami, commander of the Guards' Seventh Infantry Regiment, arrived at Eastern Army headquarters. He reported to the Chief of Staff that he had received orders over the telephone from the Guards Division and because the orders had been so astonishing he had first come to Eastern Army headquarters to secure the approval of the commander.

"What were you ordered to do?" asked Major General Takashima.

"To occupy the Nijubashi Gate area," replied Colonel Minami, "and to prevent all contact between the Imperial Palace and the outside."

There was a moment of stunned silence in the Eastern Army staff room; then the outline of the planned *coup* became transparently clear to everyone. Takashima's first counter-move was to request the Eastern Army's military police corps (Kempeitai) to dispatch a body of guards immediately to headquarters to accompany General Tanaka when he decided that his own presence was required at the scene of the rebellion. Next he ordered Lieutenant Colonel Fuha to have a look at Guards Division headquarters and report back as soon as possible. Third, he issued orders for all commanders of Guards units to report at once to Eastern Army headquarters.

Around the same time, Lieutenant Colonel Tsukamoto, of the military police corps, whom Ida had sounded out, unsatisfactorily, the previous Saturday, heard a rumor of Mori's death. He immediately sent a Kempeitai captain to Division headquarters to find out whether there was any truth in the rumor; at the same time he issued an emergency alert order to all men in his command.

Despite the fact that the air-raid warning was still in effect, most of Tokyo had gone to sleep. Although the nearby city of Kumagaya was in flames, and Tokyo itself was still without electric power, it looked as though the exhausted and hungry millions might get at least a little sleep that night.

Within the center of the triangle, three Imperial chamberlains, Toda, Mitsui, and Tokugawa, had been having a quiet talk together. They had planned to stay awake until the air-raid warning system sounded the all-clear, but as it still had not come and as there had been no sign of enemy action over Tokyo, the chamberlains decided they might as well retire for the night. It had been a long day. They still, apparently, did not know that the Imperial Palace was under siege, although the Imperial Household Minister himself had been stopped when he tried to leave the Palace at Inui Gate and had been allowed to return to the Ministry.

Once back, he had grown uneasy about the safety of Shimomura and the others who had left a little earlier, so he sent Susumu Kato, head of the Ministry's General Affairs Bureau, to make inquiries. Kato, accompanied by an officer of the Ministry police, had headed straight for the Guards command post, where, like an oblivious rabbit walking obediently into a trap, he had of course been detained, along with the policeman, swelling the ranks of the frightened and hideously uncomfortable "prisoners" to eighteen.

Captain Uehara left the command post to look for Lieutenant Colonel Takeshita, to report on the situation and to receive Takeshita's report in return; while Major Koga and Major Ishihara were still at Division headquarters, where they constituted the Division's sole liaison with the rest of Japan. This left the command post itself under the charge of Major Hatanaka and Lieutenant Colonel Shiizaki.

Although Hatanaka knew that the final success of his plan depended, almost certainly, on two dialogues he hoped were then taking place—one between General Tanaka and Ida, and the other between General Anami and Takeshita, he knew he could not delay acting until he heard the outcome of those two dialogues. Accordingly, after ordering the emplacement of light machine guns at every entrance to the Palace, Hatanaka set about questioning his prisoners.

He asked Kato where the Imperial Household Minister and Marquis Kido, Lord Privy Seal, were to be found. "Marquis Kido," Kato replied quietly, "is almost certainly somewhere near the Emperor, particularly under present circumstances. As for the Imperial Household Minister, if you get in touch with Air Defense Headquarters of the Ministry, no doubt they can tell you. It seems to me a long time has passed since I last saw the Minister and was detained here by force—so how could I possibly tell you where he is now?"

Kato was relieved to know that both the Minister and the Lord Privy Seal were safe; Hatanaka was less satisfied with the result of his interrogation and turned, with some annoyance, to his other prisoners, but all he was able to determine was that the Emperor had, indeed, made a recording of the Rescript and that no one being held in the command post would admit possession of it or knowledge of its whereabouts.

Meanwhile, in the underground shelter of the Imperial Household Ministry, four men sat huddled around a telephone. They were the Minister himself, Sotaro Ishiwatari; Masujiro Ogane, the Vice-Minister; Section Chief Motohiko Kakei; and the Minister's secretary,

241

Tadashi Ishikawa—and they were trying to get through to Imperial Guards Division headquarters. The Minister wanted to inform General Mori that Susumu Kato (of the Ministry's general affairs bureau) was missing and that he was worried about Shimomura and the others who had taken part in the Imperial recording. However, when, as sometimes happened, the telephone was answered at Division headquarters, the man at the other end would give only an unsatisfactory reply—he would say neither who he was nor where General Mori was.

Apprehension mounted in the underground shelter. Ishikawa, the Minister's secretary, was about to try the telephone once more, when a number of soldiers, wearing white bands across their shoulders, ran into the room. "Orders!" said the officer in charge, brusquely, as a couple of the men cut all the telephone wires with fire hatchets. The soldiers left without another word.

The four men, frightened and horrified, agreed at once that under the circumstances an underground room, which offered no means of escape, was not the ideal place to be. Ishikawa, the Minister's secretary, led the Minister upstairs and hid with him in a night duty room. "I'm afraid it's a *coup d'état*," Ishikawa whispered. "Doesn't it smell that way to you?"

"No question," said Ishiwatari the Minister. "Our hopes for a peaceful surrender are gone. We're in for trouble, serious trouble." He sighed deeply, then went on quietly: "It's best for you to go at once. I'll stay here—but you're young, you have a life to live ahead of you."

Ishikawa, frightened as he was, did not feel he could leave the Minister. "I'll stay a bit longer," he said.

"Better not," said Ishiwatari. "It looks like February 26th all over again."

Chamberlain Mitsui was not sure whether he was still dreaming or not when he heard a voice whispering, "The Imperial Guards

242

have occupied the Palace. All telephone wires have been cut." He sat up with a start.

The room was in blackness. A hand cautioned him to be quiet. "The Imperial Guards have occupied the Palace," the voice repeated. "All telephone wires have been cut."

Mitsui recognized the voice: it was that of Vice-Minister Ogane. The words were not a dream, then, they were nightmare reality— what everyone deep in his heart had feared, and no one had dared to believe, might happen.

Mitsui's first thought was that he must awaken Chamberlain Toda, who was sleeping in the next room, but he was too terrified to move: the marrow in his bones was ice, his legs were jelly. Suddenly the door opened, and a third man came into the room. It was Toda; he had heard Ogane's whisper.

But it was so incredible. Would the Emperor's own guards turn against the Emperor himself?

Suddenly the screech of wheels outside shattered the silence. There was a tramp of boots over the sandy paths, and an excited voice issuing commands. The men peered through the window: the soldiers outside were all members of the Imperial Guards; they wore white bands across their shoulders; and their drawn bayonets glistened in the night.

3 a.m. to 4 a.m.

"It's too late to do anything now!"
Marquis Koichi Kido

AS THE SOUND OF TRAMPING BOOTS AND shouted commands continued, Chamberlain Mitsui, a mild-mannered, short-sighted man, crawled through the dark corridors of the Ministry to Chamberlain Tokugawa's bedroom. He awakened him, delivered his dreadful message, then crept on to the small room where the two aides-de-camp slept in a pair of improvised bunks, one on top of the other.

As soon as they learned what had happened, they went at once to Chief Aide-de-Camp Hasunuma's apartment.

His first reaction was disbelief. "But Mori himself told me the Guards were safe," he said. "He also told me he might order an unexpected change of duty—probably that's what you heard."

"I'm afraid not," said Seike, one of the aides. "The Guards have occupied the Palace, disarmed the Palace police, and cut all communication with the outside. No one can come or go—it's as though we were all in prison here, including the Emperor!"

Hasunuma threw on his uniform, and the three men went at once to their office. They hoped to be able to get through to the War Ministry or to General Staff headquarters, but though, as was customary with Palace telephones, they repeatedly dialed 'O,' they were unable to get a dial tone.

Mitsui, meanwhile, having roused the other chamberlains and the aides-de-camp, decided that his next clear duty was to try to reach the Emperor, both to warn him and to offer protection. There was no chance of breaking through the ranks of soldiers guarding the front gate of the Ministry, so Mitsui crept silently through the dark halls to the north door. But with the first step he took into the black night, he was faced by a soldier and a pointed bayonet. Mitsui almost fainted.

"Get back!" said the soldier sullenly. "Orders."

After Mitsui had shut the door of the Ministry behind him, he stood trembling for a moment, then made his way stealthily around the building, to dart his head out, then back again, like a turtle into its shell: on all sides of the Ministry stood armed Guards.

It seemed to Mitsui that hours had gone by since he had been awakened by Vice-Minister Ogane, but when he looked at his watch, he discovered that it had been fifteen minutes in all. The time was 3:05.

War Minister Anami seldom drank, but tonight he seemed to be downing vast quantities of *sake*. Takeshita noticed that Anami's cheeks were flushed. Perhaps his own were too, as is the way with many Japanese when they drink alcohol.

"You know," said Takeshita suddenly, "Hatanaka is spearheading a movement to occupy the Palace, then try to get the Army to revolt and carry on the war."

Anami's expression underwent no change. "Is that so?" he remarked. "But the Eastern Army will never join a revolt."

Takeshita had feared the effect his words might have on the War

Minister, but apparently he had underestimated the power of a decision to die. Tomorrow would be a day of confusion and chaos, the Army would be vilified and its glory tarnished: but Anami would not be there to see it.

Lieutenant Colonel Ida climbed out of his car in front of the Guards command post and was met by Major Hatanaka. All the way over, Ida had been wondering how he was going to face Hatanaka with the bad news he was bringing, and when he saw the bright hope in those rebellious eyes he felt even more dispirited by the *coup de grâce* that he was compelled to give.

But Hatanaka did not need to be told. He too, as he came forward to greet Ida, had read the expression on his face.

"It's all over," Ida said bluntly. "There isn't a chance. The Eastern Army is absolutely opposed to us. If you occupy the Palace any longer, you'll find yourself fighting a battle against the entire Eastern Army."

"I'm not afraid of a battle," said Hatanaka. "I've occupied the Palace, and the Emperor's behind me—what's there to be afraid of? I even have some prisoners." He laughed. "Including Shimomura."

"Don't be a fool!" cried Ida. "How can you fight the Eastern Army? You don't even have agreement within the Guards! And when they hear about Mori's death, they'll all be against you! Can't you understand that?"

Hatanaka stared at Ida in silence, his eyes like embers, as the angry words came surging out.

Ida resumed, after a moment, in a more conciliatory tone. "Listen to me, Hatanaka. Withdraw the soldiers before dawn. Let's take the consequences together. They won't be serious—people will say it was all a midsummer night's dream. They'll be too busy with the surrender, anyway, to worry about a *coup* that didn't come off. Do you understand, Hatanaka?"

The major's shoulders sagged. "Yes," he said, in a voice so low Ida could hardly hear him, "yes, I understand."

Nevertheless, Ida decided he must now report the occupation of the Palace to the War Minister. He climbed back into his car, and as the engine started, he said softly to Hatanaka, "Remember—before dawn. . . ."

But the Hatanaka that Ida left behind was not a dispirited or defeated man. Although the blow had been a serious one, Hatanaka remained convinced of the correctness of his act: he believed that since his intention was to protect the Emperor, he was invincible so long as his enemy was Japanese. In any case, in the two hours since the Palace had been occupied, he and the other conspirators had committed no serious act of violence; they had cut wires and closed off all the entrances to the Palace, they had detained some twenty men and would be glad to have two more—the Privy Seal and the Household Minister; but beyond the unavoidable death of Mori and the fortuitous death of Shiraishi, they felt their hands were clean. Hatanaka, after Ida left, conferred with Koga and Shiizaki; they decided to continue to occupy the Palace and, if all else failed, to search every room in it until they found the Imperial recording, which would enable them to delay, or even cancel, the broadcast and so gain the time they needed to consolidate their advantage.

Chamberlain Tokugawa told the Imperial Household Minister that he knew a better place to hide than the night duty room. He came back in a moment with some keys and led the Minister, with two secretaries and two police guards, up the stairs to an anteroom used by the ladies-in-waiting. There he opened a cupboard, from which a hidden passage provided the sole means of access to an underground room the chamberlains called "the bank vault." "They'll never find you here," Tokugawa said.

Major Koga summoned Bureau Director Yabe of NHK for questioning.[18] "Did you succeed," asked Koga abruptly, "in making a good recording of the Emperor reading the Rescript?"

"Yes," replied Yabe, "we did."

"Where is it?"

"In the Imperial Household Ministry."

"When will it be broadcast?"

"At noon tomorrow. That is, today." Yabe could feel the sweat trickling down his face and the back of his neck.

"Where from? The Ministry or the broadcasting station?"

"The station."

"Then why did you leave it in the Ministry?" This seemed to be the key question that Koga had been leading up to.

"The broadcast," Yabe replied honestly, "was scheduled for seven in the morning but then was shifted to noon. We decided it would be better not to try to transport the record in the middle of the night during a possible air-raid, so we asked the Ministry to keep it—that's all."

"Are you *absolutely sure* that the record is now in the Imperial Household Ministry?" Koga asked emphatically.

"I am."

Koga was silent for a moment, then called an officer and told him to conduct Yabe to the Ministry and institute a search for the recording. "And take good care of it when you find it," Koga told the officer. "It's very valuable." But the fact that the conspirators entrusted this task to a subordinate officer suggests that their prime intention, in occupying the Palace, was not to take possession of the record but rather to change the mind of Japan about continued prosecution of the war. Getting hold of the recording was only secondary to the final aim.

Outside stood a row of some forty soldiers, with fixed bayonets. Followed by the officer, Yabe walked in front of them, through

Nijubashi entrance to the Imperial Palace

An aerial view of the Imperial Palace

The Gobunko in the Imperial Palace where the Emperor administered the affairs of state during the war

Entrance to the underground shelter in the Imperial Palace

A corridor in the underground bomb shelter

The Imperial Household Ministry

Ministry of War

Kojimachi Ward

Yotsuya Station

Han

Miya

War Minister's Official

Diet Build

Prime Minister's Official Resider

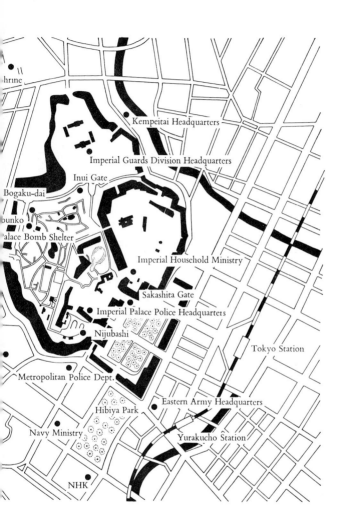

Shrine

Kempeitai Headquarters

Imperial Guards Division Headquarters

Inui Gate

Bogaku-dai

bunko

Palace Bomb Shelter

Imperial Household Ministry

Sakashita Gate

Imperial Palace Police Headquarters

Nijubashi

Tokyo Station

Metropolitan Police Dept.

Eastern Army Headquarters

Hibiya Park

Navy Ministry

Yurakucho Station

NHK

The Ministry of War at Ichigaya Heights

Official residence of the Prime Minister

The Ministry of the Navy

The Ministry of Foreign Affairs

Staff Headquarters of the Imperial Japanese Army

The Ministry of Home Affairs

Japan Broadcasting Corporation (NHK)

An aerial view of the huge airbase at Atsugi

Military Academy graduates emerging from the Imperial Palace, 1945

Chief Cabinet Secretary Sakomizu announces the Emperor's broadcast to the press, August 15, 1945

Right and below: People praying at Nijubashi before the Palace, August 15, 1945

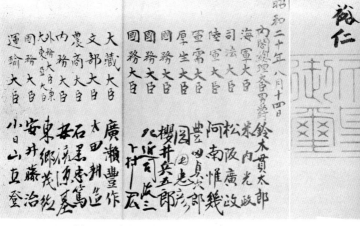

Part of the Imperial Rescript announcing Japan's surrender signed by the Emperor and members of the Cabinet on Aug. 14, 1945

皇宗ノ神霊ニ謝セムヤ是レ朕カ帝國
政府ヲシテ共同宣言ニ應セシムルニ至レル所
以ナリ

朕ハ帝國ト共ニ終始東亞ノ解放ニ協力セ
ル諸盟邦ニ對シ遺憾ノ意ヲ表セサルヲ得
ス帝國臣民ニシテ戰陣ニ死シ職域ニ殉シ非
命ニ斃レタル者及其ノ遺族ニ想ヲ致セハ五
内爲ニ裂ク且戰傷ヲ負ヒ災禍ヲ蒙リ家業
ヲ失ヒタル者ノ厚生ニ至リテハ朕ノ深ク軫念ス
ル所ナリ惟フニ今後帝國ノ受クヘキ苦難ハ

固ヨリ尋常ニアラス爾臣民ノ衷情モ朕善
ク之ヲ知ル然レトモ朕ハ時運ノ趨ク所堪ヘ
難キヲ堪ヘ忍ヒ難キヲ忍ヒ以テ萬世ノ爲ニ
太平ヲ開カムト欲ス
朕ハ茲ニ國體ヲ護持シ得テ忠良ナル爾臣
民ノ赤誠ニ信倚シ常ニ爾臣民ト共ニ在リ
若シ夫レ情ノ激スル所濫ニ事端ヲ滋クシ或
ハ同胞排擠互ニ時局ヲ亂リ爲ニ大道ヲ誤
リ信義ヲ世界ニ失フカ如キハ朕最モ之ヲ戒
ム宜シク擧國一家子孫相傳ヘ確ク神州ノ

不滅ヲ信シ任重クシテ道遠キヲ念ヒ總力ヲ將來ノ建
設ニ傾ケ道義ヲ篤クシ志操ヲ鞏クシ誓テ國體ノ
精華ヲ發揚シ世界ノ進運ニ後レサラムコトヲ期スヘシ爾臣民

*Record of the Emperor's
reading of the surrender Rescript*

Listening to the broadcast of the Rescript

People praying at the Nijubashi

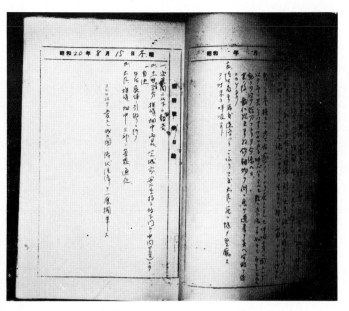

Last page of a secret diary kept by an officer at Imperial Army Headquarters. The last few lines read: "At 11:20 a.m. Shiizaki and Hatanaka committed suicide in front of the Imperial Palace. Recovered their bodies in the afternoon. Wake held for the War Minister, Shiizaki and Hatanaka. These are the events which occurred on the day of the defeat of my dear country."

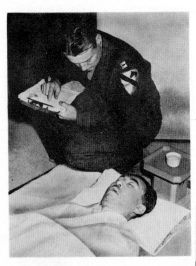

Prince Konoye takes his life by poison

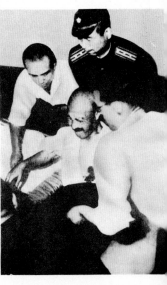

Ex-Premier Tojo moments after his suicide attempt

the dark night, to the main entrance of the Imperial Household Ministry. As he walked, he envied the crickets chirping freely and innocently in the trees. "Load rifles!" cried the officer. Yabe heard the click of the bolts. "Enter!" The search of the Ministry began.

When, a short while before, Chamberlain Toda learned that the conspirators were looking not only for the Imperial Household Minister but for the Lord Privy Seal as well, he went straight up to Marquis Kido's room on the second floor.

He told Kido what had happened and begged him to leave his quarters at once and find a hiding-place elsewhere in the building.

Kido smiled. "So what we feared all along has finally happened, has it?" he said. "But what fools they are! It's too late to do anything now!"

"Whether they're fools or not," said Toda, "they have guns and they can kill us. Don't forget the 26th of February!"

Kido shrugged. "What can we do?"

"We can hide. If they can't find us, they can't kill us."

"Hide where?"

"I've thought of a place. The doctor's office."

But as they were groping their way through the darkness, Kido suddenly stopped and said, "I left some papers in my room. I don't want them to fall into the hands of the rebels. I'm going back to get them."

Toda returned with him. They could hear the clump of boots on the floor below. Kido took the papers with him into the washroom and began tearing them up. "We'd better get rid of the most important ones," he said. Toda helped him, but the process seemed exasperatingly slow, and Toda feared that before they finished they would hear the thud of boots mounting the stairs.

But at last the papers were all flushed away. Toda shut Kido into the doctor's office and breathed a sigh of relief.

At Eastern Army headquarters, Guards commanders were reporting as instructed. There they received the following orders:

1. The Commander of the First Imperial Guards Division has been killed by insubordinate officers.

2. The First Imperial Guards Division will until further order be under the direct command of the Commander of the Eastern District Army.

3. The First Imperial Guards Division orders issued as of today's date are false. They are herewith canceled.

4. All troops surrounding the Imperial Palace are ordered to disperse.

When Chamberlain Toda returned to Marquis Kido's room, he saw an officer with a sword in his hand and half-a-dozen armed soldiers. Toda decided he would rather face his killers, so he abandoned his first idea of trying to back unobtrusively out of the room. The floor was littered with papers.

"Who are you?" the officer shouted.

"I am a chamberlain," Toda replied.

The officer turned to Yabe, who was still under guard. "Is this the one who has the record?" he asked.

Yabe shook his head. "Not that one," he said. "I don't know which one it was." It was the answer he had given several times during the course of the search.

The officer turned back to Toda. "Where is the record?" he demanded. "Where is Kido? Where is Ishiwatari?"

Toda shrugged. "How could anybody as young as I am," he replied, "know the answers to questions like that?"

The search for the Imperial recording was not rendered any easier by the fact that it was being conducted within the Imperial Household Ministry. For one thing, the building was a labyrinth of small narrow rooms that all looked exactly alike. Furthermore, the rooms had old-fashioned names that none of the soldiers could understand. To them the Imperial Household Ministry was like a foreign country: they had no idea which rooms were used by regular personnel and which by chamberlains, nor had they any idea that in the present emergency cupboards ordinarily used for the storage of bedding were now being given over to the hiding of important documents.

The Imperial Household Ministry was a complex of buildings grouped around the main office building. To complicate matters, the quarters of the chamberlains and other Palace staff were in a three-storied structure[19] situated on the side of a slope: entering from the rear, the soldiers walked straight into the third floor; those entering from the front, the first. The blackout compounded their unfamiliarity with their surroundings. Tempers grew very short.

After Chamberlain Toda escaped from the searching party, he found Chamberlain Tokugawa and together they spirited Marquis Kido out of the doctor's office and down through the third floor anteroom to the underground "bank vault," where the Imperial Household Minister was hiding with secretaries and guards. The two chief human targets of the rebels' search were now safely hidden away.

When Lieutenant Colonel Itagaki and Lieutenant Colonel Fuha, of the Eastern District Army, reached Guards headquarters, they found it in total darkness, since the air-raid warning was still in effect. As staff officers of the Army to which the Division was attached and which had vowed to put down the rebellion, they did not feel too happy about entering rebel headquarters alone and without any lights to guide them, but the Chief of Staff himself had ordered them to investigate the situation, so they had no choice but to grope their way down the dark corridors. They were challenged frequently, but insisted that as staff officers they had the right to pass.

In the Division staff room, a young officer was sitting at a desk, writing. The room was dimly lit by a small electric lamp bulb wrapped in a dark cloth. Fuha strode briskly to the desk, told the officer who he was, and demanded to know what was going on. The young officer pushed his chair back and rose. The chair fell with a clatter to the floor. The officer put his hand on his sword; his scowl was menacing.

Fuha and Itagaki were about to accept the challenge when they realized they had been sent to verify Mori's death, not to fight a duel with an insubordinate officer—who, although they did not know it at the time, was one of the leaders of the rebellion, Major Sadakichi Ishihara. It was he who was presently engaged in maintaining the Division's contact with the outside and in directing the movements of the First Regiment.

When the two Eastern Army staff officers tried to enter Mori's office, the sentry posted outside refused to let them pass, but Ishihara, who had followed the two officers, ordered the sentry to stand aside.

Mori, wearing ordinary Japanese-style clothes, lay in a pool of blood in front of his desk; there were gaping bullet holes in his chest, and his shoulder had been hacked away by a sword. Shiraishi, in uniform, had been decapitated: his body, the floor around him, and the walls above him were splattered with his blood.

Fuha and Itagaki found themselves unable to move or speak as they stared at the mutilated bodies of their fellow officers.

"I'd like to ask one favor of you," said General Anami.

Takeshita nodded.

"If I don't succeed in killing myself, will you give me the *coup de grâce*? I doubt whether it will be necessary, however—I think I am capable of taking my own life."

Takeshita was silent.

The War Minister brought out two ancient daggers that had been family treasures for quite a long time. He drew one from its scabbard and ran his finger along the edge. "This is the one I shall use," he said—for as a soldier, having respect to a soldier's honor, he would not use his sword. He handed the other dagger to Take-shita. "Keep this," he said, as he refilled the *sake* glasses, "in memory of me."

The pursuit of the Imperial recording continued, but by now the white-sashed searching parties were reacting more violently to the feeling of frustration that the labyrinthine Imperial Household Ministry and its slow-moving, hierarchical chamberlains inspired. The soldiers no longer bothered to slide the room doors open, they kicked them in with their boots, pulled drawers open, and flung the contents onto the floor.

The chamberlains, though cut off from all contact with the world and having no idea what was going on beyond the moat, or indeed beyond the building in which they were confined, never seemed to lose either confidence or gravity or their obvious sense of detachment from the undignified events that were taking place around them. What made it particularly frustrating was that the Ministry person-nel—from the Minister himself to the lowliest clerks, and including all the chamberlains—wore the same dark blue wartime uniform, the only distinction lying in the number of stars and stripes the wearer was entitled to. The soldiers never seemed able to tell one person from another.

When they questioned Yabe again about Toda, he replied, "No, no, the man who took the recording was much taller and had a much bigger nose."

Although, as a matter of fact, Toda was the tallest of the cham-berlains, the soldiers accepted Yabe's answer and went on with their increasingly frustrating, and increasingly ill-tempered, search.

The truth was, things were not going at all well for Hatanaka and his fellow-conspirators. Not only did the recording most inconsiderately fail to appear, but no word had yet come from the War Minister. Was he going to be persuaded to throw the weight of his word, his power and influence, on the side of the rebels? The outcome of Takeshita's mission was still veiled in silence, while General Tanaka had already spoken out against the rebellion and was taking steps to quell it.

Now came another setback. Colonel Haga, commander of the Second Infantry regiment, was beginning to have doubts and suspicions. Hatanaka had told him that the War Minister was on his way to the Palace to ask the Emperor for a revised decision, while Koga had assured him that General Mori was in sympathy with the plan and was about to issue further directives. Three hours had passed, and so far neither Anami nor Mori had appeared.

Haga's tone was sharp as he questioned Hatanaka again. "Where is the War Minister?" he demanded. "Why hasn't he come? What has gone wrong?"

Hatanaka looked at Koga, who had just returned from a fruitless mission to the Imperial Guards Division headquarters; Koga's glance was far from reassuring, but Hatanaka could see no choice but to continue on the path he had plotted. "I'll telephone at once," he said, "to see whether General Anami has left yet or not."

Koga, however, perceived that Colonel Haga could no longer be satisfied by assurances that every moment grew more patently false. "General Mori is dead," he blurted. "The Colonel must take command of the Guards division."

"Me?" said Haga, narrowing his eyes. "Why me? Why not the Chief of Staff?"

Koga's glance failed to meet those narrowed eyes. "The Chief of Staff," he mumbled, "is at Eastern Army headquarters. He is trying to persuade them to join us."

Haga was unsatisfied. "You say General Mori is dead. How did he die?"

Koga looked away, his face a study in despair.

"I asked how General Mori died," Haga persisted. "Major Koga must know. What was the cause of General Mori's death? I insist on knowing!"

But there was no reply. The conversation ended on this inconclusive note. Or was it inconclusive? If Haga was determined to know the details of General Mori's death, he would soon find them out, and when he did he would surely dissasociate himself from the conspirators. Had the Army rebellion ended already? Was it only the rebels themselves who were unaware that they had failed?

Lieutenant Colonel Takeshita was called away from his companionable wine-drinking with the War Minister. He went into another room to find Captain Uehara[20] waiting for him.

Uehara's smile was confident. "Major Hatanaka has sent me," he said eagerly, "to inform the Lieutenant Colonel that the plan is proceeding as scheduled."

"Is it indeed?" Takeshita asked. "Then did General Mori agree?"

"Actually no," Uehara replied, "he didn't. That's why Major Hatanaka had to kill him. The Colonel had to be killed also. Everything is going beautifully!"

Takeshita thought otherwise, but in view of Uehara's exalted state he said nothing.

"We don't know definitely yet," Uehara went on, "what attitude the Eastern District Army is going to take, but no doubt they'll join us very soon."

No, Takeshita thought, they won't join you. Anami is right: the Eastern Army is not going to rebel. The only hope for the rebels now is Anami himself. If he were to issue an order now saying that the Army was not satisfied with the decision to surrender, then the Army would rise and join the revolt. But how can I ask him to do it?

"Have you any messages," Uehara asked, "for Major Hatanaka?"

Takeshita smiled. "Not yet," he said.

He saw Uehara off and headed back toward the room where his brother-in-law waited, drinking *sake* and nibbling bits of food. General Anami was waiting for the time to stop drinking. Lieutenant Colonel Takeshita paused for a moment outside the room. Suddenly he realized how important the *coup d'état* had become to him, now that there seemed to be almost no chance of success. For the first time, he felt a deep sense of responsibility toward the conspirators.

How could he abandon Hatanaka at such a moment?

He straightened his shoulders and rejoined the Minister of War.

Now that it looked as though the Guards were going to find neither the recording they wanted nor the men they wanted, the Emperor's two chamberlains, Toda and Tokugawa, concentrated their efforts on reaching the Emperor himself.

There were three ways to get from the Imperial Household Ministry to the Gobunko. One was to take the wide road that led to the Inui Gate, then turn to the left; a second was the road from the Inner Garden Gate to the Kashikodokoro (Imperial worship hall); and the third was the new road through the Momijiyama Tunnel across the Dokan Moat. The Inui Gate road would certainly be well guarded by the insurgents, while the Inner Garden Gate road was the one Toda had tried earlier to use, from which he had been turned back. That left only the Momijiyama Tunnel route, and that too, the chamberlains decided, would almost certainly be guarded.

They looked through the window and could see the trees of Fukiage Garden looming darkly in the night. Although the Gobunko was so close, they had no way of knowing whether the Emperor had been disturbed by the insurgents or whether he was still asleep, unaware that his Palace had been isolated from the world. All the telephone wires had been cut; there was no way to call; nor was there any messenger to send.

The two men decided they would have to try to get through themselves. Their duty was plain to them, and it was no good waiting any longer in this uncertainty. They took a small flashlight and set out, Tokugawa leading the way.

The Dokan Moat was almost dry. Only a few small puddles reflected a faint glimmer of light. Toda wondered where the light could be coming from, since there was no moon.

Guards were standing at the Tsuyo Gate, but without giving them the chance to challenge, Tokugawa called: "We are Imperial chamberlains with business at the Gobunko. Will you let us pass?"

There was a moment's indecision. Then the soldiers stood aside. The two chamberlains continued on toward the Gobunko. No one said a word.

It was as easy as that! The chamberlains sighed their relief. And yet it might have been very different—for how could one guess what soldiers might do once they had rebelled against the authority that made them soldiers?

The Gobunko was dark and silent amidst the tall trees that surrounded it. Passing through the East Entrance, Tokugawa and Toda saw Chamberlain Irie, who was on duty that night, sound asleep at the duty post. Their deep relief that all was well was followed by a wild surge of anger: how dared Irie sleep so soundly after all the terrible things they had been through in the past couple of hours?

They shook him roughly awake. "How can you sleep at a time like this?" they cried.

After Irie had heard their story, he conducted them at once to Chamberlain Nagazumi, who was on duty in the audience hall, and then to Takeko Hoshina, principal lady-in-waiting. "There is no need to wake the Emperor now," they told her, "but when he does wake, see that he knows what has happened."

Actually, the Emperor *was* awake. His bedchamber, a twenty-mat room, was next door to the room where the chamberlains were holding their war council, and although they were speaking as softly as they could, so as not to disturb him, he had heard their voices. He did not, however, indicate that he was awake, because he did not want to cause any unnecessary bother. He lay and listened to the murmur of indistinguishable voices.

The chamberlains decided to bar all the doors to the Gobunko and to fasten the iron shutters over all the windows. But the shutters had become rusted through long years of disuse, and the chamberlains were unable to close them. At last they called a couple of sturdy young guards, and Chamberlain Irie, as he watched them going around the building, barring all the windows, thought how ironical it was that this was being done not against enemy troops but against Japanese soldiers—and Imperial Guards to boot.

The two men sat in silence for a few moments.

At last Takeshita told his host about the assassination of General Mori.

The War Minister had been about to take a sip of *sake*. Now he paused, glass in hand, as though he had been turned to stone. Then with a grunt, he drained the glass and put it carefully down on the low table in front of him. "One more thing to apologize for," he said sadly.

4 a.m. to 5 a.m.

*"Kill me by all means — but
I don't see what you'll gain by it!"
Yoshihiro Tokugawa*

AT FOUR O'CLOCK, MISS REIKO YASUKI, A technician in the employ of the Japan Broadcasting Corporation, heard the tramp of boots in the wide street fronting the NHK Building. Since she already knew that the Emperor's recording was to be broadcast at noon, she feared that the boots were those of enemy troops. She ran to the window and peeked out through the blackout curtains on the third floor where she was working. She was relieved to see—in the first faint flush of dawn—that the troops were wearing Japanese uniforms, and with somewhat lighter heart she went back to work.

At the same time, thirty-seven men were speeding toward Tokyo from Yokohama, by truck and private car, over National Highway No. 2. Thirty of them were wearing the uniform of the Imperial Army, five of them were students, and two were members of the

Yokohama Youth Corps. Together they called themselves the National Divine-Wind Corps (Kokumin Kamikaze Tai), and they used the name *kamikaze* because, like their namesakes, they were eager to die to advance the cause of their country and their Emperor: the cause, in this case, being a continuation of the war. They trusted that their death would prove a fuse to ignite the resistance of the nation against her enemies at a moment when all her fire seemed spent. They were armed with pistols, swords, and two light machine guns; they were led by Captain Sasaki, of the Yokohama Guards; and their immediate objective was the official residence of the Prime Minister, whom they intended to assassinate as the first step in their campaign to liberate Japan. With any luck, they would find the entire Cabinet in session—and then they would be able to assassinate the lot, and all at the same time.

Captain Sasaki had a particular hatred for the Premier, whom he saw as the arch-traitor, for he remembered Suzuki's statement when he formed his Cabinet on April 7th—only four months ago. He was ready to die, he said, in defense of his country, and when he fell in the front line, he expected Japan's hundred million to storm across his dead body—"with courageous hearts"—to ensure the preservation of the Emperor and the nation. Captain Sasaki was ready and eager to take Premier Suzuki at his word: to storm across his dead body to wage the final Battle for Japan.

Refused the cooperation of both his superior officers and his subordinates, Sasaki had managed to persuade thirty soldiers to join him, with their arms, and although they were men he had never seen before, Sasaki was eager to lead anyone who was ready to follow him. To a group of students from the Yokohama Engineering College, he had made a tearful, impassioned plea for civilian cooperation with the Army "to preserve Japan by fighting on, under a military régime, in this time of life or death. . . ." He had got five recruits.

It was just beginning to grow light as the truck and the car jolted along the pockmarked highway toward Tokyo and the first objective. In the Premier's official residence, Chief Cabinet Secretary Sakomizu was asleep at last. It had been a long and tiring day, and as he lay waiting for sleep to come, he had no confidence that the day facing him would be any less long and tiring—but at least he had attained the goal he had fought for. For him this was not a day of defeat but rather the day the war ended, the day the air-raids stopped, the day the senseless destruction of the Japanese people and their land came to a halt, the day they could begin rebuilding what had been torn down. There was so much ahead to be done! His exhausted brain throbbed as he began to anticipate the many problems to be solved—but merciful Nature took over, and he slept.

General Anami was preparing for a longer sleep. Around his belly he had wound a band of white cotton; the upper part of his body was naked.

"Have you any message," Takeshita asked, "that you want me to take to your family?"

The War Minister nodded.

"Tell my wife," he said, "that I am very grateful to her and that I have absolute confidence in her. She has done well. Yes, Ayako has done well. I have three sons, I can die in peace. Tell Koretaka to do nothing rash. I don't mind dying for I shall be going where Koreakira already is."

Takeshita had filled the glasses with *sake*.

Anami continued: "Remember me to Umezu and Suzuki." He paused; he named a few other friends, and Takeshita made a note of the names; then he asked, "How about Yonai?"

The War Minister's face, flushed with drink, turned a deep angry color. "Kill him!" he cried. "Kill Yonai!"

Takeshita was not too surprised at the outburst, for he knew how

277

much Anami disliked the Navy Minister; their personalities had always clashed—and so, in recent days, had their opinions on the question of surrender.

Takeshita said nothing. The cry—"Kill him!"—echoed through the room redolent of the sweet smell of warmed *sake*.

Toda and Tokugawa returned to the Imperial Household Ministry bearing the news that all was well at the Gobunko. Toda went upstairs to the office of the chamberlains, while Tokugawa continued on to make his report to the aides-de-camp. They said they were much relieved to hear that the Emperor was safe, but at the same time they asked Tokugawa to leave because he was talking too loudly. Tokugawa complied, with the inner reflection that aides-de-camp, after all, were military men too. Could anyone ever tell what was in the heart of a soldier?

"Halt!"

Tokugawa obeyed, thinking it was probably the same second lieutenant he had seen on his return from the Gobunko.

The officer ordered a guard standing in the corridor to bring Tokugawa along; he began to prod Tokugawa with his rifle.

The chamberlain, although slight, was not a coward. "What's the meaning of this?" he demanded. "I don't have to go anywhere with you."

"Orders," said the lieutenant curtly.

They were standing beneath the Goseimu room, where the Imperial recording had been made. Officers and men were running up and down stairs: the search seemed to be growing more frantic.

"If you have any questions to ask," said Tokugawa, "ask them here."

"We're looking for the Emperor's recording," said the second lieutenant. "And you know where it is. You know where Kido is too, don't you?"

"How should I know?" Tokugawa was standing with his back to the wall of the corridor; he threw his arms out to lend emphasis to his words. "How should I know where they are?"

A couple of other officers joined them. "Never mind," said one. "Anybody who won't answer questions, kill him!"

"Right!" said the other officer. "Kill him!"

"Kill him! Kill him!"

It sounded an unholy chorus, but Tokugawa's voice was firm as he cried: "Kill me by all means—but I don't see what you'll gain by it!"

"He's right," said an officer. "His blood will only rust our swords. Let him live."

The other officers went on their way, leaving Tokugawa with the second lieutenant, who embarked on an arrogant explanation of why this temporary occupation of the Palace was necessary. It was the same argument the Army had used back in 1936: the Emperor has been misled by the people around him; to remove them, disobedience to the Emperor is temporarily necessary; then the old, and true, Japanese order can be restored. "Have you none of the real Japanese spirit in you?" cried the officer insolently.

A couple of soldiers had stopped to listen.

"You are not the only people," Tokugawa replied, annoyed, "who are trying to preserve the country. I am a chamberlain in the service of the Emperor, and I am doing my best to serve him. We must all work together to—"

He got no further. A fist struck him full in the face, and he fell to the floor, his eyeglasses crushed beneath him. The Army had given him its reply.[21]

Lieutenant Colonel Ida's car pulled up in front of the War Minister's official residence, and Ida hopped out. He was prevented from entering the house, however, by a non-commissioned officer of the military police corps, who was standing guard outside the house and who said that no one could go in because the War Minister was preparing to kill himself.

Ida was just about to get back into the car when the door opened. It was Lieutenant Colonel Takeshita, who had come out to investigate the sound of the car. Takeshita looked flushed but not, like Ida, dishevelled. Ida's face was streaming with sweat, and his uniform was damp and caked with dust from the hot ride through the city streets.

The light was growing stronger in the eastern horizon as the two men greeted each other in somber tones, and then Takeshita led the way into the War Minister's house, whispering that he had not told Anami about Hatanaka. Takeshita apparently felt this was not the moment to involve the War Minister in the unhappy affairs of the world he was leaving.

Ida paused. He could see down the length of the corridor into the back room, where General Anami, naked from the waist up, knelt on the mats. Tears mingled with sweat on Ida's cheeks: guilt was part of his sadness too, as he remembered his own share in the night's events; no doubt the War Minister believed that with his death Army opposition to surrender would vanish.

"Welcome, Ida!" called Anami cheerfully. "Come in, come in!"
Ida entered the room and dropped to his knees.
"Come nearer!"

Still on his knees, Ida moved forward until his knees and Anami's were almost touching.

"I have decided to commit *seppuku,*" said the War Minister. "What do you think?"

Ida paused only momentarily. Takeshita was right—Anami must be allowed to die in peace, although Ida wondered then, and later, whether Anami had not in fact heard about the Palace incident and whether this was not why he was killing himself as soon as possible, in the hope that his death would prevent a general Army uprising, the consequences of which would make the abortive occupation of the Palace seem trivial by comparison. "I think it is a glorious thing to do," Ida replied.

"I am glad to hear you approve," said Anami.

Ida could say no more for a moment; his tears had choked his voice. Then, "I'll follow you," he murmured.

But the War Minister would hardly let him finish. "Don't be a fool!" he cried, in a voice of thunder. Ida felt his face being slapped hard, twice, and when he opened his eyes again, he saw Anami smiling at him. "Don't let me hear you say that again," said Anami, in the tone of a father rebuking a son. "There is no need for you to die. My death alone is sufficient. Do you understand?"

He clasped Ida firmly in his arms, and Ida felt his tears falling onto the bared breast of the War Minister. "Do you understand?" he repeated. "You must not die—do you understand?"

Ida was still determined to commit *seppuku* himself, but in order to explain why it was necessary, he would have to tell Anami about Hatanaka—and that he found impossible. "Yes," he said, "I understand."

"Good, good!" cried Anami. "You must do your best to help rebuild Japan—that takes more courage than dying!" Ida understood Anami's implication that without the courage to live and work toward a better Japan, Ida would not be able to face his ancestors and would be held in contempt by his own children. "Now, come on," said Anami, "pull yourself together, and let's drink our *sake*. I don't know how long it will be before our next *sake* party together—in some other place." He laughed heartily at his joke.

The others joined him. The drinking resumed. Anami's round face grew rosier.

"If you drink too much," said Takeshita, in a worried tone, "your hand might slip, you might not succeed in killing yourself."

"Don't worry," Anami replied genially. "I haven't drunk too much yet. Besides, drink helps because it improves the circulation—the blood will flow more quickly. And don't forget I'm a fencer! Fifth grade. No, no, I'm not likely to fail. Relax!" Anami's hearty laugh rang out.

His guests smiled, as etiquette demanded.

The two Eastern District Army staff officers, Fuha and Itagaki, returned to headquarters to report to the Chief of Staff, Major General Takashima, on the situation at the Imperial Guards Division. Takashima felt that he had been proven correct in advising the commander, General Tanaka, to wait before taking action; now, as a result of the report he had just received, he explained to Tanaka that the most important immediate step was to communicate, if possible, with Colonel Haga, commander of the Second Regiment. With luck, this could be done by taking advantage of Hatanaka's mistake in permitting a telephone line to be left open between Eastern Army headquarters and the Guards command post.

Takashima's patience was rewarded. After several abortive attempts, he finally had Haga on the wire. The connection was very bad, and neither man could hear clearly, but Takashima repeated again and again that the Division order signed and sealed by Mori was an invention largely of Koga's, that the troops around the Palace must be dispersed, and that couriers must be sent at once to Eastern District Army headquarters for new orders.

"You're not alone there, are you?" Takashima shouted into the telephone.

Haga replied that Hatanaka was standing beside him.

"Let me talk to him," said the Chief of Staff.

Hatanaka came to the phone at once. "This is Major Hatanaka," he said. "I beg the Chief of Staff to try to understand our position. Our men are zealous and eager to—"

Takashima interrupted. "I understand!" he cried. "But it makes no difference. Your situation is hopeless, you are alone, the Eastern Army will not join you. You may think you are succeeding because you hold the Palace temporarily, but you are defeated, you are like soldiers trying to defend a hopeless position in a cave with no way out. Listen to me carefully! Don't do anything rash—you will only sacrifice more lives uselessly. I respect your feelings as a private individual, Hatanaka, but as an officer in the Army you must obey the Emperor. Japan's supreme virtue is in obedience! Are you listening to me, Major?"

"I am, General! But—let me think! General!"

"Yes?"

Hatanaka's voice grew impassioned, fanatical. "I have one request to make of the General. Before the Emperor's recording is broadcast, may we have ten minutes on the air to explain our own position? The reasons for what we have done and the goals we still hope to win. . . . Ten minutes, that's all, only ten minutes to talk to the people. With the permission of the Eastern District Army!"

"You are still trying to hold an untenable position," Takashima replied. "Can't you understand that? There is no hope whatsoever. The only thing you can do now is to make sure there are no more unnecessary deaths. Have you got that, Major?"

Hatanaka did not reply. He put down the receiver and turned to Haga. His face was deathly pale, and he seemed, in the few minutes he was on the telephone, to have aged as many years. He saw that Koga and Shiizaki had joined them, but it was to Haga that he looked for understanding and support.

Haga, however, could not contain his anger. "Now I understand," he cried, looking at the three officers, "why General Anami never came. You've been lying to me the whole time! This is a rebellion —and I want no part of it. If you're going on with it, you'll have to kill me first, you—"

283

"Traitors" was the word he had been about to use, but he bit it off. He looked at the three heads bowed in front of him, and fell silent. Their plan had failed. Although they were probably determined to sacrifice themselves, they would yet have to learn that the gods may not be humbled.

Colonel Haga calmly ordered Major Hatanaka to leave the Imperial Palace.

Hatanaka raised his head and stared boldly at the Colonel.

Koga, watching him, must have understood what was happening, for Hatanaka was the kind of man who would only fight harder once he believed the entire world was against him. Like a cornered beast, he was about to turn on his adversaries no matter how great the odds against him.

Blue had begun to filter into the deep gray of the sky, and the reddish glow in the east was brightening, as a truck and a car pulled to a quiet halt in front of the Premier's official residence and the thirty-seven members of the Kokumin Kamikaze Tai slipped quietly out. Captain Sasaki ordered the two light machine guns placed facing the front entrance of the dark and silent house.

He gave the command to fire.

Kojiro Akabane, a secretary of the Planning Bureau, was the first to awaken. He looked out of a window to see the khaki-clad figures firing at the house and to hear the thud of the bullets as they hit the walls. Chief Cabinet Secretary Sakomizu decided, as he leapt out of bed, that the enemy must be attacking the city, but his younger brother, Hisayoshi, came running into the room to say that the attacking force was Japanese.

Remembering the incident of February 26th, Sakomizu's first thought was one of relief that the Prime Minister had returned to his private house, and his second was that it would really be rather short-sighted for him, for Sakomizu, having lived through the war, to be killed by Japanese soldiers after the war ended. With his brother and a police guard, he fled through the underground corridor toward the emergency exit at the back. Akabane, who was hiding in the bomb shelter, watched them through a small window: he felt, he said afterwards, as though he was witnessing a movie.

Sasaki and his men, having raked the building with machine gun fire, surged to the front gate and ordered the guard on duty to open up. As he did, he whispered to the captain: "I'm on your side—the traitors should all be liquidated. Suzuki is in his own house in Maruyama. Go and get him!"

Surprised and grateful, the captain muttered his thanks. He had some oil poured onto the carpet in the front corridor and tried to set fire to it, but the oil was heavy and refused at first to light. When at last it burst into flame, Sasaki ordered his men back into the truck and the car, and they sped away toward Maruyama.

Tomoo Sato, assistant director of the General Affairs Section, had stayed in the house, and under his direction the guards soon put the fire out.

The Premier's official residence was not the only target that morning. At four-thirty guards at the Akasaka residence of Marquis Kido were attacked without warning by a group of seven men. A fierce fire-fight ensued, during which one of the guards was wounded. The attackers, who were finally repulsed, were members of the feared "Thought Police," a super-secret section of the Kempeitai.[22]

At that same time, just a mile-and a half across the city, officers and men of the First Regiment of the Imperial Guards had surrounded the NHK Building.[23] Soldiers had been posted at all entrances; no one could come or go; Major Koga's Order No. 584 was in operation.

When Reiko Yasuki went into Studio 13, she was astonished to discover an officer and two soldiers tinkering with the equipment, for broadcasting rooms were closed to all outsiders. "We're going on the air," said the officer abruptly. "Make all preparations for an immediate broadcast."

Just then another air-raid alert from the Eastern District Army came over the loud speaker.

"We're not allowed to broadcast during an alert," said Miss Yasuki.

"The hell with you!" shouted the officer.

Miss Yasuki fled.

Some sixty NHK employes who had been on night duty were locked into Studio 1.

Yasuo Yanagisawa, assistant director of the domestic news department, looked up from his desk to find a pistol thrust into his face while the officer at the other end of the pistol demanded cooperation in making a broadcast. But Yanagisawa sensed that the officer was just as intimidated as he was himself and that he was asking rather than demanding cooperation and would not be too surprised if he didn't get it.

A few minutes later, Masanori Asakura, an employe in the business department, managed to get by the guards and out of the building. He ran through the deserted streets, in the early dawn, to the Daiichi Hotel, where Takeharu Takahashi, head of the news department, was staying.

If the NHK building was occupied, the Emperor's recording could not be broadcast. If the recording was not broadcast . . . . The possibilities were staggering, the consequences might be catastrophic. The most important thing, then, Takahashi decided, was to inform the Chairman of the Japan Broadcasting Corporation at once, but Ohashi, as he knew, had not yet returned from the Imperial Palace. What he did not know was that Ohashi was being forcibly detained.

He supposed there had been a party of some sort and Ohashi had simply stayed overnight. He got hold of Takeji Morinaga, of NHK's entertainment department, who had once worked in the Imperial Household Ministry and so would know his way around, to undertake to deliver the message to Ohashi in the Palace.

Morinaga boarded a Yamate line train at Shimbashi Station.

Within the Palace, the search was still under way, but the situation was beginning to look a little brighter, as the day brightened. A telephone line was found that had not been cut: it was a direct line between the naval aide-de-camp, Commander Noda, and Lieutenant Commander Furukawa, of the Navy Ministry, to whom Noda relayed the information that Mori had been murdered and the Palace occupied by the Imperial Guards. Furukawa promised immediate relief.

The news spread quickly. Aide-de-Camp Nakamura told Chamberlain Tokugawa that help was on the way; then, looking at the chamberlain's swollen and discolored face, warned him to be more careful of the soldiers. "They've gone crazy," he said.

"It's an honorable war injury," replied Tokugawa coldly, considering that he had sustained it as a result of being asked to leave the aides-de camp's room.

"Is the Household Minister safe?" asked Nakamura then. "And the Privy Seal?"

"Of course they're safe," said the chamberlain. "We hid them. But I don't intend to tell you where."

"Never mind," said Nakamura. "General Tanaka will be here soon, and then it will all be over. Everything will be all right."

5 a.m. to 6 a.m.

"This is what it's come to! I never thought I'd live to see it..."

Yasuhide Toda

JUST BEFORE FIVE, MAJOR HATANAKA HIM-self appeared at the offices of the Japan Broadcasting Corporation, accompanied by a second lieutenant and two soldiers. He had no trouble in passing the guards around the building, that he himself had ordered; and he went directly to Studio 2, where, brandishing a pistol, he informed Morio Tateno, an announcer, that he intended to take over the five o'clock news broadcast. Whether or not he had lost the Palace, he was not going to give up so easily—he was going to put his case before the people of Japan, asking them to refuse to accept the unconditional surrender that had been forced on them by the traitors around the Emperor, asking them to resist the irresistible tide of history.[24]

But Tateno was as firm in his resolve as Hatanaka: he would not put the fanatical major on the air even if it meant cancelling the five o'clock news, even if it meant setting his own life in jeopardy.

"But the air-raid warning is still in effect," he said. "We can't broadcast during an alert without a special okay from the Eastern Army—"

"Nonsense!" Hatanaka knew that that okay would never be forthcoming.

"Besides," Tateno went on calmly, trying to ignore the madness he sensed in the armed major confronting him, "if the broadcast is to be nation-wide, we have to advise all the other stations in the country ahead of time. It's a technical matter."

Hatanaka saw that another announcer was just then sitting down in front of a microphone, presumably to make the five o'clock news broadcast. Why can't I take his place? Hatanaka asked himself.

And the answer was: No reason at all.

With his pistol in one hand and the text of his broadcast in the other, Hatanaka glared at Tateno, trying to make up his mind what to do.

At 5:10, accompanied by his adjutant, Colonel Tsukamoto, and by Lieutenant Colonel Fuha, a staff officer, Commander Tanaka of the Eastern District Army arrived at Guards headquarters. General Tanaka had accepted his Chief of Staff's advice not to attempt to put the rebellion down before daylight. But now the sun was well above the eastern horizon: it was time to put an end to the nonsense.

The hot night was turning into a hotter day; the humidity was already rising.

Officers and men of the First Guards Regiment, fully armed, were about to leave for the Imperial Palace under the command of Colonel Watanabe, acting on Division Order No. 584. Watanabe was surprised to see the General's car drive up.

Lieutenant Colonel Fuha jumped out. "His Excellency the Commander!" he cried.

Watanabe hurried over to the car and escorted Tanaka into his own office, there to learn, for the first time, and to his horror, that General Mori was dead and that the orders upon which Watanabe had been about to act were false. Watanabe said that the orders had been issued to him by Major Ishihara, then in an adjoining room.[25]

General Tanaka ordered Ishihara in. The major's face was pale, his mouth clenched tightly shut.

Tanaka was furious. "How dare you?" he cried. "You are an officer of the Imperial Japanese Army. How dare you disobey the Emperor's command? What you have done today is high treason!"

Ishihara said nothing, he offered no excuse or extenuation—it was as though, by his silence, he desired to admit his guilt and his willingness to accept whatever punishment it deserved.

"Put him under guard!" cried the General. Fuha handed Ishihara over to a Kempeitai sergeant on sentry duty outside the door. Ishihara had awakened from his dream of glory to find he was nothing but a criminal.

Having heard that General Tanaka was on his way to the Imperial Palace, Chamberlain Toda decided he had better let Chamberlain Irie know immediately. Once again he took that precarious walk to the Gobunko through the Momijiyama Tunnel, but this time he had a guard with him. When he reached the Fukiage Gate, he was challenged by an officer, as he had expected he would be.

"I am Chamberlain Toda," he said, "on official business at the Gobunko. Kindly let me pass."

The second lieutenant curtly refused.

As Toda began to argue with him, he recalled what had happened to Tokugawa, and he wondered if the bird in the tree above was singing his death-song.

Another officer came up. "Oh, let him go. He's nobody of any importance. He won't be any trouble to us after we're inside the Gobunko."

Toda continued on his way. "This is what it's come to!" he muttered, as he scurried along the path toward the Imperial Library. "I never thought I'd live to see it. . . . Japanese soldiers attacking their Emperor!" Toda shuddered as he quickened his steps: the thought was so appalling there were no words available, no emotion adequate, to express it.

He reported to Hisanori Fujita, the Grand Chamberlain, who had arrived not long before from his quarters in the former Honmaru. He had bowed his way, so the story went, through the lines of bayoneted soldiers, beaming and exclaiming, "You're doing a fine job, men, a fine job," and so had reached the Gobunko. It had occurred to no one, apparently, that the inconspicuous little old man was the Emperor's Grand Chamberlain.

Having heard Toda's story, Fujita consulted with Chamberlains Irie and Nagazumi and with Hirohata, Lord Steward to the Empress. The question was whether, with inadequate force, they should attempt to hold the Gobunko against the marauders or whether there was less likelihood of violence if they surrendered immediately. In either case there was no way to anticipate what atrocities might be committed within the sacred precincts of the Emperor's own dwelling.

"I still can't believe it," said Fujita. He opened one of the iron shutters a crack and peeped out. He saw groups of Imperial Guards occupying strategic positions between the Fukiage Gate and the Gobunko; machine guns were being placed with their muzzles pointing squarely at the house of the Emperor.

After Ishihara's arrest, General Tanaka was able to telephone Colonel Haga within the Imperial Palace. He ordered Haga to meet him immediately at the Inui Gate. As his car drove up before the barred black gate, a sentry cried, "Who goes there?"

"The commander of the Eastern District Army," replied Tanaka.

The gate was opened.

Search parties were still swarming about in their feverish attempt to locate either the Imperial recording or the men who could tell them where it was hidden. Colonel Haga's orders to desist had not yet reached them.

At the War Ministry, the consensus of opinion was that General Anami himself had been coerced by the intransigent young officers into leading the rebellion personally. Major General Yoshio Nasu, director of the Military Service Bureau, conferred with Lieutenant General Wakamatsu, Vice-Minister of War. They decided that a soldier of Anami's proven loyalty must not be allowed to lend his name under duress to an act of treason. Nasu set off at once for the War Minister's official residence.

At the same time, there was a bitter argument going on in one of the dark corridors of Ichigaya. The participants were Colonel Arao, chief of the military affairs section, and Colonel Amano, chief of the General Staff operations section. The subject was the rebellion within the Army. Amano claimed that since it was already under way, he, as chief of operations, should be in command of putting it down; Arao countered that as a domestic affair it fell within his area of command, since he was chief of the military affairs section.

The argument continued.

The War Minister rose and put on a white shirt. "This was given to me," he said, "by the Emperor when I was his aide-de-camp. He had worn it himself. I can think of nothing I prize more highly— and so I intend to die wearing it."

Anami then pinned all his decorations to a dress uniform and put the uniform on, after which he removed it, folded it properly, and laid it in front of the *tokonoma*. "When I am dead," he said, "will you drape the uniform over me?"

Takeshita nodded, unable to speak; Ida felt his eyes fill with tears.

Anami took a photograph of his second son, Koreakira, who had died at the age of twenty-one during the China Incident, and placed it on top of his folded uniform in front of the *tokonoma*.

The telephone bell shrilled through the silent house. Hajime Suzuki, the Premier's son, sleepily picked up the receiver. "Soldiers have tried to burn down the Premier's official residence," said a voice Hajime took to be that of a police officer. "They are now on their way to his own house. Warn him, tell him to leave at once."

The connection broke.

Hajime hurried to his father's room and helped the old man dress. Then the two men, with Mrs. Suzuki, ran down to the car, which was parked in a narrow lane in front of the house. They realized, to their consternation, that the car was facing in the wrong direction, away from the main highway; the street in which it was parked was too narrow for the car to be turned. Precious, perhaps fatal, minutes would be lost, they thought, as they had to go down the narrow street, turn, and turn again to reach the highway.

The three climbed into the back of the car; in front sat the driver of the car, with the Prime Minister's nephew and his bodyguard. But now the car refused to start, probably because of the inferior quality of the gasoline then available. Some ten police officers who had been on guard duty at the house rushed down to help push. The engine finally turned over as the car began rolling downhill.

While the Suzukis were taking their roundabout way to the highway, Sasaki and his men had already driven past the turn-off, without recognizing it, and now, having realized their mistake, were on their way back. It seems quite probable that if the car had been facing in the right direction, Baron Suzuki and Captain Sasaki would have encountered one another that August dawn.

Waiting in the house for the would-be assassins was Hajime's son, a middle-school student, with an intrepid young lady named Yuriko Hara, who had been helping Mrs. Suzuki in the house.

Lieutenant General Sanji Okido, head of the secret police, came to the War Minister's official residence around five-thirty to report on the insurrection among the Imperial Guards.

Anami, when he heard the name of his visitor, asked Takeshita to see him. He did not, he said, want to speak to him himself, nor did he want Okido admitted into the back of the house, where he was about to commit *seppuku*.

After Takeshita went to the door to speak to Okido, Anami asked Ida to stand watch also near the entrance to the house. Once he was alone, the War Minister, wearing the white shirt the Emperor had given him, went into the corridor.

Although the shutters were drawn, the bright light of the early morning sun filtered through the cracks. Anami knelt in the corridor. The light etched sharp gashes across his face and chest. In choosing the outer corridor for his death-scene, Anami had compromised. To have committed *seppuku* in the garden would have meant he considered his crime so great it could be atoned for only on the bare ground. If he had stained the straw mats of the inner room with his blood, he would have been saying that he considered himself blameless. In any case, even if he might actually have preferred the penitential earth of the garden, there were people coming and going who might have tried to stop him.

Still on his knees, with his torso erect and his shoulders back, Anami removed his dagger from its scabbard.

When Captain Sasaki and his thirty-seven rebels finally found Suzuki's house, it was empty—save for the Premier's grandson and Miss Yuriko Hara. Sasaki put the point of his sword against her breast and demanded to speak to the Prime Minister. "He isn't here," replied Yuriko Hara; she had intended her voice to sound natural, but the words, when they came out, seemed to be those of someone else, spoken from a great distance. She did not even recognize her own voice, although she had thought she could face the rebels fearlessly. She had heard rumors that American troops, when they occupied Japan, would rape all the women, and she decided that she would rather die than face such dishonor. She was wearing very little make-up and a new pair of *mompe,* baggy war-time trousers for women. She was ready to die—and yet her voice, when it came out, did not sound like her voice at all. "He isn't here," she repeated, but she hardly convinced herself, let alone the would-be assassins.

Captain Sasaki ordered the house to be searched. The soldiers and the students went through every room, thrusting their swords into cupboards and closets.

"We don't want to hurt you," said one of the students. "Why don't you go outside?"

But Yuriko Hara refused.

When the search was at last completed, and it was apparent that there was no one in the house but the woman and the young boy, the soldiers angrily began to set fire to the paper-lined sliding doors. Yuriko Hara ran to the kitchen for a bucket, which she began to fill with water. "If you try to put that fire out," said a soldier, "I'll kill you."

Soon the fire caught. The flames billowed high into the pale morning light. The day was already hot; around the burning house, the heat was unbearable.

Yuriko Hara and the Premier's grandson fled to a safe distance, where they mournfully watched the immolation of a Japanese house that had withstood enemy air-raids but not the fury of frustrated Japanese soldiers. A fire engine arrived, but the machine guns held the firemen at bay.

The audience—the fire-fighters, the fire-makers, and the impotent guards—followed the bright red flames as they danced against the lurid blue sky of early morning.

When Takeshita returned, after seeing Okido, he paused in the corridor, behind the kneeling, but upright, figure of the War Minister. Then Takeshita also dropped to his knees. Anami had drawn the dagger across his belly and was now, the dagger in his left hand, looking for the carotid artery on the right side of his neck.

Anami began to sway. The dagger swept across his neck, and a torrent of blood pulsed out. Yet Anami's body was still erect.

"Shall I help you?" asked Takeshita, in quiet, almost inaudible tones.

"No." There was nothing unusual about the War Minister's voice; he might have been answering the most ordinary of questions. "Leave me."

Takeshita went out into the garden. Ida lay sobbing on the bare ground.

The Yamate line train, pulling into Tokyo Station, was almost empty; the station too seemed deserted as Takeji Morinaga crossed the great hall and headed west toward the Imperial Palace. Behind him, the sun was already mounting and much too hot; he wiped his forehead as he traversed the wide, ruined, empty avenues on his way to Sakashita Gate. There he saw machine guns pointing squarely at him, defying him to enter.

But he knew the Imperial Palace and decided he would have a better chance of getting in through the inner Sakurada Gate. Two sentries stood guard there, but present also was an Imperial Palace police officer whom he knew. The officer told him he would be fool-hardy to try to enter the Palace now, but Morinaga replied that he had special orders to deliver, no matter what.

The sweat seemed to pour down the back of his neck as he walked through the gate, but no one stopped him. Near Maruike Pond, in front of the Imperial Household Ministry, he saw a Palace policeman being disarmed by Imperial Guards, and Morinaga wondered if he was destined ever to hear NHK broadcast the Emperor's reading of the Rescript—but he had been entrusted with a message of grave importance, and so he continued on, past armed and angry soldiers, hoping that he would be able to deliver that message to Ohashi.

Major General Nasu expected the house to be swarming with impassioned officers and armed men, but when he got there, he saw only Lieutenant Colonel Takeshita and Lieutenant Colonel Ida talking quietly off to one side.

He saw the War Minister kneeling with his head toward the Imperial Palace; his body moved slightly to the right, then swayed back.

"I have come to take you with me to the Ministry," said Nasu.

"Why have you come?" The voice thundered, like the voice of a god. "Go away!" Anami shouted. "Leave me!"

Nasu looked more closely, and it was only then that he saw the blood welling from the Minister's throat, only then that he realized what Anami had done. He clasped his hands together, the tips of his fingers to his mouth, and bowed his head.

"Listen!" Takeshita's voice was no more than a whisper in Ida's ear. "I have Anami's seal. I could issue an order that would make the whole Army rebel. Shall we do it? Why not? Why should we surrender like schoolboys?"

Had Takeshita really said it? It was incredible! Or was it part of Anami's grand design? Was he only pretending to believe that his death would put an end to the Army's ambitions? No, Ida refused to believe that: the man who was dying a few feet away was not play-acting.

"False orders would soon be exposed," Ida said, tonelessly. "And do you think Anami's spirit would be content?"

"No, no," said Takeshita quickly. "I was only joking after all." But his tone belied his words. It was as though Takeshita's grief at Anami's dying, and his anger at what had made it necessary, were now forcing him to take some decisive, explosive action—and as though he did not much care what it was.

In the corridor, Anami's body swayed but still did not fall.

Captain Sasaki and his companions—their enthusiasm now fired with memories of the holocaust that was the Suzuki home—roared through the early morning streets. Sasaki had thought of next attempting to assassinate Nobuyuki Abe, Army General and former Prime Minister, but had changed his mind. His new target, and their present destination, was much better suited to their grisly purpose: Baron Kiichiro Hiranuma, president of the Privy Council.

6 a.m. to 7 a.m.

"I will explain my decision to the Imperial Guards."
the Emperor

WITHIN THE GOBUNKO, DISCUSSION CON-
tinued as to what should be done when the rebellious soldiers demanded entrance. There seemed to be no satisfactory solution to
the problem, particularly after the failure of the chief Gobunko
guard, a man named Kosuga, to return from his confrontation with
the insurgent Imperial Guards.

A short while before, Kosuga had come to say that he had had
word the insurgents intended to disarm the Imperial Palace police
force.

"But that," said Chamberlain Irie, "requires the approval of the
Chief of the Palace police. You go and tell them so."

"Yes, sir!" said Kosuga, in an energetic voice, but when he left
on his mission, he seemed less enthusiastic; and he had not returned.
The chamberlains feared he might have been killed.

They had not witnessed the scene that Takeji Morinaga, of NHK, had observed on his entry into the Palace: the Imperial police being relieved not only of their weapons but of their coats and trousers as well and left to stand in the already overheated morning sun.

The Gobunko was shut tight against the world; doors and windows were barred and heavily shuttered. No ray of light entered, no sound of birdsong or chirping of insects from the surrounding garden. The chamberlains huddled fearfully under artificial light this bright summer morning and took counsel among themselves.

Now that they had no armed police or guards to help them, they decided that the only thing to do was to let the soldiers in when they came hammering at the door and take them on a conducted tour of the Gobunko, meanwhile giving the Emperor and the Empress a chance to escape. None of the chamberlains thought it was a satisfactory solution, but none of them could devise a better one.

"Well," said Chamberlain Toda briskly, "then we had better wake the Emperor and warn him."

As Toda and Mitsui headed toward the Imperial bedchamber, each felt so weak-kneed he thought he could not take another step, yet neither wanted to reveal his anxiety and apprehension to the other; and so perhaps be ridiculed.

The Emperor rose immediately at the summons.

Mitsui made a deep bow before he embarked on his report of the occupation of the Palace and of the imminent threat to the Gobunko.

"Is it a *coup d'état* then?" asked the Emperor. "What actually has happened?"

Toda told His Majesty about the Guards' violent search for the Imperial recording as well as for Marquis Kido and the Household Minister. But so far, said Toda, the search has failed.

The Emperor was silent for a few moments. Then he said: "I will go outside myself. Gather the men together in the garden, and I will speak to them. I will explain my decision to the Imperial Guards."

The two chamberlains bowed their heads low: they did not want the Emperor to see the tears that had filled their eyes at his words.

"In any case," said the Emperor, "call the Chief Aide-de-Camp. Let me speak to him."

But Hasunuma was immured in the Imperial Household Ministry; between the Gobunko and the Ministry stood armed soldiers and loaded machine -guns.

The two chamberlains withdrew from the Imperial presence.

"You are the youngest," said Mitsui. "I think you had better go."

"But you," said Toda lightly, "are head of the General Affairs Section. I think really you should go. . . ."

Inside the Inui Gate, General Tanaka conferred with Colonel Haga. He confirmed the fact that Division Order No. 584 had been forged and that General Mori was indeed dead. "From this moment," he said, "I am in command of the Imperial Guards Division." He ordered Haga to return his men to their original station and to report back after the action had been completed.

General Tanaka then hurried across the wide road that led to the Gobunko to inform the Emperor of what had happened. He saw an Imperial chamberlain running toward him. The chamberlain, at the same time, perceived the approaching figure of a general and slackened his pace.

As they were about to pass, Tanaka said, "Is the Grand Chamberlain in the Gobunko?"

"No," said the chamberlain.

"And the Chief Aide-de-Camp?"

"No," said the Chamberlain.

"The Emperor then?"

"Yes," said the chamberlain. "The Emperor is in the Gobunko."

General Tanaka laughed. "Why do you keep trembling?" he said. "The revolt's over—you have nothing to worry about. Here!" He handed his calling card to the chamberlain, who read it, sighed, bowed, and handed the General one of his own cards. Once again the two men exchanged bows.

The chamberlain's name was Mitsui. "We're safe then!" he murmured, with another deep sigh of relief.

"I find it very strange," said Tanaka, "that neither the Grand Chamberlain nor the Chief Aide-de-Camp is with the Emperor."

Mitsui smiled. "Ah, but the Grand Chamberlain," he said, "*is* with the Emperor. The Chief Aide-de-Camp is not—I am on my way now to the Ministry to fetch him."

When Chamberlain Irie opened the Gobunko to General Tanaka, he saw the sun shining behind the General, and he thought it had never looked so bright or splendid.

"Everything is all right now," said Tanaka firmly. "I deeply regret that so much inconvenience has been caused."

Premier Suzuki thought that everything was all right too, as he took shelter in his sister's house in Nishikatamachi in Hongo. But when his son Hajime had telephoned back to the Premier's house after their arrival to say they were safe in Hongo, he realized that he had been speaking to one of the rebel soldiers and so had inadvertently given away their hiding-place.

Hajime hung up at once. The Suzukis decided that they had better move on again. This time they headed for the house of some friends who lived next door to the Premier's brother, General Takao Suzuki, in Shiba.

Nor was everything all right at NHK; inconvenience was still being caused by Major Hatanaka, who continued to brandish his pistol and threaten wholesale death unless he was allowed to explain his actions and his motives to the people of Japan. Yet his tone was not belligerent or authoritative: it had shifted closer to appeal.

The NHK people repeated that they could not make a broadcast during an alert without the approval of the Eastern District Army. As an added precaution, they had disconnected the line between the NHK Building and the broadcasting tower, so that even if Hatanaka had forcibly seized a microphone, he could not have put his case on the air.

Meanwhile he continued his hour-long intimidation of the radio staff. He seemed to be reaching the point of no return, veering from despondency to exhilaration in a moment's time, from the realization that he had failed to the certainty that he could never fail. While the radio people wondered, fearfully, what he was going to do next, he received a telephone call.

It was from an officer of the Eastern District Army general staff.

The NHK personnel listened as he poured forth, once again, all his reasons for believing that Japan could be preserved only through continuance of the war. But his tone was no longer that of a man convinced that he was right and ready to act on his convictions; a note of fear had crept into his voice, his cheeks seemed sunken and his lips bloodless, as he halved his original demand: he was ready now to settle for five minutes of radio time.

Announcer Tateno caught a glimpse of the script that Hatanaka had prepared. It began: "Our troops are now guarding the Imperial Palace. . . ."

Hatanaka listened for a moment to the officer at the other end of the line. "Very well," he said at last, "it can't be helped." He put down the receiver, looked up at the ceiling, then seemed to lose his balance. He looked as though he was going to faint. Finally he wiped his eyes with his fist, turned to the other officers in the room, and said: "We've done everything we could. Let's go."

The rebels departed, and NHK was free to resume its preparations for the broadcast of the Emperor's voice speaking to his people.

When Lieutenant Colonel Shiizaki, still in the Imperial Palace, learned that General Tanaka had the situation in hand, he drew his sword from its scabbard. His face contorted into the grimace of a madman, he swung the sword with all his might against a pine tree. The sword shivered for a moment in the bark before Shiizaki withdrew it.

To Takeji Morinaga, who was watching, it seemed that the aura around Shiizaki had suddenly lifted; ecstatic hallucination had given way to realistic despair. Morinaga felt an involuntary tremor shake his whole body.

A few minutes before seven, Captain Sasaki and his Kokumin Kamikaze Tai pulled up in front of Baron Hiranuma's house. "He is one of the chief collaborators!" Sasaki cried. "He would like to deliver our sacred country into the hands of the enemy." Without knowing who was in the house, Hiranuma or his family or servants, they set fire to it and, after watching for a few moments, piled back into their vehicles and headed home to Yokohama. The hot morning sun beat ruthlessly down.

All that remained of Hiranuma's huge house was part of the garage.

7 a.m. to 8 a.m.

"Let us all listen respectfully to the voice of the Emperor."

Morio Tateno

WHILE PREMIER SUZUKI LAY RESTING IN Shiba, his son Hajime managed to get in touch with Chief Cabinet Secretary Sakomizu, with the inspector general of the Tokyo Police Department, and with the Welfare Minister, among others. Thus, the Premier learned, at long last, that the Imperial Palace had been occupied and that General Anami was dead.

Lieutenant Colonel Takeshita, as he drove to the War Ministry, gazed up at the sun, but his thoughts were still back at the house he had just left. More than an hour after he had committed his act of *seppuku,* General Anami still knelt in the same place, his body still erect. The blood still flowed from his wounds.

"Aren't you in agony?" Takeshita whispered.

But there was no reply. The War Minister seemed to have lost consciousness.

Takeshita took the dagger that lay beside him and thrust it deep into the right side of Anami's neck. The body fell.

Then Takeshita telephoned the War Minister's house in Mitaka and spoke to the Minister's wife, who was Takeshita's elder sister. She was prepared for the news and took it calmly, one solace, at least, for Takeshita. She agreed to come at once to the official residence and look after what needed to be done.

At Ichigaya, Takeshita reported first to General Wakamatsu, the Vice-Minister. He gave him the details of Anami's death and of the two documents that the Minister had left behind.

" 'For my supreme crime,' " Wakamatsu repeated. "What do you believe he meant by that?"

Takeshita supposed that Wakamatsu was asking whether Anami had been involved in the aborted *coup d'état,* whether that was the "supreme crime." He felt the truth must be made known, so that Anami's name should not be stained by a crime of which he was not guilty. "I did not," Takeshita replied, "ask him directly what he meant, but I know what his intention was: as the Army's chief representative, he wanted to take on himself all the responsibility for the Manchurian Incident, and the Greater East Asia War, and Japan's defeat. He wanted to bear the blame and beg the Emperor's pardon."

In the silence that followed, Takeshita had the thought that all the officers of the Army ought to share the blame—for their interference in political affairs and their arbitrary decision to plunge the nation into war. They ought to share the blame and the punishment both, Takeshita thought; but he said nothing.

The men locked up in the Guards command post near Nijubashi were aware that dawn had come because their watches told them so and because, whenever the front door opened, they could see officers outside, sheltered from the bright morning sun, sipping tea.

They themselves had been without light or air for almost six hours; they had been forbidden to smoke or talk; they had not been offered so much as a glass of water; and they were completely ignorant about what had happened within the Palace and outside it, to their radio stations, their newspapers, their ministries, and—not least of all—their Emperor.

But probably the strongest emotion they felt was thirst. They had been cooped up in a hot, humid, airless room all night long; they had felt the sweat pouring from their bodies; their tongues were like parched and swollen blotting paper, their throats so dry they couldn't close them.

Every time the door opened and he saw the officers sipping tea, Kawamoto would feel a surge of anger, not only for himself but for the older men, who must be suffering more than he, but then he would try to put the anger out of his mind, for he knew that it would only make him feel thirstier.

Shortly after seven, some soldiers entered the detention room. "Will you kindly come this way?" said one, who was probably a corporal. "We hope you will forgive us for keeping you waiting such a long time."

As the prisoners filed out of their prison, Kawamoto shouted: "Water! Give us water!"

Outside the prison, the air, though hot, was fresh and sweet; birds were singing; the sun rode freely in the sky. The men thought they had never seen a garden look so green. Around the command post, which had been bristling with armed Guards the night before, a few soldiers loitered, stretching and yawning in the morning sun. The yawn was infectious: and some of the prisoners realized, for the first time in their lives, what a delicious experience a yawn can be.

Morinaga was waiting for the chairman of the Japan Broadcasting Corporation to deliver his report. He had been interrogated at length by the insurgents about his "special orders," but he had refused to divulge them to anyone but Chairman Ohashi. Now here was the chairman himself, to whom he reported the news of the occupation of NHK, but by that time word was circulating that General Tanaka had raised the siege of the Imperial Palace—which, combined with the sweet smell of life and freedom, made other news seem pale.

Tanaka himself was, at that moment, bowing deeply before the Grand Chamberlain. "I beg of you," he said, with another bow, and then another, "to convey my profoundest apologies to His Majesty. I cannot express my sorrow at the discomfort my delay may have caused him." And another bow.

As Fujita returned the bow, he decided to request the Emperor to grant General Tanaka an audience.

After the General left the Gobunko he went directly to the Imperial Household Ministry, which was still surrounded by armed Guards. "Make way!" shouted Tanaka. "I am the commander of the Eastern District Army."

The Imperial Guards made way.

At 7:21, NHK broadcast a special announcement.

"His Imperial Majesty the Emperor," said announcer Tateno, "has issued a Rescript. It will be broadcast at noon today. Let us all respectfully listen to the voice of the Emperor."

He paused.

Then he repeated, still more solemnly: "Let us all respectfully listen to the voice of the Emperor at noon today."

After a moment, he continued, more briskly: "Power will be specially transmitted to those districts where it is not usually available during daylight hours. Receivers should be prepared and ready at all railroad stations, postal departments, and offices both government and private. The broadcast will take place at twelve o'clock noon today."

He wiped the sweat from his face and then repeated: "The broadcast will take place at twelve o'clock noon today."

Within the Imperial Household Ministry, Lord Privy Seal and the Household Minister were still hidden in the "bank vault." Soldiers were still searching both for them and for the recording that the Emperor had made.

Major Koga sat on a chair, alone, in one of the offices, staring straight ahead at nothing. The only expression on his face was one of blank despair.

When General Tanaka at length found the Chief Aide-de-Camp, he repeated his bows and his apologies. Then he told Hasunuma the whole story of what had happened, and Hasunuma, for the first time, was fully aware of the extreme danger in which he had for a short while been placed. He expressed his gratitude to Tanaka. "But how sad I am," he said then, "that General Mori is dead."

"We have lost a very valuable man," General Tanaka replied. "I am not unaware of my responsibility in the matter."[26]

Not without considerable ceremony, General Tanaka took his leave of the Chief Aide-de-Camp and was driven back to the Inui Gate. He was content with his total victory over the insurgents—but the flames of rebellion, though under control by now, had not altogether died.

Some twenty minutes earlier, three colonels—Ida, Arao, and Shimanuki—had sat in conference in the Ministry of War, pondering the futility of their earlier actions. Ida, particularly, was sobered by the chilling memory of General Anami in his death agony. The three men now decided to try to break the chain of events that had started some twenty hours before.

Immediately after reaching a decision, the three officers commandeered a car and headed toward the Inui Gate of the Palace. As the car ground to a dusty halt, the three jumped out and ran toward the guardhouse, but instead of Hatanaka they were confronted by General Tanaka. They halted, unsure what the General's presence at the Palace meant—and Tanaka was equally uncertain of their intentions.

He took no chances. "Get back into the car and away from here at once!" he barked. "Get out!" The repentent colonels left.[27]

Yoshiro Nagayo, the author, after he heard the NHK announcement, wrote in his journal to this effect:

I can't believe it! A couple of days ago I said there was no other way to save Japan from destruction. In fact, I thought—and said—so a couple of years ago: the only way to avoid a revolution and preserve the country was for the Emperor himself to broadcast to the people. It was our last, our only, chance. But I never really believed it could happen! I was sure that too many obstacles would be put in the way of an Imperial broadcast. And now in a few hours it's about to come true. I know it could not have been easy. And I know also that it will mark a turning-point in the history of Japan.

8 am to 9 a.m.

"There's no place for an old man like me any more."
Baron Kantaro Suzuki

THE CHANGING OF THE GUARD TOOK PLACE at eight o'clock as always. A battalion of the Second Regiment, officers and men, flag flying high, marched out through the Inui gate. There was nothing on the soldiers' faces to show that they had any idea that they had just taken part in a *coup d'état* that had not come off. What they had done, after all, was just follow orders.

General Tanaka, in tight-lipped silence, watched the regimental banner as it disappeared beyond the Inui Gate. One battalion remained on guard within the Palace—which was the way things were supposed to be. Life was returning to normal—or as normal as it could be in the heart of a country that had just surrendered to the enemy, a country whose people did not yet know that they had admitted to their first defeat.

Chamberlain Mitsui hurried down the steps to the "bank vault," where a heavy iron door still guarded six men against an adversary who had ceased to exist. Mitsui struck the door three times with his fist, which was the agreed signal.[28]

There was no reply.

Mitsui then took off one of his shoes and hammered it three times against the door. This time the door was opened.

Ishikawa, the Minister's secretary, peered out.

"All's well," said Mitsui.

Ishikawa was delighted, not only because they were safe but also because he could now have something to eat. He was famished. He had wanted to go out during the night for a bite of food, but the Imperial Household Minister, Ishiwatari, refused to permit it. "Minister," he said, as he followed Ishiwatari and Kido out of their underground dungeon and up the stairs, "what are we going to do about breakfast?"

Ishiwatari looked at him coldly. "This is not the time for breakfast," he said.

At 8:10, the Grand Chamberlain was received in audience by the Emperor at the Gobunko. Fujita was horrified to see how wan and tired the Emperor looked as he sat back, exhausted, in his chair.

"Fujita," the Emperor said quietly, "what did they want? Why couldn't they understand what was in my mind?"

The Grand Chamberlain had no reply to make. There was silence. Sunlight glanced brightly on the busts of Lincoln and Darwin that stood behind the Emperor.

His Majesty then received Marquis Kido, Lord Privy Seal, and Sotaro Ishiwatari, the Imperial Household Minister, in a brief audience; and when the two men left, the Gobunko was wrapped in silence: there was no clanking of swords, or marching of boots, or shouting of orders, no enemy planes roaring overhead, only the rustle of birds winging through the trees, and the hum of insects.

Captain Sasaki had returned to Yokohama, after burning a couple of houses, but he still felt restless—he still felt something ought to be done to prevent the catastrophe of surrender. He decided to visit Captain Kozono at Yokosuka, not knowing that Kozono had been in Atsugi for a good many hours now, nor that the base there had still not agreed to surrender along with the rest of Japan. Sasaki's intention was to report to Kozono on the night's activities and to enlist his cooperation in something still more spectacular.

But before he got to Yokosuka, he was stopped by a Navy patrol. The lieutenant commander in charge refused to let him continue.

"Do you agree that the Navy should surrender?" asked Sasaki.

"I am following orders," replied the other officer.

"Don't you realize," Sasaki shouted, "that that means the end of the Imperial Navy?"

"You better go back where you came from," said the young lieutenant commander, in a patronizing tone, backed by his men.[29]

Chamberlain Okabe, when he reached the Imperial Palace at eight-thirty to begin his day's work, heard about the busy night his fellow-chamberlains had had. His first thought was the Imperial recording. Was it safe? He rushed to the office where it had been hidden, to find Chamberlain Mitsui and Director Kakei of the General Affairs Section huddled in conference. They looked so serious that Okabe took fright at once.

"Something's happened!" he cried.

Mitsui looked at him sadly over his glasses. "This morning," he said slowly, "this very morning, at dawn—"

"Where is it now?" Okabe interrupted, growing more agitated.

Mitsui pointed to the little safe. "Right there," he said, as his face broke into a grin.

But there still remained the problem of getting the recordings safely to the broadcasting studio. The first lap of the journey—to

the General Affairs Section of the Imperial Household Ministry—
was perhaps the most hazardous, for the Ministry was full of dark,
narrow, winding corridors, and although the insurgents had theore-
tically all left the Palace, one could not be sure that some fanatical
officer was not lurking somewhere, waiting to snatch the records
away.

The three men finally agreed on a procedure suggested by Okabe.
The first pair of records, stamped COPY, was to be put in a tray
and carried respectfully, even ostentatiously, through the corridors
by Kakei. The second pair of records, stamped ORIGINAL, Okabe
was to put in the bag that contained his lunch-box. A few minutes
after Kakei left, Okabe slung the bag casually over his shoulder and
marched off down the corridor. They had agreed to meet in the
General Affairs Section.

General Tanaka, having returned to Eastern District Army headquarters, issued another order. "Major Hatanaka," he said, "seems
to be at NHK. Have him put under guard at once. Under no circumstances is he to be allowed to broadcast."

Colonel Inadome relayed the order to the Kempeitai, and had
hardly put the telephone down when it rang again. He heard the
excited voice of Colonel Fuha: "The records the Emperor made
have disappeared!"

Inadome sat by the telephone and took down the information as
it came in; there seemed to be an awful lot of it.

Premier Suzuki was just finishing breakfast. Hajime decided that
this was a good time to bring up an inevitably painful subject.

"The Emperor's reading of the Rescript," he said, "will be
broadcast at noon. That means our work is done. Shouldn't you
tender your resignation now? Then the Cabinet can resign en
masse."

314

The Premier agreed at once and asked Hajime to write out a draft of the resignation. Paper, brush, and ink were brought, and after a few minutes Hajime read what he had written:

After I received the Imperial command to form a Cabinet, I devoted all my efforts, night and day, to save Japan from defeat. However, I have failed. I have now received the Imperial Rescript terminating the war. I do not know how to express my deep apology. . . .

Suzuki heard his son's draft through to the end, then said, "Excellent, excellent! So be it."

After a moment he added: "There's no place for an old man like me any more.

"I can't bear," he went on, "to think that I had to request the Imperial decision twice.

"The future of the country lies with the young men now."

The drama in which Suzuki had played such a leading role was ended. The old man folded his hands in a gesture of relief—and resignation.

The black despair which had overwhelmed the officers of the War Ministry was lightened by the news of Anami's death. The calm bravery with which the Minister had committed his act of *seppuku* served as a kind of inspiration to his subordinates and gave them hope for the future. Anami had lived, and died, like a Japanese, a *samurai,* a man to be respected. The Ministry mourned him, honored him, and found in his death a source of strength to go on living.

315

9a.m. to 10a.m.

"Put them both under guard at once."
Lieutenant Colonel Makoto Tsukamoto

WHEN CHIEF CABINET SECRETARY SAKO-mizu got to the house where the Prime Minister was still in hiding, he congratulated him on his escape from assassination. Then he began to give the Premier a detailed account, so far as he knew it, of the night's peculiar goings-on.

Suzuki cut him short. "I am planning," he said, "to submit our resignation en masse at today's Cabinet meeting."

Sakomizu was surprised and delighted: surprised because, although he knew the resignation had to come, he did not expect it to come quite so soon; delighted because he was so terribly tired. After he had discussed the agenda with Suzuki, he took his leave with lighter steps than when he had arrived.

Four months ago, at the time he assumed the post of Chief Cabinet Secretary, he had weighed 145 pounds. Now he was down to just over 127. He was rather pleased, as a matter of fact, about the loss.

Director Shimomura of the Information Bureau, with his secretary, Kawamoto, had drunk some light tea after their release from detention and then had headed directly for the Prime Minister's official residence. Shimomura supposed that the Cabinet was already in session, deciding its own fate at all events; the fate of the country had already been decided.

Yet the building, when they arrived, seemed ominously quiet. Was it too in the hands of insurgents? Shimomura told Kawamoto to go in and see whether State Minister Sakonji was in his office—Sakonji's office was next door to Shimomura's. Kawamoto hurried inside and in the front hall slipped and fell on the heavy oil that Captain Sasaki's Kokumin Kamikaze Tai had poured around.

Kawamoto rose, covered with oil, and looked around. Fire had damaged the front hall, but beyond that Kawamoto had no idea what had happened—or what was happening now.

Lieutenant Colonel Tsukamoto, of the Military Police Corps, who had been alerted to the possibility of a *coup* a few days back by Colonel Ida himself, received a distressing report. It said that two officers, one on horseback and the other riding a motorcycle, were distributing leaflets outside the Imperial Palace urging people not to accept the surrender order but to go on fighting.

Tsukamoto remembered saying, in his discussion with Ida, that he believed a revolt would be meaningless unless the entire Army took part and that once the Emperor announced his decision there could be no question of not obeying it. He remembered seeing the desperate and angry faces of Hatanaka and Shiizaki.

Tsukamoto called in a subordinate officer. He told him about the two men who were handing out seditious leaflets just outside the Imperial Palace. "Put them both under guard at once," he said.

Admiral Yonai, the Navy Minister, was on his way to the War

Minister's official residence. He sat silently back in his seat. Then, after a deep sigh, he murmured to his secretary, "We've lost a very valuable man."

When the car arrived, Mrs. Anami and an adjutant conducted Admiral Yonai into an inner room, where the body of the War Minister was lying. It was covered with a quilt; there was no blood to be seen, and the face of the Minister was serene, showing no trace of the agony of his last hour.

Yonai went up to the body and bowed his head; then, still silent, he sat down on the straw mats that covered the floor and looked for a long time at Anami's face.

Then he rose, left the room, followed by his secretary, and went back to his car. He still had not said a word. As they rode in silence, Yonai's secretary was thinking about a bit of paper he had seen lying on a mat near Anami's body. A few words had been written on the paper in bright black India ink—perhaps a first version of Anami's death-poem—and by comparison with the ink, the few drops of blood that had splashed onto the paper seemed pale.

"Yes," said the Navy Minister, after his long silence, "we have really lost a very valuable man."

Behind the War Ministry, great clouds of smoke were blackening the morning sun. The burning of classified documents had been resumed—but no matter how many went up in smoke, there always seemed to be more coming out. The flames rose higher.

10 a.m. to 11 a.m.

"I am on my way to the broadcasting Studio."

tomoo Kato

A PLENARY SESSION OF THE PRIVY COUNCIL had been scheduled for eleven o'clock within the Imperial Palace, at the underground Conference room of the Gobunko. Chief Cabinet Secretary Sakomizu, having left the Premier, had come to the Palace to make preparations for the Privy Council session. He went first to the Imperial Household Ministry, where, at the entrance, he met Director Kato of the General Affairs Bureau. Kato was wearing puttees and carrying a ration bag slung over his shoulder. He seemed extremely nervous. Clasping his bag tightly, he said, as he passed Sakomizu, "I am on my way to the broadcasting studio."

He got into a car of the Tokyo Metropolitan Police Department.

In an antechamber used by advisers to the Privy Council, Sakomizu caught sight of the Council's president, Baron Hiranuma. He was shocked by how much Hiranuma seemed to have aged in the few hours since he had last seen him.

"Forgive me for asking, Your Excellency," he said, "but is there anything seriously wrong with your health?"

Hiranuma laughed. "When my house was attacked this morning," he replied, in a blurred voice unlike his usual one, "I got away and ran into the house next door, but I forgot my teeth. They got burnt with the rest of my house. Now I'll have to buy another house—and another set of teeth."

It had been a disastrous night for a lot of people.

Kato reached the NHK Building safely, with the "original" of the Emperor's recording; the "copy" was brought by Section Chief Kakei in a car belonging to the Imperial Household Ministry. This was put away in a reserve underground studio, to be used in case anything happened to the "original."

Because of a shortage of vacuum tubes, transmission from about seventy per cent of Japan's emergency broadcasting stations had been curtailed from August 1st. This was now restored, for the reading of the Imperial Rescript, and instructions had also been issued to transmit power to districts which had not customarily been receiving it during the day time. NHK's own power had been increased from the usual ten kilowatts to sixty.

Announcements were made repeatedly that the Emperor's voice would be heard at twelve noon. Programs that had no connection with the Imperial broadcast were cancelled.

The Emperor himself was extremely busy that morning. In addition to dealing with a number of letters and other documents relating to the termination of the war that required his attention, he granted audiences to Marquis Kido, various Cabinet ministers, and directors of the Imperial Household Ministry. Of all those whom he received he asked the same question: he wanted to know how they felt about the Imperial decision to end the war.

The chamberlains on duty were deeply touched by his reiteration of this question, by his evident desire to know what his people really thought.

Half an hour before the Privy Council meeting was to start, Chamberlain Tokugawa installed an old RCA portable radio in a small anteroom to the underground conference chamber. He checked the reception, which was satisfactory despite the fact that the room was underground, and arranged a special seat for the Emperor beside the radio, for it was here that His Majesty would listen to his own voice, recorded twelve hours earlier, proclaiming the first defeat in Japan's long history.

Tokugawa sat waiting for the minutes to tick by: they seemed to do it very slowly.

At Kodama Air Base, Major General Nonaka ordered all personnel to assemble to hear the noon broadcast. He was of the opinion that the Emperor was going to urge the armed forces to make a supreme effort to overcome the enemy—a decision with which he was very much in accord. He had watched the failure of his men's attack the previous night, he had seen the city of Kumagaya go up in flames, and he was determined to do better next time. That there would be a next time Major General Nonaka had no doubt.

Captain Kozono, at the Atsugi Air Base, was not so certain. He had delegated the job of assembling the men to a subordinate, while he himself sat cross-legged on his bed waiting for twelve o'clock. Then he would know whether he was going to be forced to act in defiance of the Emperor or not—whether, in fact, he was going to have to commit treason in order to preserve his country.

The command posts at both Kodama and Atsugi were hot; in the glare of the sun reflected from the concrete runways, they seemed hotter still. Major General Nonaka and Captain Kozono made frequent use of their handkerchiefs as they waited.[30]

There was no waiting for Colonel Inadome, as he sat at the telephone in the staff room of Eastern District Army headquarters. First the Tokyo Metropolitan Police Department called to ask how many soldiers were guarding the Prime Minister's official residence. Inadome's reply—"Thirty men and one officer"—seemed to satisfy them. Then came a call from Cabinet Councillor Yamashita to say that the Imperial recording was safe, after all. NHK telephoned to complain that the guards they had asked for had not arrived. Inadome replied they had been sent. When he checked, he discovered that the guards had got the address wrong. He had to make other arrangements immediately. It seems quite possible that Colonel Inadome was the busiest man in Tokyo that morning.

Premier Suzuki was putting on his long morning coat, which had not been forgotten despite all the alarms and excursions. He would then go to the Imperial Palace, where, after he had had an audience with the Emperor, the plenary session of the Privy Council would begin. That would be followed by a Cabinet meeting; an en masse resignation would be proferred; and Suzuki's long day would be done.

11am to 12 noon

"A broadcast of the highest importance is about to be made."

Nobukata Wada

SEVENTEEN ELDERLY GENTLEMEN FILED down the damp and narrow stairway that led to the underground conference room of the Gobunko. They had come to complete the work that, twenty-four hours before, had been begun by twenty-four men. Those twenty-four hours had been blank for most of the people of Japan, busy for some, for some exalted, for others tragic, frustrating, terrifying, ecstatic, even sublime—and now they were about to end. Everything was about to end, all the horror of war, and the passion of partisanship, and the love and hatred that entwine to create the phenomenon of patriotism. Japan, after fifteen years of war, was about to taste the fruit of peace—and see whether it was sweet. Japanese boys and girls of fifteen had no idea what that fruit was like: they had never tried it.

The late War Minister had declared that before the Imperial Rescript could be promulgated, it would have to be approved by the Privy Council. The late War Minister was about to see his demand fulfilled. Baron Hiranuma, the President of the Privy Council, led the way down the narrow stairs, followed by the vice-president and the other members of the Council, along with Premier Suzuki, Foreign Minister Togo, and Director Murase of the Legislative Bureau.

Colonel Ida's "midsummer night's dream" had ended with the end of night. In the bright light of day, Major Hatanaka, riding a motorcycle, and Lieutenant Colonel Shiizaki, astride his horse, were distributing leaflets to an astonished populace outside the Imperial Palace. This is what the bemused people who received those leaflets read:

We, officers of the Imperial Japanese Army, who, this morning of August 15th, 1945, have risen up in arms, declare to all officers and soldiers of the Armed Forces and to the Japanese people:

That our intention is to protect the Emperor and to preserve the national polity despite the designs of the enemy;

That our prime concern is neither victory nor defeat; nor are we motivated by selfish interest;

That we are ready to live, or die, for the sole just and righteous cause of national loyalty; and

That we devoutly pray that the Japanese people and the members of the Armed Forces will appreciate the significance of our action and join with us to fight for the preservation of our country and the elimination of the traitors around the Emperor, thus confounding the schemes of the enemy.

The two officers thrust their declaration into the hands of the passers-by—but the latter did not pause; they passed by.

At eleven-twenty, the Emperor entered the underground conference room, attended by Chamberlain Koide, and within ten minutes the plenary session of the Privy Council had begun.

Baron Hiranuma rose and, after a profound bow, began to read the communication that the Emperor had sent him:

We have commanded Our government to inform the Governments of the United States, Great Britain, China, and the Soviet Union that the government of Japan has accepted the terms of the Potsdam Proclamation. Although this is a question that should have been considered previously by the Privy Council, the government has been seriously pressed for time and therefore requested the presence of the President of the Privy Council at their prior deliberation. . . .

After Baron Hiranuma finished reading the Imperial communication, he rolled it up, raised it high above his head, like a baton, and made a deep bow in the direction of the Emperor. The others in the room, having executed the same gestures, resumed their seats; the silence in the conference chamber was absolute.

Then Baron Hiranuma cried, "The Prime Minister!"

Suzuki rose and sighed deeply. His expression was as unreadable as ever, yet there was no one present who did not know what he was thinking. It will soon be over, it has all come to this. . . .

On the greensward in front of the Imperial Palace, between the Double Bridge and Sakashita Gate, Major Hatanaka's exalted and frustrating war came to an end. Using the pistol with which he had killed General Mori, he put a bullet through the center of his forehead. The Palace he had tried to capture and hold, the Palace that had fired his imagination to attempt deeds far beyond his ability, the Palace that was the symbol both of power, which he professed to disdain, and of the unity of Japan, which he affected to adore: this was the background for his final deed of desperation.

At the same time, Lieutenant Colonel Shiizaki put a sword into his belly, and then a bullet into his head.[31]

Beneath the molten orange mid-day sun, the grass in front of the Imperial Palace was stained with human blood and brain; the men who resisted peace with all their strength had found peace at last.

Beside the coffin in which lay the body of General Mori, at Imperial Guards headquarters, Major Koga committed his final act. Earlier than morning General Tanaka had said to Major Koga, "Let us die bravely—that is the supreme virtue of a Japanese officer." Despite the fact that his fellow-officers had been expecting such an act and trying to circumvent it, Koga slipped away from them and fulfilled General Tanaka's instructions: he cut his stomach open in the design of a cross. By the time the other officers came into the room, Koga was dead.[32]

The NHK Building was being closely guarded, both inside and out, by Eastern District Army soldiers as well as the Kempeitai.

At eleven-thirty, the recording that the Emperor had made was carried from the office of Chairman Ohashi to Studio 8, where it was to be broadcast. Waiting were Ohashi, Kato, and Yamagishi of NHK; Shimomura and his secretary Kawamoto, of the Information Board; and Kato and Kakei of the Imperial Household Ministry. Most of them had spent the night imprisoned in the hot, steamy little Guards command post, sleeplessly wondering what was going to happen to them next. Although they had changed, the fresh clothes they had put on were already soaked with sweat.

The announcer, Wada, sat at a table in front of the microphone; he was worried, and he looked it; his face was pale and tense with an awareness of the responsibility that would soon be his. Beyond a glass partition, sat the engineers, also terrified that something might go wrong which could be blamed on them. Suddenly one of them realized that no test playback of the recording had been made in the studio. They held a hurried discussion, and although they all agreed that to play the record over before the broadcast was a kind of lèse-majesté, not to play it might have far more disastrous results.

Suddenly the Emperor's voice was heard in the studio. All the men waiting there looked terrified, as though at some unexpected phenomenon of nature, and even after they realized that it was only a test run, they remained uneasy until the test ended.

They would have been far more uneasy if they had known what was happening outside the soundproofed studio. To Lieutenant Colonel Shigetoyo Suzuki, a staff officer of the Eastern District Army, the behavior of a Kempeitai lieutenant seemed suspicious. The man was standing in the corridor outside Studio 8, staring at the ceiling as though in a trance. Suzuki walked over to him. "Don't go to sleep," he said; "the Emperor's broadcast will be on the air very soon."

As though released from his spell, the lieutenant of police drew his sword and shouting, "There won't be any broadcast—I'm going to kill them all," started to rush for the studio.

Suzuki leapt on the man and pinned his arms behind him. As he continued to struggle, Suzuki cried, "I'll kill you if you don't stop!"

Then he turned him over to the Kempeitai, and the lieutenant was led away. He had been in command of twenty men. Would they, Suzuki wondered, appalled, have followed him into the studio if he had given the order?

All over the country, the people of Japan were marking time while the clock ticked toward noon. Like characters in a crowded film that has suddenly stopped, they were waiting to hear the voice of the Emperor, so the film might start again. But it would be a different film, once the Emperor had spoken. A few knew it, more guessed it, many were puzzled and uncertain—but most, certainly, were ready to welcome an end to the death and destruction, the hunger and despair of the past months, so long as their country and their Emperor could be preserved.

The life of the capital ground to a halt. Everywhere people were huddled about their radios: at the War Ministry, at Eastern District Army Headquarters, at NHK, within the Imperial Palace itself. Downstairs, in the underground shelter, the Emperor had withdrawn to the small anteroom that the chamberlains had arranged for him.

"A broadcast of the highest importance," said announcer Wada, "is about to be made. All listeners will please rise."

The nation of Japan got to its feet. It may be surmised that the only able-bodied human being in the country who did not rise was the Emperor himself. He sat in his chair, so tense that the chamberlains were frightened. His head was bowed.

"His Majesty the Emperor," said the announcer, "will now read his Imperial Rescript to the people of Japan. We respectfully transmit his voice."

The strains of "Kimigayo," the Japanese national anthem, followed.

Then, after a brief pause, out of the sky came the long-awaited, the revered, the troubled but peaceful Voice of the Crane:

"To Our good and loyal subjects. . . ."

Notes to the Text

1. Deleted were the following statements:
   The Japanese military forces, after being completely disarmed, shall be permitted to return to their homes with the opportunity to lead peaceful and productive lives.
   We do not intend that the Japanese shall be enslaved as a race or destroyed as a nation. . . .

2. The diary of Musei Tokugawa, which lists the events of the day in minute detail, does not mention the name Potsdam. The diary of Jun Takami, the noted author, for that day is as follows:
   I read the newspapers by the light of a candle. The political upheaval in Britain. The Potsdam broadcast. The Yomiuri and the Mainichi newspapers call the Proclamation "ridiculous."

3. Hissho Gakuto Renmei was a voluntary students' organization formed when the tide of war turned against Japan. During their rest-days, the students helped clean up bomb-damage and performed other such tasks of rehabilitation until Captain Sasaki persuaded them to take other action.

4. According to some accounts—based probably on Shimomura's diary—the Emperor wiped his face with a white glove. But his attendants say that it was out of the question for the Emperor to have worn white gloves on an occasion like the present one.

5. As no stenographer was present at the Imperial Conference, no official transcript exists, but many of the participants subsequently wrote down their recollections of the Emperor's words. Shimomura's account of the speech (on which we have largely based our

text) seems to be the most faithful since it makes use of the accounts of three other ministers. Shimomura also asked Premier Suzuki to go over it.

6. As it turned out, Ikeda's plan backfired. The Soviet troops, when they occupied Manchuria, confiscated all matériel as "trophies of war"; it could not therefore be used for purposes of reparation. Ikeda's plan, nonetheless, contributed greatly to the liberation of Asia.

7. After the Army conference ended, Wakamatsu took the document to General Kawabe, commander of the Air General Forces, and persuaded him to sign it.

8. *Rekidai Shochoku Shu, Naikaku Kokuyu Shu, Kanwa Dai Jiten,* and *Kojirin.*

9. Councillor Hideoto Mori of the Overall Planning Board was reported also to have prepared a draft of the Rescript; if so, he also refrained from presenting it.

10. The words that follow are based on a deposition made by Colonel Arao on August 16th of the questions he asked Lieutenant Colonel Ida and of Ida's replies. Use was also made of Ida's diary.

11. Coincidentally, the number of characters in the Imperial Rescript—815—matched the date of the broadcast: the 15th day of the 8th month. After his retirement, Admiral Yonai made it a daily practice to write out these 815 characters and send the copy to friends.

12. These identifications have been substantiated, but the identity of the third officer has never been proved. Both Takeshita and Ida were lieutenant colonels, but neither seems to have been present at that time.

13. The origin of this Note seems to be somewhat mysterious. It was certainly cabled by the Foreign Ministry, presumably on the authority of Yoshinaga Ando, who says in his diary that he was requested to send it by Major General Nagai, "of the Military Affairs Bureau." However, Nagai had been injured in an air raid the month before and had been replaced; he could not, therefore, have made any official request of Ando.

14. Although Tokyo was blacked out, most of the strategic centers, such as the Imperial Palace, the War Ministry, and NHK, had their own auxiliary power generators.

15. There is some question whether Mori actually intended to go to the shrine or whether this was only a tactic to delay the insurrectionists. It is quite possible that Mori, a devout man, had both purposes in mind.

16. Mystery still shrouds the deaths of General Mori and Lieutenant Colonel Shiraishi—understandably enough, since these were the sole acts of murder committed during that rebellious night. The presumption that Hatanaka shot Mori, while Uehara decapitated Shiraishi, is generally accepted; but the exact number of men present in Mori's room at the time of the murders is uncertain. Some investigators are of the opinion that there may have been other witnesses in addition to Lieutenant Colonel Shiizaki.

17. Anami is said to have composed this death poem as long ago as July, 1942, when he was commanding the Second Manchurian Regional Army and was making preparations against the possibility of a Soviet attack.

18. According to the records of Hiroshi Shimomura, among others, it was Hatanaka who questioned Yabe, but Yabe himself is certain that the officer who interrogated him was wearing a staff officer's sash. Thus it would have to have been Koga, since Ishihara, the only other staff officer involved, was at the Division's headquarters at that time.

19. This is one reason accounts differ as to the room in which the Emperor made the recording, some claiming it was a second-floor room and some a room on the third floor. Both could be correct.

20. The identity of the officer who called on Takeshita at that point is not certain. According to Takeshita, it might have been Uehara because there was no other suitable liaison man available. Uehara apparently returned to the Air Academy, and at dawn flew over the Imperial Palace to encourage the insurgents who were still occupying it. Takeshita's assumption, therefore, might be correct.

21. Although Yoshihiro Tokugawa says that his assailant, a Sergeant Wakabayashi, did not strike him very hard, the other chamberlains say that Tokugawa's face was heavily discolored for several days, so the blow could not have been a light one. Some fifteen years later, Wakabayashi called on Tokugawa to apologize for having struck him and brought a tea kettle which he said had been made out of a bronze mirror, an important family possession.

22. This was probably the gunfire that many residents heard during the early morning hours, although reports as to the time it took place vary. Some thought the sounds originated from the Palace, but these fears were later proved groundless.

23. Accounts vary. Some say that it was the Seventh Infantry Regiment of the Imperial Guards that occupied NHK, but Regiment Commander Teisaku Minami categorically denies it, so quite probably it was the First Regiment which, in accordance with Order No. 584, occupied the broadcasting station.

24. There is no proof that the major who insisted on being allowed to broadcast was, in fact, Hatanaka. Some accounts incline toward Major Komatsu, on the theory that Hatanaka did not have time to get to NHK, but that seems to be false: after Hatanaka was ordered to leave the Imperial Palace by Haga, he would have had ample time to go the short distance to the NHK Building. Further, Colonel Inadome and others mention that General Tanaka, on his return from the Imperial Palace, said that Hatanaka was at the broadcasting station and ordered him to be arrested there. The NHK personnel present at the time were divided in their opinion: on being shown a photograph of Hatanaka, not all agreed that he was the major in question.

25. The rebels apparently intended that Ishihara was to oversee the First Regiment and Koga the Second. The plan was fifty percent successful: Chief of Staff Takashima, despite persistent efforts, was unable to make contact with the commander of the First Regiment.

26. General Tanaka, as commander of the Eastern District Army, was also responsible for both the Imperial Palace and the Meiji Shrine, both of which were damaged by bombs during enemy raids. Tanaka asked to be allowed to resign his post, but the Emperor refused to accept his resignation. After August 15th, Tanaka was determined to commit suicide as soon as possible. On August 24th, he put down an attempt by military students to occupy the Kawaguchi broadcasting station, and that same night, at eleven-ten, put a bullet through his heart. He left a number of farewell letters to friends and fellow-officers, in which he said he was committing his act "on behalf of all his officers and men."

27. By the night of the 15th, Lieutenant Colonel Ida was still determined to commit suicide. He bade farewell to his wife and left for the War Ministry, telling her to come the following morning to collect his body. Colonel Arao, aware of Ida's intention and guided by General

Anami's injunction against any further suicides, ordered a strict watch to be kept over Ida that night. In the morning, when Mrs. Ida came to the Ministry and saw her husband alive, she wept for the first time.

28. Mitsui does not recall having made such an agreement, but Ishikawa is convinced that that was the arrangment and that Mitsui was a party to it.

29. On the evening of the 15th, Sasaki's student-warriors voluntarily gave themselves up at Kempeitai headquarters in Kudan, but headquarters was in chaos. A number of men had deserted, and a huge pile of documents was being burnt. The students were told to report to the Tokyo Police Department, since the police would be interested in hearing their stories. "You won't be punished," said a Kempeitai lieutenant. "Tenno Heika Banzai," shouted the students as they left: long live the Emperor!

At Police headquarters, they were detained and tried. Five year sentences were commuted to a year and a half, which five of them spent in Chiba prison.

Captain Sasaki himself went into hiding for fourteen years—the period of proscription. After this legal period ended, Sasaki is reported to have gone to Hajime Suzuki, the Premier's son, to apologize; and Suzuki is reported to have comforted him with the words: "At a time like that, people would have thought you were a coward if you hadn't done something of the sort."

30. At both Kodama and Atsugi, a chaotic kind of insurrection continued for several days—at Atsugi until the day before General MacArthur landed. Despite the fact that Captain Kozono had to be put into the psychiatric ward of Yokosuka navy hospital, his men continued to plan, and to make attempts to carry out, attacks on enemy forces. At Kodama, after the Emperor's broadcast, pilots packed torpedoes onto their planes and made ready to take off; it was all Major General Nonaka could do to persuade them to obey the Imperial command to desist. An aborted attempt was also made by the Mito Army Air Division, on August 17th, to spearhead a revolt.

31. Some accounts of this final day insist that Hatanaka and Shiizaki were arrested by the Kempeitai and released after they had pledged their word to commit *seppuku*. Men who were in the Kempeitai at the time, however, deny that the two officers were ever arrested. Masataka Ida wrote in his diary: "When they heard of the suicide of the War Minister, Hatanaka and others also took their own lives."

On the afternoon of the 15th, Lieutenant Colonel Takeshita went to recover the two bodies. In the pockets of both were their death statements. Shiizaki's, written in large characters, said: "Both life and death are a communication with God." Hatanaka's was a poem: "I have nothing to regret now that the dark clouds have disappeared from the reign of the Emperor." The two bodies, along with that of the War Minister, were laid in the officers' assembly hall at Ichigaya, and a silent wake was held throughout the night of the 15th. On the morning of the 16th smoke rose once again from the grounds of the War Ministry, as the bodies of the Minister himself and the two rebels were consumed.

Captain Uehara, of the Air Force Academy, the presumed murderer of Lieutenant Colonel Shiraishi, tried vainly to stir up continued armed resistance throughout the day and night of the 15th. On the 16th, he took his own life.

Colonel Oyadomari was also determined to commit suicide after the war ended, despite General Anami's prohibition. The date he chose was September 2nd. On September 3rd (the day that Japan signed the instrument of surrender aboard the Missouri), one of Oyadomari's subordinates called and found four bodies in the Oyadomari house. Two of them were children: they had been poisoned. Mrs. Oyadomari had apparently shot herself in the temple, and then the colonel had put the pistol into his own mouth and pulled the trigger. A few days before, Oyadomari's son, Tomokuni, who had just entered primary school, told one of his schoolmates with a smile that he would soon be going to a better place.

32. Shortly after the Imperial broadcast, the telephone rang in the house of ex-Premier Tojo. Tojo himself answered, and after listening for a few minutes, put down the receiver and turned to his daughter standing beside him. "Makie," he said, "Hidemasa will return home in about an hour. Are you prepared for my news, Makie? He has killed himself." "Yes, Father," replied the widow of Major Koga, "I have been prepared for some time. Now Hidemasa will be a major forever. His glory will never be tarnished."

A List of the Participants in Japan's Longest Day

The ranks and titles given are those current on the day of surrender. Japanese names are fairly easy to pronounce; vowels sound much as they do in Italian, while consonants, in the romanization in general use, are not very dissimilar from those of English, save that "g" is always hard. Words tend to be accentless, every syllable occupying much the same length of time, with the exception the long "ō" and "ū" (marked in the list with a macron), which double the time, and of "u" and "i," which are sometimes almost silent when they follow "s," "sh," and "k."

H. M. the Emperor

*Abe, Genki (Minister of Home Affairs)

Anami, General Korechika (Minister of War)

*Arakawa, Daitarō (Director of Technical Bureau, Japan Broadcasting Corporation)

***Arao,** Colonel Okitsugu (Chief of Military Affairs Section, Ministry of War)

Doihara, General Kenji (Inspector-General of Military Education, Ministry of War)

*Fuha, Lieutenant Colonel Hiroshi (Staff Officer of the Eastern District Army)

*Fujita, Hisanori (Grand Chamberlain)

Haga, Colonel Toyojirō (Commander of the 2nd Regiment, Imperial Guards Division)

Harada, Major General Susumu (Commander of the 3rd Brigade, Tokyo Guards)

Hasunuma, General Shigeru (Chief Aide-de-Camp)

Hata, Field Marshal Shunroku (Commander of the 2nd General Army)

Hatanaka, Major Kenji (Military Affairs Section, Ministry of War)

Hayashi, Major Saburō (Adjutant to Minister of War Anami)

Hiraizumi, Kiyoshi (Professor at Tokyo University)

Hiranuma, Kiichirō (President of the Privy Council)

Hirose, Hōsaku (Minister of Finance)

*Hoshina, Vice Admiral Zenshirō (Director of the Bureau of Naval Affairs)

***Ida,** Lieutenant Colonel Masataka (Military Affairs Section, Ministry of War)

*Ikeda, Sumihisa (Director of the Overall Planning Bureau)

*Inadome, Colonel Katsuhiko (Staff Officer of the Eastern District Army)

*Inaba, Lieutenant Colonel Masao (Military Affairs Section, Ministry of War)

*Irie, Sukemasa (Chamberlain)

Ishiguro, Tadaatsu (Minister of Agriculture and Commerce)

Ishihara, Major Sadakichi (Staff Officer of the Imperial Guards Division)

*Ishiwatari, Sōtarō (Minister of the Imperial Household)

*Itagaki, Lieutenant Colonel Tōru (Staff Officer of the Eastern Army)

*Kakei, Motohiko (Chief of General Affairs Section, Imperial Household Ministry)

*Katō, Susumu (Director of General Affairs Bureau, Imperial Household Ministry)

*Kawamoto, Nobumasa (Secretary to Information Bureau Director Shimomura)

***Kido,** Marquis Kōichi (Lord Keeper of the Privy Seal)

Kihara, Michio (Assistant to Sakomizu)

Kobiyama, Naoto (Minister of Transportation)

Koga, Major Hidemasa (Staff Officer, Imperial Guards Division)

Konoye, Prince Fumimaro (Ex-Premier and Jūshin)

Kozono, Naval Captain Yasuna (Commander of the 302nd Air Corps)

*Machimura, Kingo (Superintendent-General, Tokyo Metropolitan Police)

*Matsumoto, Shunichi (Vice Minister of Foreign Affairs)

Matsuzaka, Hiromasa (Minister of Justice)

Mikasa, Prince (Brother of the Emperor)

*Minami, Colonel Teisaku (Commander, 7th Infantry Regiment, Imperial Guards Division)

*Mitsui, Yasuya (Chamberlain)

Mizutani, Colonel Kazuo (Chief of Staff, Imperial Guards Division)

Mori, Lieutenant General Takeshi (Commander of the 1st Imperial Guards Division)

*Morinaga, Takeji (Entertainment Section, Japan Broadcasting Corporation)

Murase, Naoyasu (Director of the Legislative Bureau)

Nukada, Lieutenant General Mamoru (Director of the Personnel Bureau, Ministry of War)

Ōgane, Masujirō (Vice Minister of the Imperial Household)

*Ōhashi, Hachirō (Chairman of the Japan Broadcasting Corporatoon)

Ōhta, Kozō (Minister of Education)

Okada, Tadahiko (Minister of Welfare)

Okamatsu, Shinjirō (Chief of Air Defense Section, Imperial Household Ministry)

*Okamoto, Suemasa (Minister to Sweden)

Oyadomari, Colonel Tomomi (Information Department, Ministry of War)

Sakonji, Seizō (State Minister)

*Sakomizu, Hisatsune (Chief Cabinet Secretary)

Sakurai, Heigorō (State Minister)

*Sasaki, Captain Takeo (Commander of the Yokohama Guards)

Satō, Tomoo (Chief of the Cabinet's General Affairs Section)

*Shibata, Toshio (*Asahi Shimbun* Reporter)

Shiizaki, Lieutenant Colonel Jirō (Military Affairs Section)

Shimomura, Hiroshi (Director of the Cabinet's Information Bureau)

Shiraishi, Lieutenant Colonel Michinori (Staff Officer of 2nd General Army)

*Soga, Captain Otokichi (Adjutant to Regiment Commander Colonel Haga)

Sugiyama, Field Marshal Gen (Commander of the 1st General Army)

*Suzuki, Hajime (Son and Secretary to Prime Minister Suzuki)

Suzuki, Baron Kantarō (Prime Minister)

*Takashima, Major General Tatsuhiko (Chief of Staff of the Eastern District Army)

*Takeshita, Lieutenant Colonel Masahiko (Military Affairs Section, Ministry of War)

Tanaka, General Shizuichi (Commander of the Eastern District Army)

*Tateno, Morio (Japan Broadcasting Corporation Announcer)

*Toda, Yasuhide (Chamberlain)

Tōgō Shigenori (Minister of Foreign Affairs)

Tōjō, General Hideki (Ex-Premier)

***Tokugawa,** Yoshihiro (Chamberlain)
 Toyoda, Sadajirō (Minister of Munitions)
 Toyoda, Admiral Soemu (Chief of Naval Staff)
*Tsukamoto, Lieutenant Colonel Makoto (Military Police Corps)

Uehara, Captain Shigetarō (Air Academy)
 Umezu, General Yoshijirō (Chief of Army Staff)

 Wada, Nobukata (Japan Broadcasting Corporation Announcer)
 Wakamatsu, Lieutenant General Tadaichi (Vice War Minister)

 Yasui, Fujihara (State Minister)
*Yasuki, Miss Reiko (Technician of the Japan Broadcasting Corporation)
Yonai, Admiral Mitsumasa (Minister of the Navy)
*Yoshitake, Makoto (*Asahi Shimbun* Reporter)
 Yoshizumi, Lieutenant General Masao (Director of Military Affairs Bureau, Ministry of War)

Asterisks denote those who were interviewed by members of the Pacific War Research Society. Others interviewed include: Sadatoshi Tomioka, Yoshio Nasu, Yoshio Ozaki, Hirokichi Nadao, Nagaaki Okabe, Shigetaka Yamagishi, Takao Aso, Haruo Konuma, Takeharu Takahashi, Takeo Seike, Shigetoyo Suzuki, Yūzaburo Katō, Kōjirō Akabane, Michio Uda, Yuriko Hara, Isamu Furukawa, Hiroo Yanagisawa, Tsuneo Fujii, Fumio Sudō, Kiyoshi Tsukamoto, Yōzō Miyama, Ryūzō Kimura, Shunichi Nagatomo, Toshio Nakano, Masao Hirai, Tatsuo Hisadomi, Yasukichi Kondō, Komonta Sano, Tadashi Ishikawa and about twenty soldiers of the Imperial Guards Divison.

imperial role in decisions

Now available in Kodansha International's new paperback series:

Black Rain 黒い雨 by Masuji Ibuse

The Dark Room 暗室 by Junnosuke Yoshiyuki

The Lake みずうみ by Yasunari Kawabata

War Criminal 落日燃ゆ by Saburo Shiroyama

A Dark Night's Passing 暗夜行路 by Naoya Shiga

Botchan 坊っちゃん by Natsume Soseki

Japan's Longest Day 日本のいちばん長い日 by The Pacific War Research Society

A Haiku Journey: Basho's *Narrow Road to a Far Province* 奥の細道

The Waiting Years 女坂 by Fumiko Enchi